THE ROOTS OF AMERICAN

ECONOMIC GROWTH, 1607-1861

THE ROOTS
OF AMERICAN
ECONOMIC GROWTH
1607-1861

An Essay in Social Causation

By STUART BRUCHEY

Professor of American Economic History
Columbia University

HARPER TORCHBOOKS

HARPER & ROW, PUBLISHERS

NEW YORK AND EVANSTON

ACKNOWLEDGEMENT

I wish to express my thanks to Robert W. Fogel and to the Johns Hopkins Press for permission to make use of data from Professor Fogel's forthcoming book, *Railroads and American Economic Growth: Essays in Econometric History.*

TO ELEANOR

For Making All Things Possible
With love and admiration

Contents

List of Tables

Introduction to the
Torchbook Edition

The Rise of the New Economic History

Four years have passed since the completion of the manuscript of this book in January 1964, and in that interim scholarly inquiry has brought new light to some of the areas with which it is concerned. In addition, in formal reviews and private communications friends have called errors to my attention, and I am glad for the present opportunity to correct them. The new findings are very largely the product of the "new economic history," a phrase that was just coming into vogue at the time the manuscript was finished. Because of the importance of the work being done under the aegis of that school it seems worthwhile to trace its rise and assess its strengths and weaknesses.

The term "new economic history" appears to have been used first in an article published in 1960 by Lance E. Davis, Jonathan R. T. Hughes and Stanley Reiter.[1] Deploring the fact that the total

[1] In two essays written in 1957 Alfred H. Conrad and John R. Meyer first formulated the new approach, then demonstrated its utility in relation to a specific historical problem. See John R. Meyer and Alfred H. Conrad, "Economic Theory, Statistical Inference, and Economic History," *Journal of Economic History,* XVII (Dec. 1957); and Alfred H. Conrad and John R. Meyer, "The Economics of Slavery in the Ante-Bellum South," *Journal of Political Economy,* LXVI (April 1958). For guidance through the thickets of the new economic history I should like to express my appreciation to Professor Robert W. Fogel, the mimeographed output of whose Workshop at the University of Chicago provides a continuing source of information concerning work in progress throughout the country.

amount of quantitative work in the field was small, the authors called for a greater application of statistical and data-processing machine methods to the study of the past. By the spring of 1963 Douglass C. North, whom Davis calls the "chief propagandist and entrepreneur" of the movement, was proclaiming the existence of a state of "revolution." The revolution, North wrote, "is being initiated by a new generation of economic historians who are both skeptical of traditional interpretations of U.S. economic history and convinced that a new economic history must be firmly grounded in statistical data."

Not only statistics but economic theory as well is central to the work of the school. Acknowledging that many of the outstanding studies of the past abound in quantitative data, Robert W. Fogel points out that older scholars made little or no effort to transform the original data in a way that would make it shed light on "rigorously defined concepts of economic analysis." Moreover, the older historians "limited themselves almost exclusively to measuring things that could be measured directly." In contrast, the new historians try to reconstruct economic measurements "which might have existed at some time in the past but which are no longer extant." As an example, Fogel cites Paul David's effort to infer from extant data on output, employment, and wages information that is now missing on the growth of the stock of capital in Chicago between 1870 and 1893.

Other statements by Fogel and other leaders define even more precisely the objectives and techniques of the school. Pointing out that economic history "has always harbored scholars with a keen interest in the applications of theory and statistics to historical problems," Fogel, writing at the end of 1963, looked upon the movement as "the contemporary continuation of this theoretical-quantitative tradition, fortified by the methods developed and the experiences gained in recent empirical studies of economic growth, by the increasingly powerful tools of mathematical economics and econometrics, by the increasingly varied models of economic theory, and by the improved understanding of the possibilities that exist for the *adaptation* of models to the analysis of problems and situations other than those that prompted their invention." By December 1966, while continuing to insist that the "methodological hallmarks of the new economic history are its emphasis on measurement and its recognition of the intimate relationship between measurement and theory," Fogel had added a vigorous defense of the use of hypothetico-deductive models to answer counterfactual questions.

Counterfactual assertions, Fogel insisted, abound in old as well as new economic history:

They are present in discussions which either affirm or deny that tariffs accelerated the growth of manufacturing; in essays which argue that slavery retarded the development of the South; in debates over whether the Homestead Act made the distribution of land more equitable; in the contention that railroads expanded interregional trade; and in virtually every other discussion which makes a legal, social, technological, administrative or political innovation the cause of a change in economic activity. All of these arguments involve implicit comparisons between the actual state of the nation and the state that would have prevailed in the absence of the specified circumstance.[2]

It followed that the difference between the old and new history was not the frequency with which one encountered counterfactual propositions "but the extent to which such propositions are made explicit." The advantage of explicit statements is that they can be tested. Since counterfactual propositions are merely inferences from hypothetico-deductive models, it follows that they can be verified in at least two ways. The first involves the determination of whether the asserted proposition follows logically from its premises. The second requires a determination of whether the assumptions of the model are empirically valid. "Most of the revisions of the new economic history," Fogel believes, "follow from a demonstration that one or both of these conditions for valid inferences have been violated." In his judgment, *the fundamental methodological feature of the new economic history* "is its attempt to cast all explanations

[2] "The New Economic History, Its Findings and Methods," *Economic History Review*, XIX (December, 1966), p. 655.

of past economic development in the form of valid hypothetico-deductive models."

With these views Lance E. Davis is in essential agreement. In an article published in England at the end of 1966 he defined as follows the objectives of the new history:

First to state precisely the questions subject to examination and to define operationally the relevant variables. Second, to build explicit models that are relevant to the questions at hand. Third, to produce evidence (frequently quantitative, but at times qualitative) of the world as it actually existed. And finally, to test the model (a logical statement of assumptions and conclusions) against the evidence (the world that did exist) and the counterfactual deduction (the world that did not exist).[3]

Thousands of pages have been written about the British Industrial Revolution, Davis pointed out, yet the term still lacks an operational, that is to say, a testable, definition. The same lack exists for the populists, robber barons, and monopolists of the late nineteenth century in the United States.

If the robber barons were "bad," then we must have an idea "good"; if the railroads were a revolutionary force in American history, then the world with railroads must have been quite different than some world without railroads; and if the Industrial Revolution led to the impoverishment of the working class, then the workers must have been worse off than they would have been had there been no Industrial Revolution.[4]

"In short," Davis concluded, "any argument carries with it some assumptions about a counterfactual world—a world no one has ever seen, but a world . . . which might have been." Like Fogel and Davis, Douglass C. North also stresses the importance of counter-factual propositions, although preferring to call them "hypothetical alternatives." Suggesting that "a more scientific history" would follow from the use of "methods of scientific inquiry" developed by the social sciences, North in 1966 held forth the prospect of a

[3] Lance E. Davis, "Professor Fogel and the New Economic History," *Economic History Review, ibid.,* p. 657.

[4] Davis, *ibid.*

body of historical knowledge that would be "something more than a subjective reordering of the facts as man's perspective changes with each generation."

In the proclamation of revolution, in the missionary fervor with which the followers of the new movement seek to overthrow the long "tyranny of persuasive rhetoric," in the burning conviction that its methodology is scientific and will produce an understanding of the past that will be immune from the ravages of time, one sees a reflected image of the mood of contemporary economics. Indeed, from its beginnings in the late eighteenth century, as I point out in the opening chapter, economics has sought to carry the rigor and power of the natural sciences into the area of the social sciences. Given this emulative tradition, the reaction of economics to the phenomenal scientific and technical developments of a century that has discovered the secrets of atomic fission and fusion, that engages in the exploration of space, and that devises high-speed data-processing machines to cope with massive amounts of numerical information, is hardly surprising.

Increasing mathematization and increasing stress upon the quantitative dimension are hallmarks of contemporary economics. In the exuberant language of presidential address, George J. Stigler reminded the membership of the American Economic Association at the end of 1964 that "The age of quantification is now full upon us. We are now armed with a bulging arsenal of techniques of quantitative analysis, and of a power—as compared to untrained common sense—comparable to the displacement of archers by cannon." In contrast to the revolution heralded by Douglass North, the dimensions of which confined it to a palace guard of historians, Stigler's revolution sweeps through armies of economists. "The growth of empirical estimation of economic relationships," he averred, ". . . is a scientific revolution of the very first magnitude—indeed I would consider the so-called theoretical revolutions of a Ricardo, a Jevons, or a Keynes to have been minor revisions compared to the vast implications of the growing insistence upon quantification. . . . I am convinced," Stigler concluded, "that economics is finally at the threshold of its golden age—nay, we already have one foot through the door."

That the new economic history should respond in kind to such contagious enthusiasm is to have been expected. "Vibrant is the word," Robert Fogel told his audience at the same meetings in December 1964, "that best describes the present atmosphere in economic history." Pointing to John Clapham's *Economic Development of France and Germany* as an example of an "older descriptive and literary social history," George G. S. Murphy suggested in 1965 that "Considerations of charming the reader aside, we could replace such a [book] by a statistical abstract." For Sir John Clapham, the chickens had indeed come home to roost. A distinguished economic historian of the most traditional kind, he yet insisted that historians ask the questions: how large? how often? how long? how representative?

While every young movement sends its advance scouts to indefensible frontiers, I nevertheless believe that both the approach and contributions of the new school are valuable. The field of economic history, formerly diminished in yield through an overcultivation of familiar crops, displays now a surprising fertility. Eager young men in increasing numbers are subjecting themselves to the necessary discipline and acquiring techniques which will enable them to practice in the new mode. Some older men too are joining in. Can anyone disagree with George R. Taylor's judgment, expressed at the end of 1966, that the progress made in the last ten or twelve years has been greater than at any comparable period in the past, and that a considerable part of the credit for this must go to the new economic history? While my own training has been in history, it now seems to me desirable that students entering the field of economic history take work in statistics and in theory. The amount to take will be subject to debate, but one cannot deny that without some familiarity with the newer techniques it will be impossible to assess a great part of both current and future scholarship.

These techniques, however, are not the only ones desirable. Their great strength is their ability to make possible a rigorous quantitative analysis of the short-run behavior of economic variables. Their great weakness is their inability to cope with the long-run behavior of non-economic variables. Some of the leaders of the new school are frank to acknowledge the limitations of their technology. The new economic history, Lance Davis has remarked, "may not say much but at least the reader is aware of what has been said." The latter is all to the good. But what do we do about highly important problems that require the saying of much more than a given set of techniques permits?

The business cycle is not the growth cycle. In analyzing the former one may safely hold as constant the tastes, technology, values, political and legal systems, and social structure of a people; in analyzing the latter one cannot. The longer the time period involved, the greater the probability of change in the data which, from the point of view of purely economic analysis, it is desirable to hold safely impounded in the category of *ceteris paribus*. It is the thesis of this book that the causes of long-run economic change are multiple, that they are not simply economic but broadly social, that they are interrelated, are not always reducible to quantitative modes of expression, and require collaborative study by the social sciences generally, not by economics alone, if they are to be understood.

As a tool for causal analysis, the counterfactual proposition is far more efficient for problems of the short run than for those of the long. Suppose, for example, that the question at hand is the degree of responsibility to be credited President Franklin Delano Roosevelt for the liberal social legislation of the 1930's. (Historians will recognize the example as an instance of the familiar problem of determining the relative importance of historical individuals and historical forces in the production of historical events.) Since the period during which this legislation was enacted spanned only a few years, we are concerned here with a short-run problem. In the effort to answer it, a historian creates a counterfactual situation by performing a mental exercise. He imagines the absence of the President from the historical scene and proceeds to ask whether labor laws, tightened control of the banking system, social security, and other legislation would then have been passed. By removing the President from the scene he is able to focus upon the paths of development which might have been taken by other trends and forces. In the absence of the President, which elements would have developed differently from the ways in which they did in fact develop? in what direction? how far?

In his search for answers, he may well consider a number of historical forces, of western European as well as American origin, that were "bending the times" in the direction of the legislation in question; in addition, he may take into account the heightened role of government in the United States before and during World War I, as well as the fact of the Great Depression. His answer, it is clear, will represent a judgment, a judgment from which some other student, who may weigh and balance the pertinent factors somewhat differently, might dissent. In a word, it is not "scientific knowledge" that results from the use of the counterfactual, but merely a sharpened sense of the numerous variables pertinent to the inquiry and, hopefully, an abridgment and sharper definition of areas of disagreement. It is not possible to know for certain the causes of social change. While repeated comparisons of similar cases may strengthen one's explanatory hypotheses the latter must remain far less secure than the statistical probabilities that may reward the search for causes within the realm of the natural sciences.

But even the relatively modest achievements possible to the social sciences are more difficult to attain when the technique of the counterfactual is employed for the analysis of long-run problems. The reason, of course, is that when one performs a mental exercise that removes from the historical scene an element present in it for a long period of time, one can be far less certain of the ability to remove it *in toto*. If the element is of sufficient importance to justify historical inquiry, the probability is great that in a period of twenty or thirty years or more it intertwined itself with numerous institutions and trends in ways of thinking, valuing, and acting. President Roosevelt had been in office fewer than a half-dozen years before most New Deal legislation was passed, and to imaginatively create a version of the historical scene that would have obtained in his absence is a relatively manageable task.

But what if we consider, like Robert W. Fogel, the relationship of railroads to economic growth, and, beginning with the known size of the Gross National Product as of 1890, proceed to ask what was the contribution to it made by the railroad? The subjunctive world of what might have been can then be populated only with great risk and uncertainty, and wide areas of disagreement will survive the exercise. For in the many decades that the railroad belonged to the historical scene it intertwined its presence with so much that belonged to that scene that almost anyone's effort to imagine the consequences of its absence must be grossly inadequate.

To continue with the same illustration, Fogel himself acknowledges that "No evaluation of the impact of railroads in American development can be complete without a consideration of the cultural, political, military, and social consequences of such an innovation." But is it not inadmissible to divorce from one's consideration of *economic* consequences the effect of railroads on social and cultural change, to reason as if one believed that the greater ease with which people could move and information could flow had no effect on the values and incentives of men, and on the efficiency with which economic and business life were conducted? Furthermore, as Julius Rubin has pointed out, Fogel's failure even to mention the subject of industrial organization means that he implicity equates the size of railroad organizations with those of canal, turnpike, and wagon companies, and thereby ignores the effects of that experience with large-scale organization and finance which for a long time was provided only by the railroad. He also makes light of the fact— and here I cite a telling criticism of Fogel's work by George R. Taylor—that "the pattern of population distribution and of production and marketing of commodities under a transport system using waterways and roads would surely have developed differently and more efficiently if not confined within the particular pattern molded by railroad development. But this raises important questions as to market organization, external economies, etc., which place in doubt

the meaningfulness of Fogel's whole linear programming approach."
Surely it is clear that the longer the time period the wider the area
of disagreement flowing in the wake of the counterfactual. To dress
one's characterization of the world of the subjunctive in quantitative
garb fails to conceal an extent of nudity whose accompanying degree
of embarrassment must depend on the point of view. As a historian,
I can only applaud Julius Rubin's suggestion that deeper insight
into the relationship between railroads, industrialization, and economic growth may be obtained from reflecting on the fact that
industrialization in Britain was virtually completed before the
coming of the iron horse, than from considering Fogel's meticu-
lously elaborate but necessarily incomplete calculations.

Fogel's failure to cope with the imponderables of causality is by
no means atypical of the new economic history. In a thoughtful
inquiry into the relationship between *American Railroads and the
Transformation of the Antebellum Economy,* Albert Fishlow also
omits from his consideration variables upon whose importance a
more broadly-conceived social science approach would insist. Unless all social and psychological change can be associated with the
railroad, how can the transformation of the economy be understood
apart from all other participating variables? In a pioneer study
of the *Economic Growth of the United States, 1790 to 1860,* Douglass C. North took the frank position that his book was "based on
the proposition that U.S. growth was the evolution of a market
economy where the behavior of prices of goods, services and productive factors was the major element in any explanation of
economic change." While conceding that "institutional and
political policies" often accelerated or retarded growth, North
insisted that their influence was modificatory rather than fundamental.

It may be that a similar distrust of the pertinence of variables
exogenous to the price system, particularly activity by government,
has informed a number of other studies undertaken by new economic historians. Robert P. Thomas denies that British imperial
policies were very costly to the colonists during the decade 1763–

1772. In one study Albert Fishlow found that popular education successfully preceded an extensive system of publicly-supported and controlled schools, while in another, the book just mentioned, he contrasted the failure of publicly-supported railroads in the 1830's with the success of privately-financed lines in the Middle West in the 1850's. Lance Davis and John Legler appear to have equated the low expenditures by American governments in the nineteenth century with their importance in economic development. For Conrad and Meyer, the economic nexus is alone sufficient to account for the flourishing of slavery in the antebellum period. Morton Rothstein, in a prospectus of a study now under way, registers his belief that the antebellum Southern plantation elite shared the capitalist mentality of their more northerly confrères of the Chesapeake region of the eighteenth century. Finally, in his studies of the economy of India in the nineteenth century, Morris David Morris severely, although reluctantly, downgrades the importance of religious and cultural factors as retardative influences on economic growth. If these studies may be viewed as straws in the wind, they suggest the possibility that economists will place increasing weight upon sheerly economic variables and apply to their analyses of growth tools more fit for short-run change. If so, the development will be a regrettable one.

I think the need is clear for a collaborative effort on the part of the social sciences to work out theories of growth that will include all the variables pertinent to its explanation. What I have in mind is not a single theory that would be so highly generalized as to lose its meaning in specific applications, but rather sub-theories, so to speak, more limited explanatory frameworks that will reflect the numerous yet potentially definable subsets of conditions in which accelerating rates of per capita output growth have been discerned. The justification for an emphasis on subsets will be clear if one looks at any economy as a whole, certainly any economy that has passed beyond the subsistence level of development. What one sees, of course, is that it is composed of a number of geographical regions, economic sectors (such as agriculture, trade, and manufacturing), industries, and business firms. Even if the economy as a whole is undergoing growth, not all its components are growing at the same rate. If overall growth is taking place, it is only because the growth of some components is more than compensating for the failure of others to grow or to grow at the same rate.

While as we shall see there is lively current debate over the dating of acceleration of American economic growth, it is indisputable that the acceleration occurred in a nation that was far from being economically unified. Richard A. Easterlin has supplied tentative yet highly valuable estimates of regional differentiation in the growth of per capita income. Is it not a plausible hypothesis that these differences were associated with regional differences in the distribution of value emphases, psychological drives, vertical social mobility, political leadership, degrees of market dominance, urbanization and other configurations affecting ease of transmission of innovations in technology, administration, and law—to name some of the considerations that seem pertinent?

In their valuable study of *British Economic Growth,* Phyllis Deane and W. A. Cole make an observation that serves to point up my suggestion here: "While we have reasonable confidence that we have discerned the main features of the growth process and that our measurements, though rough, are generally of the right order of magnitude, the details of the picture are extremely doubtful; *and it is the details that may be crucial in suggesting the causal connections of the process.*" [5] The closer to the relevant details we can approach in the American case the more we shall close in on the root causes of growth.

It may be that drawing cultural regions or some other organizational framework, whose relevance may be suggested by both intra- and international comparisons, will bring us closer to the objective we seek. Fundamentally, it is individual men whose decisions make for growth, and in my view we need to be able to trace the complex interactions between men, between various groups and institutions, and between various ideas and values alive in the regions,

[5] Emphasis supplied.

sectors, and subcultures of the society. Scholars whose penchant is toward quantitative rigor may continue to prefer narrow questions that generate narrow answers and leave us to wonder about the bulk of the problem under review. But I shall continue to believe that history is fact selected and explained by judging men. I know of no way in which a body of knowledge about the past can be made fast to a rock of ages and secured against the changing needs of changing times.

While the larger significance of the conclusions reached by members of the new school must await the theoretical formulations to which I have adverted, some of them already compel modification of positions taken in this book. At the time I was writing it, literally nothing was in print concerning historical rates of growth during the colonial period, and in view of the paucity of quantitative evidence it seemed probable that a definitive treatment of the subject would forever remain impossible. That impossibility still seems likely, but George R. Taylor has since published a persuasive qualitative argument for the thesis of a more rapid rate of growth after the early decades of the eighteenth century. I was inclined to locate the acceleration in the later decades and associate it with the beginnings of industrialization. In that, I think I was wrong. Important recent work by Aubrey C. Land also provides good evidence of improving living standards between 1690 and 1770, which strengthens Taylor's case, as against mine, still more.

On the subject of antebellum growth rates, recent work by Paul David plays havoc not only with theses advanced by Rostow, Martin, North, Taylor, and Fogel, but also with my own assumption of a close temporal association between industrialization and acceleration in the growth rate. While both industrialization and urbanization grew after 1790, with especial rapidity between 1820–1840, the estimated per capita rate of growth was not immediately affected thereby. David's hypothesis, suggested by comparison with the British case, that a necessary lapse of time occurred before the structural transformations associated with rapid industrialization made their impact felt throughout the entire economy, may prove a highly fruitful one. Multiple regional and international comparisons may permit a charting of the time path of structural transformation so that it will be clearer precisely what accelerating and impeding forces are at work in the transmission of new impacts.

Although I do not believe I would much modify my emphasis on the importance of the role of government, the recent work of Robert P. Thomas must arrest any headlong assumption that the economic well-being of the colonists during the last dozen years of the colonial period would have been markedly superior if they had been free from the constraints of the English Navigation Acts. Whether Thomas' findings are equally applicable to conditions that obtained during the preceding century and a half, however, remains to be proved. A little calculating is a dangerous thing. Furthermore, I am not altogether persuaded by Thomas' effort to minimize the annual cost to the colonists of the Navigation Acts. Thomas' estimate of that cost ($2,370,000) is remarkably close to the "low" estimate of $2,500,000 made by Lawrence A. Harper many years ago. One difference between the two scholars is that Harper compares his figure to the annual per capita expense of operating the national government during the last six years of Washington's administration—and so emphasizes its importance—while Thomas compares his to an estimate of per capita income—and so minimizes its importance. A wag is reported to have reacted to Thomas' minimization with the comment that had John Hancock realized that, there would have been no Revolution. The importance of the role of judgment can hardly be more clear.

Except for his handling of the question of quality, the already-mentioned work on education by Albert Fishlow is persuasive. Fishlow's minimization of the importance of government in the field of internal improvements, however, seems to me to lay insufficient stress on the necessity of governmental aid in surmounting the Appalachian barrier. My emphasis on the importance of the Hamiltonian program for the revival of national credit still appears pertinent, in part because imports of capital funds from abroad, while relatively small, may have made important marginal contributions to a developing country in need of capital. In addition, one must not lose sight of that program's important contribution to the formation of a framework of security in which investment might thrive. Finally, I would pay tribute to recent articles by Aubrey C. Land and to a report of work in progress by Morton Rothstein, which suggest that I underemphasized the extent to which the planting elite of both the eighteenth and nineteenth centuries was market oriented. The presidential address of Thomas C. Cochran before the Organization of American Historians convinced me that I paid far too little attention to the importance of land speculation as a source of income to small farmers in the colonial period.

New York City, October 1967

Preface

To say that economic growth involves far more than economics is to utter a truism. Most students of growth, it seems safe to say, now view that process as one which cuts across the boundaries of the disciplines within the social sciences. Growth implicates political science, sociology, social psychology, and much else besides economics and economic history. In this book I attempt to apply this broad approach to American economic growth and to place the process within the mainstream of American history.

I am aware of the presumption implied by that effort. The area is vast and the terrain difficult: if in some places it is hardly known, in many others it is covered by a tangled growth of monographic and journal literature. Indeed, without a conceptual compass of some kind one would lose one's way. After a brief introduction of the subject of the book I further discuss in the opening chapter the need for such guidance and try to make clear what it is that has directed my own path.

Within the area of pertinence indicated by my compass I have tried to supply some guidance to the literature, at least to the extent of identifying many of its contributors, whose works are partially listed in a selective bibliography. In part, therefore, the

book is an extended commentary on that literature. While I have
made frequent use of such printed primary sources as the Journals
of the Continental Congress and the works of Jefferson, Hamilton
and others, my research in manuscript sources has been in the main
confined to mercantile and banking records. One additional dis-
claimer should be entered for the benefit of all except economists,
who will not need to be told: my training and interests are those of
the historian.

More specifically, my interest lies in the causes of social change,
of which economic change may be viewed as one aspect. Many students of economic growth approach its problems in ways which
differ from the path I have chosen. Devotees of what is sometimes
called the "new economic history," their interest centers in the
economic analysis of quantitative phenomena. The current prestige
of the natural sciences and their mathematical tools, together with
the availability of high-speed computers to handle masses of data
beyond the previous capacity of the individual researcher, are recruiting increasing numbers of younger scholars trained in the use
of these techniques. Their analytical precision, their ingenious
efforts to fill gaps in the data by indirect measurements that are
guided by the logic of economic theory, compel admiration, for
they often result in the drawing of more defensible lines between
what is probable and what is not.

Quantitative methods made undoubted contributions: but their
limitations are also clear. In the words of Carter Goodrich, "attempts to deal with causation, to consider what factors lead to
development in one situation and stagnation in another, necessarily
become qualitative in their nature." Since my own interest lies precisely in the problem of causation a resort to qualitative techniques
would have been compelled by that consideration alone. Yet an
observation once made by Frederic C. Lane should be added: both
the quantitative method, and the machines which are an extension
of that method, are extensions in turn of the basic technique of
historical criticism. What will always remain for determination is

the question: is a particular statement, whether qualitative or quantitative, true or false?

. . . .

To Professor Lane I shall always owe far more than I can ever repay for teaching me that the whole man is at the center of all our studies. This is the meaning of humanism, the *raison d'etre* of the university. I wish to thank him here more specifically for his helpful comments on an early outline for the present volume. To several colleagues I owe thanks for the stylistic and organizational improvement of various chapters. Richard E. Sullivan gave me the benefit of a very careful reading of Chapters two and three, and Dean Paul A. Varg also contributed much to the lessening of the imperfections of those chapters. To Arthur E. Adams I am indebted for helpful criticisms of Chapters four and five. Robert E. and B. Katherine Brown listened in patience to a reading of Chapter one and made useful comments on it. I have benefited from conversations with John W. Baldwin of Johns Hopkins, and with Marvin R. Cain, Bernard A. Kemp, and W. Paul Strassmann of Michigan State.

The incisive editorial comments of John Higham and Carl N. Degler did much to improve the style and enrich the substance of the entire manuscript. Scholars are especially aware of the great chain of academic being, and the most cursory reading of these chapters will reveal the extent of their indebtedness to the thoughts and findings of others. But those who have poured forth their learning and other aids must not be blamed if the receptacle proved too small to hold the fullness of their offering. To my wife, finally, to the extraordinary clarity of her thought, and to her great and patient giving, the book owes much of any merit it may possess.

I am indebted to Michigan State University for helping finance the costs of research, to Richard E. Chapin and Henry C. Koch of the Michigan State University Library for many generous aids, and to Edie Starr for excellent typing. The grant of a faculty fellowship by the Social Science Research Council made it possible to complete the manuscript more expeditiously.

I

The Matter of Method

The world of the mid-twentieth century is one in which two-thirds of mankind live in want. Poverty is, of course, nothing new: most of the people who have ever lived have probably been poor. Yet the problem of want in the contemporary world wears a different face, and even the occupational skepticism of the historian cannot prevail against the need to recognize its newness. Poverty today is accompanied by a multinational consciousness of its existence, by the beginnings of an organized will to alleviate it, and by the availability of the means of success. The means are a growing body of scientific knowledge and the widening technology that rests upon it, including not only machinery and processes but techniques for the organization and management of human and other resources.

While science and technology promise enormous increases in the productivity of economic effort, their use to this end requires the massive support of an aspiring nation. Not surprisingly, therefore, in one underdeveloped country after another in Latin America, the East, and Africa during the years following World War II there have arisen educated leaders determined to teach their peoples that the preconditions of higher levels of living depend greatly upon the human will. This is not to minimize the great difficulties that stand in the way: incomes so low as to afford only a marginal possibility of capital formation out of domestic savings; illiteracy, poor health, and undeveloped skills; resistant customs, institutions, and values. It is only to suggest that these difficulties may not loom so large once a determination to raise standards of living has permeated the populations of the depressed areas.

The factor of social will has been underestimated in most discussion of the conditions necessary to economic development. Yet its importance is as clear in the historical experience of mature Western economies as it is in the case of backward nations. It is clear in the West today. Despite the advanced technologies that are available to the West, the foreseeable future holds little or no promise that rates of growth will advance as rapidly as they did in the nineteenth century. Part of the reason for this, of course, is that Western man has increasingly preferred the uses of leisure to the multiplication of material possessions. This preference is certainly not to be deplored. The relative decline of materialism holds rich promise for the cultivation of the spirit of man. Yet it is undeniable that many in the West are concerned over lagging growth rates. And it is this concern, together with efforts by underdeveloped peoples to rise from age-old conditions of poverty, that has created world-wide interest in problems of economic growth. Competition between China, Russia, and the West for political influence in the underdeveloped regions only sharpens an edge already honed by nationalist aspirations.

The quickened growth that is the objective of both study and policy is no mere spurt in economic activity, such as that which might follow from an unusually good harvest, or that which comes with an upward movement in the business cycle. The business cycle traverses its run from peak to depression to peak in from four to nine years. The growth in which the contemporary world is interested is not a temporary phenomenon but one that is sustained over the long run. Analyzing the course of the long run, some students have found growth cycles of ten, others of approximately sixty years in duration. It is not impossible that cycles of one hundred years may someday be discovered. About this aspect of growth, as about so many other features of the phenomenon, much has yet to be learned, especially concerning the nature of the relationship between short-run business cycles and the "long swings" of growth.

Scholarly opinion concerning the proper measure of growth reflects the dual interest in both mature and underdeveloped economies. Almost everyone agrees on the need to employ national income as an index, but some favor the use of that index alone. More strictly, they would define growth as an annual increase either in the total real net output of goods and services (net national product) or in its monetary equivalent, national income. Others emphasize the importance of population change, and prefer to divide national income by the size of the population in order to obtain a figure for income per person. The former are mainly concerned with the need to speed up the lagging growth rates of the economies of the West, where levels of living have long been high and population increases have provided only short-run threats to those levels. The latter have in mind mainly the difficulties of initiating growth in underdeveloped countries where increases in income are so small that they tend to be swallowed up by even larger increases in population, with the result that levels of living already pitifully low are depressed still more. Income per capita supplies the best available measure of economic welfare, and it is in this sense of output (or income) per capita that the term "growth" (or "development") is used in the pages that follow. I shall use the term "expansion" to designate increases in output that appear to owe their existence to increases in population. Needless to say, if an increased number of people is required to produce an increased amount of goods and services, the processes of production have not made it possible for anyone to be any better off than he was before.

The severity of both aspects of the contemporary problem of growth makes it understandable that students, in their efforts to cope with them, should turn for guidance to past experience. Two formidable obstacles confront the search for historical origins: the problem of evidence and that of causation. Involving, as it does, rates of output (income) over periods of time, economic growth is clearly a quantitative concept. The problem of evidence is simply that the statistical data necessary for the establishment of either the existence or the rate of growth are available for scarcely a dozen of the more than one hundred countries of the world. Derived from census returns and other fragments, these data exist only for the more advanced countries, and even in these cases the data are for only short periods of time. Even for the United States, figures upon which estimates of national income may be securely based commence only in 1869. Some students are therefore doubtful that we shall ever possess sufficient data upon which to rest reliable estimates of output during the earlier years of the nineteenth century, to say nothing of the eighteenth and seventeenth centuries. Others, less pessimistic, are studying movements of productivity in agriculture and other sectors of the economy. The most widely used index of productivity—which is a measure of the efficiency with which resources are converted into the commodities and services that men want—is physical output per manhour. Studies of productivity may well be moving into the center of research efforts to trace the probable course of early American growth.

It is precisely here that the even more difficult problem of causation enters. While the *fact* of an increase in productivity requires quantitative evidence in its support, many of the *causes* of increased efficiency are wholly or partly unmeasurable. Under most reasonable assumptions it is true that the use of more machinery per worker will increase output per worker, so that a causal chain reaching from investment to profits, savings-income ratios, prices, costs, and other elements in capital formation may be forged from quantifiable links of an economic nature. But it is also true that causes of a different order may be found in changes in social structure and mobility, in sharpened incentives, in contributions to efficiency made by improved economic organization, by new knowledge, better training and health, and by other sociocultural or political factors.

Strictly speaking, as William N. Parker has suggested, social changes of these kinds made their own contributions to the inputs.

But can these contributions be separated from each other, measured, and compared in "importance" both with each other and with contributions simultaneously made by economic inputs? I for one do not see how they can be. How does one measure the effects of an increase in vertical social mobility upon incentives to produce? And separate those effects from the contributions made by other inputs? Or again, while social expenditures on education and health provide a useful index to the available quantity of those inputs, how does one cope numerically with the contributions made by improvements in their quality? Even if one abstracts expenditures on medical and educational research and development and compares changing ratios of these to total expenditures on education and health, is it not reasonable to assume that research and development in some particular area may be far more responsible for the rise in productivity than those activities in other areas? One thinks, for example, of the importance of vaccination in the late eighteenth century, or of the movement for free public schools in the second third of the next century, a movement which may be justly conceived of as a form of educational research and development. Is it not clear that when one begins to assess the relative importance of the components of a total expenditure, when one breaks open the crust of what is after all a grossly external and enumerative index, he is engaged in the process of making historical judgments? Surely the need for such judgments is inescapable, for the numerous social factors contributing to an increase in productivity shift their positions of relative importance as historical change occurs in the context in which they appear. It therefore seems to me that decisions concerning relative importance, whether expressed in numbers or words, are fundamentally historical approximations resting on judgment.

The point may be otherwise expressed. At any given moment of rise in productivity numerous influences conspire to bring the rise about. But to associate specific portions of a numerical result (the productivity increase) with each of its multiple causes appears impossibly complex. Would the effort to do so not make for a merely meretricious exactness, a kind of *reductio ad absurdum* of quantomania? Economists and other social scientists are surely justified in seeking to quantify whatever may usefully be quantified. But many of the important contributions to productivity, and hence to growth, cannot be so reduced.

The fact that the economic causes of growth are more easily quantified than are other causes makes it difficult to assess the relative importance of the two categories. This is because it is tempting to assign a greater weight to that which is ponderable, to regard it as somehow more "fundamental," and other things as secondary or "derived." As an alternative, it is tempting to label non-economic factors as "important" and then in the ensuing discussion of total causes to permit them to carry an inconsequential burden of responsibility for producing the results under analysis. It does not follow that these temptations should not be resisted. As Alexis de Tocqueville noted long ago: "The mind is easily imposed upon by the affectation of exactitude which marks even the mis-statements of statistics; and it adopts with confidence the errors which are appareled in the forms of mathematical truth." Simon Kuznets, a twentieth-century economist who has been a pioneer in the field of national income accounting, would agree: "Concentration on quantifiable factors in formulating hypotheses may mean a definite bias in the selection and too high a price for a statistically testable hypothesis." Nevertheless, what is undoubtedly a leading tradition in the history of economic thought tends to discount the economic significance of anything that cannot be numerically expressed.

The late eighteenth-century world into which classical economics was born was a world dominated by a belief in the superiority of natural over man-made law. From its first systematic formulation of principles by Adam Smith and David Ricardo, the dominant classical strain has sought to draw up canons comparable in their uniformity and universality to the laws of nature. Classical economics was mechanistic; it was built in the image of Newton's classical mechanics. And since the laws of motion in classical

mechanics, to employ the words of Gregor Sebba, "establish deter-
minate functional relationships between measurable variables,"
classical economics "assumed that a modern economy can be
represented by a general mechanistic model capable of mathematization and presumably prediction." From its beginnings, economics
has sought to carry the rigor and power of the natural sciences into
the area of the social sciences. Its "models" are essentially statistical
hypotheses concerning the quantifiable features of a mechanistic
world.

Nevertheless, models are, or at least are capable of being, useful
tools of analysis. Being small machines that represent big machines,
they simplify the real world by abstracting from its complexities
those causal factors (variables) that are believed to be most significantly related to the problem under scrutiny. By clearly specifying the nature of the variables, the way in which they are related to
each other, and the identity of other factors ("data") assumed to
be relatively fixed or constant, and which may therefore be taken
as given, they supply frameworks within which the possibility of
disciplined thought is enhanced.

Depending on the method by which the variables are chosen for
inclusion, models may be classified as "real" or "ideal" types. A
"real" model is one that is constructed in the closest possible
proximity to historical evidence. An "ideal" model is a deliberate
mental construct, the distinguishing feature of which is its purpose-
ful exaggeration of some of the elements found in the real world in
order to achieve logical unity. It is the ideal type that is most
familiar to the economist. The model of a free-enterprise economy,
for example, exaggerates features of the real world, for it assumes
a condition of perfect competition: the existence of numerous firms,
perfect markets, perfect knowledge, and freedom of entry or exit
from business. The model nevertheless serves as a standard by
which the nature of real-life deviations from it can more clearly
be seen. At the same time, it permits a prediction of the reaction
of competitors to changes in market conditions.

Whether ideal or real, a model is an hypothesis, and the purpose for which it is constructed is to provide an explanation of situations or phenomena whose common features are assumed to be more important than their distinctive ones. Were every phenomenon unique, there would be nothing to explain; description alone would suffice, and generalization would be impossible. A model makes a preliminary identification of those elements of uniformity, a tentative statement of the way in which they are related to each other. But whether it be employed in natural science or in social science, its utility depends upon its power to explain the empirical data to which it is applied. If in one application after another the hypothesis succeeds in explaining the data, the supposition that its variables truly reflect the causes operative in the real world may more confidently be held. From preliminary hypothesis it may rise to higher levels of probable validity, to the dignity of "theory" or "law." Maximal validity, maximal power of prediction and hence of control of the forces making for change, is the goal of physical and social science alike. The essential difference between the two areas of inquiry is thus not methodological; it lies in the far smaller degree of success which a multiplicity of variables permits to the social sciences. Take three observations of a comet and a cat, the great nineteenth-century English scientist Thomas Huxley used to say, and it will be safer to predict the date of the comet's return than which way the cat will jump. The longer the time span, the wider the problem, the more numerous will be the variables of jumping, so to speak.

The economist's models are more efficient instruments for analysis of the quantifiable short-run determinants of income than of the causes of growth. In income analysis, long-run factors of a sociopolitical nature may be held constant, regarded as given. Economic growth, however, as sociologist Bert F. Hoselitz has put it, "is a process which affects not only purely economic relations but the entire social, political, and cultural fabric of society." In the dynamic world of growth, unlike the changeless, timeless world of short-run analysis, the data previously assumed as given are in constant motion as factors making for change. It is indeed the element of time, as the nineteenth century economist Alfred Marshall observed, that is "the source of many of the greatest difficulties in economics." And the difficulty here is this: how can short-run models incorporate the long-run, non-quantifiable elements of economic growth?

Some economists, it must be said, have recently tried to devise models sufficiently comprehensive to include all factors impinging upon growth. Irma Adelman, for example, has suggested that the mathematical symbol "U_t" be used to represent "the entire social, cultural, and institutional complex of society." The "form of the equation governing the rate of social and cultural change," Professor Adelman adds, however, "cannot be specified without a complete theory of the historical process . . . a staggering requirement indeed." Indeed. Walt W. Rostow has also attempted to provide a link between long- and short-period factors. But he readily acknowledges that this "multiplies vastly the number of variables and reduces the possibilities for strict theoretical statement." Other leading economists agree with this assessment. None of the numerous factors pertinent to growth, Evsey Domar has written, "could properly be taken as an independent variable, and the required system of simultaneous relationships, whether expressed in symbols or in words, would be impossibly complex and probably useless." So vastly ambitious an objective as a general theory of growth, Simon Kuznets has said, may be "forever beyond reach." What may forever abort the attainment of a general theory is the distinct possibility that the common features of growth combine in ways that are significantly determined by the unique historical experiences of the nation in which they occur.

The inference is clear that the more rigorous the model, the higher its degree of technical success may be, but the greater its inability to explain growth. Such a model necessarily omits too many of the significant causes of growth. While supplying a technique for precise analysis of part of the problem, it leaves us wondering about the whole. It follows that an inquiry into the causal origins of growth ought not to commence with a highly generalized, highly abstract model to frame the analysis. To force a translation of qualitative factors into the language of numbers is to guide us to reality in the way of parody. To apply formal economic analysis to the complexities of long-run change is to invite the rigor of *rigor mortis*.

On the other hand, to proceed without the guidance of any hypothesis at all is impossible. A leading historiographical tradition, it is true, would deny this statement of necessity and place its emphasis upon the uniqueness of particular events. Admittedly, there is a fundamental sense in which the emphasis is not mistaken. To every event there belongs a temporal singularity, a contextual particularity, and it is because of this that all historical being possesses a quality of never-quite-the-sameness. But it is equally true that the essence of a thing is not altogether its separateness. There is essential sharedness as well as essential singularity, and if this were not so, all experience were a succession of differentiated particulars, without meaning because nothing would be recognizable. "No man is an island," said John Donne; nor is any thing.

Because all things possess characteristics that are similar to some other things, it is possible to group these similarities and bestow upon them a name that marks them off from groups sharing other characteristics. This name is a concept. Its nature is general rather than particular; the name "chair," for example, denotes those common qualities which make for "chairness" rather than those qualities which describe a particular chair. And, as Plato knew, we are able to recognize a chair only because it shares in the characteristics essential to the concept.

It is in this equally fundamental sense that not only historical research but all thought must begin not with the particular but with the general. Concepts must precede percepts. Investigation begins with a problem (or problems) to be solved. Was there democracy in the colonial period? Did commercial banking exist? Did economic growth take place? There can be no gathering of evidence to answer these questions without a preliminary understanding of the nature of the concepts. To be sure, the evidence may lead us to reformulate an inadequate concept, in the way, for example, that Bernard Bailyn was obliged to recast a faulty concept of education in the course of his investigation of the educational experience of the colonial period. But it remains true, as Morris R. Cohen once expressed it, that "Without an anticipatory idea or hypothesis we do not know what specific facts to look for and cannot recognize what is relevant to the inquiry."

Some devotees of historical tradition would counter with the claim that while they make use of concepts, they do not employ hypotheses, preferring to present a simple narrative in which the facts are permitted to speak for themselves. But facts must be chosen before they can speak. The records of the past contain great multitudes of facts, but historians give voice only to those they consider to be of interest or importance. Even within the compass of a subject found interesting or important, a constant process of selection is ordinarily required to weed the rank growth of available facts. Some of them "matter" and others do not. Those that do are judged to relate in some significant way to the phenomenon under investigation, helping, for example, to "explain" it. But relations are never perceived; they are conceived. The historian perceives only sequences; it is his mind rather than his eye that determines how the facts are related to each other. In a word, the criteria by which he selects some facts and rejects others as irrelevant are not inherent in the data; they are supplied by the historian. In every historical narrative, therefore, the beads of fact are strung on threads of hypothesis that vary in their degree of visibility.

While thus in history as in economics a scaffolding of hypothesis must frame the ultimate structure, too great a degree of rigidity or elaboration risks distortion or omission of significant structural elements. An intermediate position between imputed universality and untotalizable fact, between the embrace of mechanics and what Thomas C. Cochran has well called the "tyranny of persuasive rhetoric," therefore seems appropriate. This seems to me best provided by Simon Kuznets' hypothesis that the modern economic growth of the past two centuries has been the product of industrialization.

It is true that some countries—for example, New Zealand and Argentina—have relied upon sales of agricultural or pastoral surpluses in world markets to raise their people's levels of living. Others, such as Australia and the United States, were once so-called "empty" countries permitting both increasing population and welfare even before the advent of industrialization. Yet the generalization appears valid that substantial and sustained increases in both population and output per capita have required the process of industrialization, the application of science and technology to problems of production. "The predominant problem of economic growth in our day," Bert Hoselitz has recently written, "is the overcoming of economic stagnation, which normally takes place through a process of industrialization." Both directly and indirectly industrialization has been the source of numerous gains in productivity which have not accrued to the same degree in its absence, and these larger gains have made for higher and more sustained levels of growth than the lesser ones associated with preindustrial change. A quick preliminary look at American experience will serve to identify some of the sources of these gains.

Perhaps above all, industry afforded far greater scope than any other economic sector for the efficiencies generated by continued technological progress. Improved transport itself, it should be stressed, owed much to the presence and growth of the industrial sector, and to some extent, at least, the same was true of agriculture. Industrialization contributed to the growth of occupational specialization and joined hands with transport improvements to make possible a greater degree of specialization of economic sectors and geographic regions. It permitted economies of scale, and generated external economies: as unit costs of production fell, a reduction in product prices brought "external" economies to other producers using those products. Nor is this all. In conjunction, once again, with improved mechanisms of transport, it quickened the pace of urbanization, and this, in turn, quickened that exchange of ideas which is so favorable to innovation. By helping to create numerous occupational opportunities, industrialization also increased the means by which individuals might move from one level of income and status to another; and the increased vertical mobility of society that resulted—an increase to which other factors to be discussed also contributed—generated competitive pressures, enhanced by urban living, to work hard and save. Finally, through its impact upon transportation, urbanization, social structure, and occupational opportunity, industrialization helped spread throughout American society values favorable to growth. In a word, it both sharpened incentives and multiplied the means of achieving greater efficiency in productive effort. It did not do these things alone or with results capable of precise statement in quantitative terms. But it made for a causal difference that is grossly visible in any comparison between the America of 1740 and that of 1840.

This method of comparison—of early America with later America, of American experience with that of other nations—makes it possible to conduct a causal inquiry by affording a means of coping with what would otherwise be the nearly illimitable tyranny of conditions necessary to economic growth. There is a fundamental sense in which it will always be true that each necessary condition is, in the words of John Stuart Mill, "equally indispensable to the production of the consequent." By definition, a necessary condition is precisely that. We accord primacy as precipitant to the spark, but without the powder, its dry condition, the smallness of the space in which it is confined, atmospheric conditions, and so on, there would be no explosion. And, strictly speaking, this only begins the matter. What conditions necessarily anteceded the production of the spark, of the powder, of the smallness of the space, and so on? And what conditions, in turn, preceded these? The conditions of any event, even a relatively simple one like an explosion, must beat their way back into the past via a process of "infinite" regression until they disappear in the mists of the unknowable—unless, like Aquinas, one can persuade himself that an uncaused first cause is the necessary condition to all subsequent causation.

True as these ancient reflections are, they contribute little to the solution of human problems. It helps little to realize that everything is the cause of everything else, that a nearly illimitable number of conditions is equally important not only for the production of one event but also of every other event. Some method of delimiting the problem of causal inquiry is clearly useful, and as R. M. MacIver suggests, "the basic method is a form of the method of comparison, the successive analysis of comparable situations in order to demarcate our phenomenon and to segregate the particular complex of things to which it immediately belongs."

Applied to the problem at hand, the method of comparison permits us to look out over the history of the past two centuries and observe that some nations experienced rapid economic growth while others did not. The question immediately arises: what explains this? What did the growing countries have that was lacking, or present in less significant amounts, in those that grew less rapidly? And the answer seems clearly to be: industry, together with a constellation of conditions that made it possible. Not only in the United States before the early decades of the nineteenth century, but also in the case of Great Britain before roughly the 1760's (although the British case is disputed), of France before the 1830's, Germany before the 1850's, Russia before the 1890's, Turkey before the 1930's, and so on, rates of growth were slow before the pace of industrial development began to accelerate.

If, then, industrialization is properly to be associated with rapid and sustained economic growth, the further question arises: what conditions were necessary to industrialization and sufficient to explain its advent? Once again comparative analysis, a search this time for features common to the experience of industrializing countries, suggests the answer. In all cases industrialization depended on the necessary condition of continuous technical progress and, underlying that, a series of new scientific discoveries. Yet science and technology were necessary conditions, not sufficient ones. Industrialization also required both physical and human capital, entrepreneurial skills and incentives, the willingness and ability of businessmen and workingmen to adopt new machines and processes, and the existence of markets to absorb their output at prices sufficient to cover the production costs of marginal producers. These requirements, combined with the necessary condition of increased technological knowledge, constituted the sufficient condition for industrialization and, hence, of modern economic growth.

The task before us, then, is not that of tracing the origins of industrialism to its remote beginnings and finding the paths by which it spread from one country to another in recent history. It is that of tracing the historical emergence of its necessary and sufficient conditions in the United States. What aided and what inhibited the emergence of those conditions? In what attitudes and values, institutions, processes and events, did they have their roots? Our enquiry, it is necessary to add, can by no means be confined to economic phenomena alone but must range among political, social, and cultural sources of change as well. While the contribution of industrialization to those increases in productivity that made for growth was greater than that of any other constellation of conditions, this contribution implicated numerous processes of social change as both cause and effect. A causal enquiry into social phenomena may safely ignore many effects but not all of them. Some bend backward, as it were, to enter the causal complex at a later stage of its development, and thus they become pertinent to the enquiry. What these are, we shall see in the chapters ahead.

II

The Dependent Years: I

The Question of Colonial Economic Growth

In his recent testimony before the Joint Economic Committee of Congress, Raymond W. Goldsmith made some observations concerning early American economic growth that not only deserve to be taken into consideration in any discussion of the subject but also form a convenient point of departure for the present one. Goldsmith raises a basic question: is it possible for the economy to have grown at the same rate in its earlier years as that at which it has grown since the significant beginnings of industrialization? Apparently placing these beginnings in the late 1830's, Goldsmith calculates that in the 120 years between 1839 and 1959 the *average* annual rate of growth in gross national product per head amounted to 1⅝ per cent. He thinks it extremely unlikely this rate obtained much before 1839. The assumption that it did, he points out, implies a halving of national income every 43 years, with devastating consequences for average income per person. Estimating the latter at about $400 (in present valuation) in 1839, he shows the arithmetic necessity of it being about $145 in 1776, $80 in 1739, and less than $30 in 1676. Income at such levels, he argues, even under the simpler conditions of colonial America, is too low to have sustained life. At present prices for individual commodities, he doubts that an income below $200 would have been sufficient even in the early eighteenth century. Colonial incomes must therefore have been higher, and if they were, the rate of growth must have been smaller than 1⅝ per cent. Goldsmith questions whether it was as much as 1 percent in any fifty-year period before 1839.

By a process of logical inference Goldsmith thus reaches two conclusions: that average income was not impossibly low during the colonial period, and that its rate of growth was comparatively slow. He believes that industrialization and the advent of the railroads sharply accelerated the rate "not very long before" 1839. Now it may be debated whether a sudden acceleration or "takeoff" in the level of income occurred in the 1830's, or whether the process of growth described a more gradual cumulative rise beginning sometime in the eighteenth century. But it seems to me that the weight of probability must fall, with reservations to be noted, on the side of Goldsmith's two conclusions. It is unlikely that the probability can ever be converted into certainty, for the surviving evidence is likely to remain too scantily quantitative to specify income sizes and rates of change.

Other obstacles also make it difficult to cope with questions concerning income and growth in the colonial period. Perhaps the most important of these is that indices of national income are unable to provide for the value of economic activities that bulked large in early America, as they do in other undeveloped economies. Especially important in this connection are goods made in households for family use rather than for sale, and the value of barter exchange. Indeed, the values it is possible to assign manufacturing and exchange undertaken in a later period when both are market-oriented and expressed in monetary terms, necessarily makes it appear that income for that period, and hence its rate of growth, is higher than in fact it is. Thus Goldsmith's minimal estimate of the colonial growth rate is probably somewhat low and the specified rate of its later acceleration somewhat high. If so, the resulting narrower gap between them would make for a smoother, more gradual process of growth rather than one of abrupt transition from preindustrial to industrial conditions.

This probability is also strengthened by another consideration. It seems clear that comfortable standards of living in the colonial period were compatible with cash incomes of surprisingly small size. "We live here very plentifully without money," said William Fitzhugh of Virginia in the last quarter of the seventeenth century. And if we accept the validity of the following remarks made by a South Carolina backwoods farmer, it will be evident how little cash was required by rural people even in the early nineteenth century:

At this time, my farm gave me and my whole family a good living on the produce of it; and left me, one year with another, one hundred and fifty silver dollars, *for I never spent more than ten dollars a year*, which was for salt, nails and the like. Nothing to wear, eat or drink, was purchased, as my farm provided all. With this saving, I put money to interest, bought cattle, fatted and sold them, and made great profit.[1]

Now there may well be in this account some element of exaggeration, for the Carolina farmer goes on to deplore, in this communication to a newspaper, changes from the old frugal ways which now require him to open his purse for such extravagances as gauze, "ribands," silk, tea, and sugar! But we shall see how widespread was the possibility of such a standard of living as he describes.

Colonial Economic Expansion

Such statistical remains as have survived the colonial period strongly indicate a remarkable and almost continuous expansion of population (Table I), urbanization (Table II), westward movement, agricultural production, foreign trade, and shipping. The figures for population and urbanization are rough estimates, the latter especially so. Those for population suggest, particularly clearly in the eighteenth century, the oft-noted tendency for popu-

[1] Quoted in Lewis C. Gray, *History of Agriculture in the Southern United States to 1860* (Gloucester, Mass., 1958), I, 452. Italics supplied.

TABLE I

ESTIMATED POPULATION OF THE ORIGINAL THIRTEEN COLONIES BY REGIONS, 1630–1770[1]
(White and Negro)
(in thousands)

	1630	1640	1650	1660	1670	1680	1690	1700	1710	1720
New England[2]	2	13	23	33	52	68	87	93	115	171
Middle	—	2	4	5	7	15	35	53	69	103
Southern	2	11	23	36	52	68	88	105	147	192
Total	4	26	50	74	111	151	210	251	331	466

	1730	1740	1750	1760	1770
New England	217	290	360	450	540
Middle	147	221	296	428	556
Southern	265	395	514	716	994
Total	629	906	1,170	1,594	2,090

[1] Individual Colonies rounded to nearest hundred; regional totals rounded to nearest thousand.
[2] Plymouth Colony counted separately till 1691, then merged with Massachusetts; Maine counties included with Massachusetts, 1660–1760.
Source: *Historical Statistics of the United States, Colonial Times to 1957* (Washington, D.C., 1960), p. 756.

Table II

Estimated Population of Five Leading Port Cities, 1630–1775

	1630	1640	1650	1660	1680	1690	1700	1710
New York	300	400	1,000	2,400	3,200	3,900	5,000	5,700
Philadelphia	—	—	—	—	—	4,000	5,000	6,500
Boston	—	1,200	2,000	3,000	4,500	7,000	6,700	9,000
Charleston	—	—	—	—	700	1,100	2,000	3,000
Newport	—	96	300	700	2,500	2,600	2,600	2,800

	1720	1730	1743	1760	1775
New York	7,000	8,622[1]	11,000	18,000	25,000
Philadelphia	10,000	11,500	13,000	23,750	40,000
Boston	12,000	13,000	16,382[1]	15,631[1]	16,000
Charleston	3,500	4,500	6,800	8,000	12,000
Newport	3,800	4,640[1]	6,200	7,500	11,000

[1] Actual census.
Source: Bridenbaugh, Carl, *Cities in the Wilderness* (New York, 1938), pp. 6n, 143, 303, and *Cities In Revolt* (New York, 1955), pp. 5, 216.

lation approximately to double every 20–25 years, a trend that is marked after 1660. They also exhibit the tendency of the southern colonies, from Maryland to Georgia, to grow more rapidly than those of New England after the close of the seventeenth century. Increasing numbers of Negro slaves explain the phenomenon. Relatively few before about 1680, their subsequent increase was so rapid that in 1770 they formed 40 percent of the population of the five original southern colonies. In any estimate of national income they would constitute one of the forms of capital.

The evidence concerning commodities and shipping, conveniently available in *Historical Statistics of the United States,*[2] pertains in the main to the eighteenth century. One exception is tobacco: in 1616 England received merely 2,500 pounds from America, a figure that rose to more than 28 million in 1688. In 1771, Great Britain received from the colonies 105 million pounds. Not surprisingly, in 1770 the value of tobacco among total American exports to all destinations was nearly double that of bread and flour, with fish, rice, indigo, and wheat following in order of importance among articles valued at £100,000 sterling, or more.

Among eighteenth-century data are those for rice, which reveal an eight-fold increase in quantity exported from Charleston to Great Britain between 1725 and 1774. Data available on other exports, some of them identified with particular ports of origin, inform us for varying periods of time of the quantities or values of such items as whale oil, timber and timber products, pitch, tar, and turpentine, furs, silk (South Carolina and Georgia), iron in pigs, bars, and castings, and a few wrought-iron products (anchors, scythes, and axes). In 1775 the value of all colonial exports to England was about seven times that of 1697. The outgoing tonnage of major ports also increased. Boston's doubled between 1714–17 and 1772, New York's almost doubled between 1715–18 and 1754, Charleston's rose one and one-half times between 1731

[2] U.S. Bureau of the Census, *Historical Statistics of the United States, Colonial Times to 1957* (Washington, D. C., 1960).

and 1772, and that of Philadelphia more than tripled between 1730–34 and 1770–74. In 1772 domestic production of iron totalled 27,600 tons, of which 8,213 were exported and the remaining 19,387 consumed directly in the form of cast-iron products or goods finished from pig and bar iron. Most commercial manufacturing was closely articulated with the needs of foreign trade, consisting of naval stores manufactories, ropewalks, canvas and sailmaking shops, sugar and salt refineries, anchor and chain forges, cooperage establishments, lumberyards, breweries and distilleries, gristmills, blacksmiths, shoe and carpenter shops, cargo warehouses, and shipbuilding yards.

The essential question is whether this considerable economic expansion is equivalent to economic growth. Did output per unit of labor input rise so that the amount of goods available per person also rose, thus permitting rising standards of living for the whole society? Or was the economic expansion the product of an increasing population? While a definitive answer to these questions seems to me impossible I suggest the hypothesis that some increase in output per person did occur: what gave rise to it were productivity gains deriving from a favorable land-man ratio, and from increased capital in the form of slaves. It is also probable that the pull of expanding foreign markets on subsistence agriculture, by reducing unemployed or underemployed resources, also contributed to growth. Nor must one rule out the possibility that some contribution began to be made by the apparent increase in the amount of industrial production in the later eighteenth century. Because of obstacles to capital formation and technical efficiency that will be discussed later, much of the increase in total output seems to me attributable to population increase. The net effect, then, was this: while "average output per capita" rose, in general it rose slowly and not by very much. This is a consequence quite compatible with evidence of significantly rising standards of living among some parts of the population. In part, my thesis will be that these people were relatively few in number, that their own higher standards of living represented consumption preferences which, by reducing the rate of capital formation, kept both their own and society's standards from rising even higher and more rapidly, and that for most people, including them, resources were significantly underemployed.

Land

Given the overwhelmingly agricultural character of the colonial economy, it is clear that land (natural resources) formed by far the most important constituent of capital. But not raw land, not unimproved land. The quantity and quality of natural resources depend not alone upon nature but upon man as well. Scanty resources did not prevent the Venetians from playing a dynamic role in the economic development of Europe from the twelfth to the seventeenth centuries, nor tiny Holland from surging to the forefront of "capitalist" development in the seventeenth century. The resources of the United States support at unprecedentedly high levels of living a mid-twentieth-century population that presses the two hundred million mark. Prior to the arrival of the Europeans, these resources supported something fewer than one million natives, and far less well. And the early years of Virginia are marked by a bitter struggle to obtain a dependable supply of food: by January of the second year of settlement at Jamestown, 67 of the original 105 colonists were dead of disease and malnutrition. Resources, in a word, belong as much among the consequences of economic growth as among its causes.

"Knowledge," the eminent English nineteenth-century economist Alfred Marshall wrote, "is our most powerful engine of production; it enables us to subdue Nature and force her to satisfy our wants." Once the Virginians, and colonists elsewhere as well, had learned from the Indians how to plant maize, once they had determined the fitness and limitations of the country for various crops, they had begun to accumulate their first capital: a store of experience that would make their pathway easier in the future. Only then could the land and its resources begin to affect their welfare. To understand the relationship between land and colonial standards of living requires an examination of two problems: (1) to what extent land was available to the settlers, and (2) what disposition they made of its product.

Motivated by a desire to promote British trade, reward political favorites, discharge debt, and rid the nation of its "surplus" population, the British Crown made vast grants of land in the American wilderness to trading corporations and private individuals. It is this fact, in addition to the early utopian ideals of some of the grantees and the systems of land tenure both numerous and complex, that explains the wide discrepancies found in the sizes of individual holdings. These range from the early Virginia headright of 50 acres to the 47 million acres granted William Penn, from the generally small farms of New England to the great manors of Maryland and the Carolinas. The degree of equality in land ownership was indeed, observes the leading authority, Marshall Harris, "far from perfect."

It came closest to "perfection" under the New England town system. Here lands that had been granted initially by the General Court to a group of settlers to permit the seating of a new town, were subsequently divided after 1635 by the towns themselves into home lots. Some of these lots were as small as one-quarter acre, others as large as 22 acres. New England was a land of small proprietorships and family farms, and nowhere was there to be found the extensive manors or plantations of the middle and southern colonies. In the latter colonies small farms alternated with large estates, a consequence not so much of the original headright system as of the system of land disposal by sale, which paved the way for widespread speculation and engrossment. Indeed, by 1782 Robert Morris could say to the Continental Congress:

Yet a large proportion of America is the property of great landholders, they monopolize it without cultivation, they are (for the most part) at no expence either of money or personal service to defend it, and keeping the price higher by monopoly than otherwise it would be they impede the settlement and Culture [cultivation] of the Country.[3]

[3] *Journals of the Continental Congress,* 1774-1789, ed. Gaillard Hunt (Washington, D. C., 1914), XXII, 429-47. Letter dated July 29.

Despite the existence of wide inequality in the sizes of holdings and of some leasehold tenures in all the colonies, it seems that relatively few people who wished land were unable to obtain it. Under the headright system, according to Harris, land ownership was not denied any person because of race, creed, or previous economic or social condition. Under the sale system, which soon replaced headrighting in most places save New England, prices varied from time to time and place to place. Harris does find, however, a "distinct long-term rising trend" in the price of raw land. Lewis C. Gray concludes that most of the available "good" land in the southern colonies had been taken up by the time of the Revolution. In Maryland, Clarence P. Gould finds that between 1720 and 1730 prices appear to have averaged about five shillings per acre; between 1763 and 1765 "medium" land brought approximately £ 1 an acre, with more desirable offerings commanding from £ 2 to £ 3. It is possible that to some extent these increases participated in a secular price rise which Arthur H. Cole and others have traced in various commodities from 1720 to the end of the Revolutionary period. The scantiness of surviving statistics, uncertainty about their comparability, and the great length of the period to which they relate make generalization extremely precarious. But Harris ventures the judgment that the price of land was "not too high for the settler."

On the whole this seems a reasonable conclusion. The demand for settlers far exceeded the supply. The interests of imperial trade required colonists to provide raw materials and to buy finished goods. The gains of proprietors depended upon their ability to dispose of their land grants. Individual colonies competed with each other for emigrants in order to provide a widened tax base for essential community services and protection at the frontiers against the French, Spanish, and Indians. Easy attitudes toward squatting, gifts of land, sales with payments deferred—all bespoke the need for people. And bespoke, too, the other half of the equation—the existence of a vast domain. Fundamentally, it was the favorable land-man ratio that made possible in all the colonies a wide distribution of individually owned and privately operated farms.

The produce which nature returns to the work of man, Alfred Marshall once wrote, is her effective demand for population. If we place the land-man ratio in the light of Marshall's observation, we may see more clearly its pertinence to colonial welfare. The population supply was far less than nature's demand for people, and she treated them well. It was a situation in which the erosive power of diminishing returns might indefinitely be postponed. Let us put the minimum case: families on the land are unlikely to have starved. While this question will be examined later in somewhat more detail, it is pertinent here to cite the judgment of Carl Bridenbaugh that pauperism in the "more rural communities [was] almost nonexistent" in the seventeenth century. How small it must have been for the population as a whole throughout the colonial years is evident from the fact that even at their end scarcely one person in ten lived in a city.

Production for Subsistence and for Markets

Granted the widespread ownership of landed capital in colonial America, we have now to determine the nature of that capital. Was it producer's capital, which farmers used to raise market crops, or was it a kind of consumer's capital, employed for family sustenance rather than for purposes of sale? How high levels of living rose above subsistence depended upon the extent to which rural families were able to raise an agricultural surplus and exchange it for manufactured goods. The question, then, is this: to what extent were farm families self-sufficient, and to what extent were they linked to a market economy? Self-sufficiency, it should be made clear, usually had a dual aspect. It entailed not only production of crops for family consumption rather than sale, but also of clothing, utensils, furniture, and other household manufactures.

Complete self-sufficiency was rare. In the main it was only to be found in hilly and mountainous regions, especially along the stony ridges of New England, and on the most inaccessible reaches of the frontier. Farmers constantly sought a marketable product, not only to exchange for such indispensable articles as ammunition and salt but to better their standards of living. Relatively few farm families could have remained untouched by commercial intercourse, even if only that of the visits by wandering peddlers to remote hamlets. Most of these families were in comparatively easy reach during the seventeenth century, for even at its end, with the main exceptions of farmers who had gone up the Connecticut and Hudson river valleys, settlement both North and South was confined to land within about fifty miles of the coast. Rivers like the James, Potomac, Delaware, Hudson, and Connecticut served as the principal lines of penetration into the interior. And in much of the South settlers along the river courses could send their produce in flatboats to the coast. In the eighteenth century almost all of the settled backcountry of South Carolina and Georgia was connected with Charleston and Savannah by inland navigation or by wagon roads.

The more westerly penetrations of the eighteenth century appear to have included country stores. William B. Weeden mentions such a store in the "rural Connecticut" of 1704. Gray speaks of "numerous local stores" in Virginia and Maryland after settlement had pushed into the Blue Ridge Mountains and entered the Valley of Virginia. Many had been established by Scottish and other outport merchants who entered the backcountry when they discovered that the Tidewater tobacco business was largely in the hands of London merchants. The "few small local stores" that grew up in various parts of South Carolina in the eighteenth century were branches of Charleston firms or acted as agencies for Charleston merchants, selling imported commodities to the planters in exchange for their crops.

The case of Jonathan Trumbull well illustrates the middleman function of the rural store. Better known as Connecticut's patriot governor, the Trumbull of mid-century maintained a country store at Lebanon, where he bartered gunpowder and flints, pots and pans, looking glasses, copies of Watts' *Psalms,* and numerous other items brought from Boston, for the flaxseed, deerskins, grain, furs, potatoes and other produce of the surrounding countryside. How small might be the hamlets in which stores located is illustrated by Colonel John May's record of a visit to the Ohio country in 1789. Surprised by coming upon five log cabins in a clearing of fifty acres, a place called Mingo Bottom, the Colonel entered in his diary: "Yet small as the settlement is, here is a store, with a very good assortment of goods, to the value, as I suppose, of £ 1,000."

How far west were these stores to be found? What were their precise locations in relation to settlements and to roads and rivers connecting with the coast? In what numbers did they exist, and what was their scale of operations? If we had answers to these questions, we would be able to draw more meaningful conclusions concerning the commercial impact of rural markets on upcountry agriculture. Yet it is surely reasonable to assume that no storekeeper could function unless he were able to transport country produce to the coast and manufactured goods back home. To the extent that settlement moved away from the rivers and main roads it must have moved to a higher degree of compulsory self-sufficiency. Thus, in referring to the eighteenth-century Germans who streamed down both sides of the Blue Ridge Mountains into the New South, or southern half of the Old West, Gray says: "Both their peasant training and their remoteness from markets inclined them toward a diversified system of farming involving a large measure of self-sufficiency."

The phrase "large measure" is the key one here. It is the measure that matters, the degree of self-sufficiency. For if complete isolation from all markets was rare, so too was a complete commitment to commercialized agriculture. Numerous specialized farms or plantations devoted large parts of their resources to the production of one or two crops for foreign markets. In this category fall the tobacco farms and plantations of tidewater Maryland, Virginia, North Carolina, and Georgia, and the large grain farms of Pennsylvania, western Maryland, and the Valley of Virginia. Other familiar staples are the indigo of the Carolinas and the rice of South Carolina, which accounted for one-half to two-thirds of the value of the colony's exports during the eighteenth century. Yet in the southern heartland of highly commercialized agriculture, planters raised corn, wheat, and other foods for their slaves and employed many of the latter in the manufacture of cloth, hogsheads, bricks, and other products. Most colonial agriculture falls between the extremes of high self-sufficiency and high commercialization. In all probability it falls closer to the self-sufficiency end than to the other.

It is true that a flat conclusion of this nature does violence to the change that occurred from time to time and from one region to another. Thus, in the early colonial period a considerable amount of self-sufficiency existed even in the southern Tidewater because of the irregularity of commercial intercourse. In Virginia in the 1680's the entry and exit of tobacco planters from the market appears to have fluctuated with the price of the crop. Soil erosion from overcropping, especially with tobacco, often compelled the farmer who was unable or unwilling to move either to allow his tired land to go fallow or to put in subsistence crops. But not always so: increasingly after the mid-eighteenth century, one-time tobacco planters in parts of Maryland were shifting from tobacco to wheat destined for export.

A patch of tobacco was the crop of the little man wherever it could be grown: next to cattle it was the principal money crop of backcountry farmers. But it took "a family" a month to clear an acre of trees and underbrush. And the weed required intensive and careful labor, from the preparing of seedbed to hoeing, cutting, curing, sorting, packing, and marketing, the latter often by rolling the hogsheads to shipping centers. Larger planters could more easily than small farmers afford the labor first of indentured servants and then, especially after about 1680, of slaves. Most small farmers had to depend on the labor of their families, which thus tended to be large. However, the late eighteenth-century Virginia wills examined by Robert E. and B. Katherine Brown disclose numerous small farmers with one or two slaves.

Yet even at the end of the colonial period there remained a large amount of farming that was self-sufficient to a high degree. That its greatest concentration was to be found in New England should occasion little surprise, for here is a region in which the alluvial coastal plain, extending from tidewater to fall line, forms a narrow belt of thin, rocky soil. Inhospitable in climate, the area early became one of small, diversified farms. The area was capable, to be sure, of exporting livestock, timber supplies, corn and other foods to West Indian and other markets, but it was far richer in cod and whale fisheries, in a ranging commerce, and in the ship-yards that produced the means of carrying the commerce. Not until the coming of the railroad, and in some cases the automobile, would the subsistence farmers between the three major rivers of New Hampshire, in the hill country north of Lake Winnipesaukee, and in similar parts of Massachusetts and Connecticut, enter the market economy.

Subsistence farmers in many other parts of the country were on or near transportation routes to be developed much sooner, for example, along the Mohawk in New York and in the upper Dela-ware regions of New Jersey and Pennsylvania. It is in the South, perhaps the most heavily commercialized agricultural region of the country, that the existence of a significantly high degree of self-sufficiency is surprising. Yet Lewis C. Gray, the historian of southern agriculture, says: "In the colonial period especially, it is probable that the great majority of inhabitants were engaged in types of economy that approximated the principle of self-sufficiency." For the new nation as a whole the length of time in which a significant degree of self-sufficiency would continue to exist is suggested by Rolla M. Tryon's conclusion that household manu-facture remained important until about 1830.

Scarcities of capital and labor and inadequacies of transporta-tion were mainly responsible for this result. Its consequences are

fraught with meaning for the economy as a whole. By circum-
scribing the ability of most farmers to concentrate a larger share
of their resources on production for market, these scarcities kept
incomes per capita low. Low incomes necessarily limited farmer's
demands for manufactured goods. Since most people were farmers,
the limited ability of farmers to buy narrowed the domestic market
and thus helped prevent the growth of domestic manufactories
large enough to produce economies of scale. Only the low unit costs
of enterprises of larger scale might have competed with those of
England, which produced goods for wide foreign markets.

To be sure, shortages of capital funds and high wages also
helped restrict the growth of large-scale manufacturing, but these
shortages would have been less severe had the level of agricultural
output and income been higher than it was. While Gray believes
that in the case of tobacco the greater use of the plow and other
instruments of tillage "resulted in some increase in product per
man" between the early seventeenth and the later eighteenth
centuries, the general quality of these instruments is indicated in
Curtis Nettels' judgment that the farmer's tools "would have been
familiar in ancient Babylonia." Some improvement in agricultural
techniques occurred, particularly in the case of upcountry Germans.
But as was repeatedly to happen in subsequent years, these had
little impact on agriculture as a whole. The generally primitive
state of agricultural technology limited output per capita (and
hence income per capita), and it was this, together with poor
transport facilities, that severely restricted the size of the domestic
market.

The Planters: Sources of Operating Capital

I have referred to the larger planters as men who could more
easily "afford" large estates, servants or slaves, tools and implements for clearing land, and other necessary means of devoting
their resources more fully to commercial production. What were
the sources of the operating capital with which they made and then

worked the fixed capital of land? Where did they obtain the purchasing power they were able to convert into these two forms of "real" capital? Their main sources appear to have been three-fold: British loans and investments; equipment, supplies, and claims to American land brought by emigrants from England; and earnings from planting "ploughed back" into the land. While it is impossible to quantify these sources so as to display their relative significance, it appears that the two British channels deserve most emphasis.

Great quasi-public trading companies, privileged, chartered, and joint-stock, had served as the initial funnels through which English capital funds and labor sought to exploit the new-world opportunities opened by voyages of discovery and exploration. Overwhelmed by heavy costs of settlement and blinded by fools-gold schemes for easy wealth, they had failed to return profits to their investors. So too had failed the subsidiary colonizing associa-tions which in some instances grew out of them. The private planta-tion, a method of uniting English capital, the labor of indentured servant or slave, and the resident management of the planter, emerged from these early failures. "Venture" and "capital," pre-viously united in the person of an English absentee investor, split off from each other: the venturer now came in person to America to manage his enterprises and drew upon English capital in the form of mercantile credit. Some of these early enterprisers, Gray believes, "undoubtedly brought with them all or a part of the requisite capital." Certainly the "ambitious younger sons of middle-class families" who came to Virginia in the wave of the second generation of emigrants between 1640 and approximately 1670 brought "material advantages" with them. The recent researches of Bernard Bailyn have shown that they brought with them family claims to land in the colony, inherited shares of the original Com-pany stock, or "a variety of forms of capital that might provide the basis for secure family fortunes."

Probably upon most planters, however, as upon colonial enter-prise generally, pressed the scarcity of capital funds and labor that characterizes a newly-opened country. Even as late as 1680, in reply to the question "What obstruction do you find to the improvement of the trade and navigation of your Corporation?" the Governor of Connecticut specified the "want of men of estates to venture abroad, and of money at home for the management of trade, and labor being so deare with us." Scattered evidence suggests that interest rates were high. Gray reports they ranged from 8 to 10 per cent on well-secured loans in South Carolina during the greater part of the colonial period. Just before the Revolution the legal rate was lowered to 8 per cent in both that colony and Georgia. Massachusetts in 1641 restricted the rate to 8 per cent so that there would not be "usury amongst us contrary to the laws of God," but it lowered the rate to 6 per cent in 1693. However, in the judgment of Victor S. Clark, the costs of capital funds in relation to profit margins were not "excessive." That the productivity of funds was higher in America than in Britain in 1765 is suggested by James Habersham's remark to an English correspondent that 8 per cent could be "as well if not better paid by a Carefull Person either in the commercial or planting way here, than £ 5 per Ct. [5 per cent] with you."

It is this greater marginal efficiency of capital funds that attracted British loans and investments to America, in shipbuilding, iron works, the seventeenth-century fisheries, trade, manufacturing, and southern agriculture. Immediately after the Revolution John Lord Sheffield remarked that the "greater part of the colony commerce was carried on by means of British capitals," with "at least four-fifths" of the importations from Europe being "at all times made upon credit." "The greater part both of the exportations and coasting trade of America," Adam Smith asserts in *The Wealth of Nations* (1776), "is carried on by the capitals of merchants who reside in Great Britain. Even the stores and warehouses from which goods are retailed in some provinces, particularly in Virginia and Maryland, belong many of them to merchants who reside in the mother country." Victor S. Clark says further: "Until the very end of the colonial period, speculative enterprises in

America, including the most important manufacturing undertakings, were financed very largely with English or German money, though occasionally wealthy colonists cooperated in these projects." That the achievement of political independence did not automatically bring to an end American dependence upon British capital, particularly in the case of the southern planter, is clearly seen in the following evaluation made in June 1792 by William Heth of Bermuda Hundred, Virginia, for the benefit of Alexander Hamilton: "The trade of this state is carried on chiefly with foreign capital. Those engaged in it, hardly deserve the name of merchants, being the factors, agents and Shop-keepers of the Merchants and Manufacturers of Gt. Britain—and their business to dispose of the goods of that, for the produce of this country, and remit it to the order of their principals with whom the profits of the trade of *course* centre.—"

Because of the cheapness of land and the ability to obtain headright claims to it by importing servants or slaves, the amount of funds required by the southern planters was not as large as it was to be in the later pre-Civil War period. Gray reports that about the year 1775 the establishment of a tobacco plantation of two thousand acres involved an expenditure of approximately £ 1,000 for slaves, £ 300 for buildings and furniture, £ 60 for implements and arms, £ 50 for a small sloop, £ 265 for livestock, £ 40 for land fees, and £ 100 for orchard and small miscellaneous items. The total came to £ 1,915 sterling. At about the same period the cost of a rice or indigo plantation of "moderate" size amounted to approximately £ 1,000 more. Leila Sellers presents an estimate of about £ 2,500 for a South Carolina rice plantation of two hundred acres (£ 100), forty "working hands" (£ 1,800), annual wages of an overseer (£ 50), and various tools and supplies.

English merchants customarily provided these supplies on one-year credit, with the planter's crop serving as security for the advance. In the early years of settlement, credit purchases of servants and slaves were of less importance to Virginia and Maryland than to South Carolina and Georgia. The two tobacco colonies very largely used indentured servants for the first three-quarters of the seventeenth century, and the initial costs of servants usually amounted only to about one-fifth those of slaves. But the indebtedness of the tobacco planters mounted in the late seventeenth and eighteenth centuries with the increasingly rapid introduction of slaves.

Were figures for British capital exports to America available, they would undoubtedly show the mainstream flowing into the plantation agriculture of the southern mainland and British West Indies. The southern planter, according to Gray, borrowed "much" of his capital funds, and in the British West Indies "most of the estates" were burdened with heavy encumbrances to persons residing in Great Britain. British law flowed in the wake of British capital in an effort to protect profit margins on these investments. While this body of law will be examined more closely later, it should be noted here that the profits to be won by transshipping tobacco from Great Britain to the Continent led to the "enumeration" of that article in the Navigation Acts. And if tobacco was thus forbidden by law to be shipped by colonial merchants to any point outside the British empire, so too was rice (to which, however, limited concessions were made after 1750) and indigo. However, it was not colonial merchants but English merchants, not colonial shipping but English shipping (and after the Act of Union of 1707, that of the Scots as well) that dominated the greatest trade route of the colonial period, the route which ran back and forth across the Atlantic between Great Britain and her southern and West Indian colonies. As late as 1769–71 four-fifths of the traffic crossing the Atlantic was carried in British bottoms. In a word, British mercantile houses provided the credit required for production and marketing, and with the aid of laws enacted to promote the interests of the merchants and the navy of Great Britain, the same houses provided almost the entire machinery of marketing itself.

Geography facilitated this dominance in the case of the tobacco colonies. The numerous navigable rivers of Maryland and Virginia diffused trade throughout the two provinces, long preventing its concentration in port cities under the control of native merchants. There was no need for the intermediation of natives: English ships simply penetrated the country to the wharves of the larger planters, unloaded their supplies, and put on tobacco for the homeward voyage. The cargo was consigned to the same merchant who had shipped the supplies, and it represented payment on account of obligations thus incurred as well as previous ones. Many smaller planters and farmers less favorably situated with respect to navigable waters purchased supplies from the larger planters and sold or consigned their tobacco to them. With the movement of tobacco away from the Tidewater into the Piedmont after the early eighteenth century, the consignment system gradually gave way to a method of direct purchase. Finding English merchants in control of Tidewater business, Scottish mercantile houses dispatched factors to supervise the general operations of chains of stores opened in the backcountry of both provinces. The stores seem to have offered merchandise on credit to any grower "from whom a purchase of at least 300 hogsheads of tobacco could be made annually," the typical scarcity of currency in the backcountry making it natural to resort to a system of bookkeeping barter. One of the most recent students of their practices, James H. Soltow, makes clear that the planters' accounts were supposed to be settled at the close of the crop year. But it was sometimes a difficult policy to enforce, and some balances remained unpaid as long as four or five years.

South of Virginia the shoal channels of the inland streams did not obstruct navigation by small craft but prevented ocean-going vessels from penetrating inland. It was a situation inviting both urbanization and the rise of a numerous group of small native middlemen, known at the time as "country" factors. Charleston emerged after 1670 as the commercial funnel for an agricultural district embracing South Carolina, parts of North Carolina, Georgia, and, after 1763, East and West Florida as well. At Charleston, and also at smaller ports in the district, country factors served as retail middlemen between planters and larger wholesale merchants, buying from the former and selling to the latter. Sometimes, however, they imported goods from colonies to the north, from the West Indies, and even from England. Despite the differences between the Carolina country and the region of the Chesapeake, "the masters of business," the men in "command of the shipping and wholesale trade," to use the language of Leila Sellers, were, in both areas, the factors of British merchants. It was they who provided indentured servants, slaves, and other supplies to planters on credit and directed the exportation of the planters' staples.

British credit thus came to southern agriculture through a number of channels, sometimes directly, sometimes circuitously, in the latter case being extended first to a resident factor, storekeeper, or colonial merchant and then by one of them to the planter. Larger planters, who had themselves obtained credit directly from an English mercantile house—on a "wholesale" basis, as it were— often proceeded to "retail" it to the smaller planters and farmers in their neighborhoods. To what extent was the shortage of capital funds in the hands of the southern planters owing to their intimate dependency upon the British?

The Planters: The Question of Capital Losses

From contemporaries through Washington, Jefferson, and Calhoun to modern students, much has been written on both sides of the question whether an inordinate part of the profits of agriculture were siphoned off from the planters by the merchants, principally English and Scottish, who supplied them with credit and dominated their marketing mechanism. Were planters given too little for their crops and charged too much for the supplies they received in exchange? Were they made to bear the burden of illicit handling charges, not credited for duties refunded on crops re-exported to the Continent, and otherwise victimized? How difficult it is to generalize will be obvious. Unquestionably there is some truth in all the allegations; the problem is, how much? It seems to me that the most any student of the debate can do—and fair-minded ones from Gray to Soltow have done so—is to admit that the merchants had the upper hand, wished to employ it to their own advantage, and sometimes succeeded in doing so but at least as often were forestalled by the existence of competition among themselves.

It would nevertheless be difficult to conclude that the situation was as favorable to the planters as would have been the case had they developed their own marketing facilities instead of depending upon the shipping, insurance, and other services provided in the main by British merchants. It is true that statistical estimates of the commerce of the southern colonies indicate an excess of exports over imports throughout the colonial period. The trade balance amounted approximately to £ 147,000 a year as early as 1700, and for the period 1700–73 the total balance was almost £ 11,000,000. But these figures are deceptive in that they omit entirely the large cost of imported slaves and omit as well the costs of freights, insurance, commissions, taxes, interest on debts to the British, and other "invisible" items of trade. In a word, the lower returns to investments attributable to the subordinate market position of the planters were probably considerable.

If losses through market subordination reduced the net proceeds from southern exports, the planters' own propensity to consume, mounting in social urgency with the advancing eighteenth century, limited still more the amount of permissible capital formation. The better textiles, furniture, plate, and other refinements that helped lift the material basis of life above the level of the first frontier century represent an understandable choice of alternative uses of income. Yet much of the income so converted appears to have reflected a conscious emulation of an old-world gentry by that of the new. The purchase of consumption goods on credit, says Gray, was in "considerable measure" in the nature of "conspicuous and competitive" expenditure. If it is fair to cite Jefferson's familiar plaint that "long experience has proved to us that there never was an instance of a man's getting out of debt who was once in the hands of a tobacco merchant and bound to consign his tobacco to him," it is also fair to call attention to the consumption component of that debt.

To characterize the planter as a man more interested in consumption than in production, as unconcerned with ways of increasing his income, would be misleading and unfair. One thinks of the first William Byrd, who, arriving in Virginia about 1670, thereafter became planter, colonizer, wholesale exporter and importer, retail storekeeper, Indian trader, prospector for ores, and miller, among other things. The activities of his contemporary, William Fitzhugh, were almost as diverse. One thinks of Robert Carter of Corotoman, an earlier eighteenth-century Virginian whom Louis B. Wright characterizes as "an industrious and astute businessman," maintaining a "shrewd oversight of his tobacco sales, his purchases of commodities or securities, his land transactions, and the multifarious details connected with his great plantations." And there are many others, such as Robert Carter of Nomini Hall, whose diligent pursuit of multiple business activities is justly well remembered. Lewis C. Gray makes perfectly clear that on efficient estates planters used something like an elementary form of scientific management in organizing their labor force. "Many" of the planters of Virginia and Maryland, he says were "zealously engaged in accumulating large fortunes, living mainly on the produce of their estates and reinvesting most of their income in land and slaves." One may agree with James H. Soltow on "the business-mindedness of a significant portion of the tobacco producers."

On the other hand, Gray records that "Many planters kept no systematic accounts," although perhaps the majority either personally or via overseers kept records of monetary receipts and disbursements, inventories of stock and equipment, and various supplementary memoranda. Of strict "cost accounting," he notes, "there was very little in the South." One may add that there was very little in any field of colonial enterprise anywhere. Inadequate records, together with "long delays in exchange between Englishmen and Americans," Evarts B. Greene believed, often left the planter ignorant of the exact state of his balance. The system "certainly did not promote sound business methods." In 1785 Jefferson himself remarked that the planters were "careless of their interests . . . thoughtless in their expenses and in all their transactions of business." It is specifically to the Chesapeake tobacco trade that Jacob M. Price refers in attributing its dominance by "outsiders" to "the failure of the planters to think like capitalists or to live like prudent speculators." My own inclination is to cast in that character a more considerable area of the colonial South. So far as the tobacco colonies were concerned, the increasing change in the 18th century from the older consignment system to one of direct sale to resident Scotch factors appears to have been of crucial importance. Under the newer system the planter, no longer the owner of the tobacco shipped to Europe, had no need to maintain a detailed correspondence concerning the quality of it, or of the incoming merchandise he desired in return. Nor need he any longer concern himself with the numerous costs of shipping, importation, and sales, nor with insurance and freight. Having a lesser need to concern himself with matters of trade, the planter was more likely to develop an attitude of disdain for it. Jefferson's characterization certainly suggests that many did so. Many became absentees and learned to discount the value of labor in a society where it was done by slaves. In none of these respects would the passage of time introduce substantive change. Cotton would replace tobacco, and New York merchants and bankers those of Great Britain, but the economic life of the South would continue to be dominated by "outsiders," and there would remain both dependency and slavery, the attitude toward labor, and the entrepreneurial consequence of these combined facts. Regardless then of the direction in which the balance of typicality may fall, it appears true that there existed within the planter group as a whole a significant amount of underemployed resources, not least of which was the resource of entrepreneurship. Had the goal of profit maximization permeated the group, had it employed systematic accounting to enhance its control of productive resources, had it made a determined effort to gain control of the marketing mechanism, its level of income would have been higher. Granted these business objectives and techniques, a larger proportion of its income would have been "ploughed back" into production, increasing the rate of new capital formation, and this would have raised average investment and income for the economy as a whole. That the value system of only some of the planters can be described in these terms is to be noted and not deplored. All systems, all values, have their opportunity costs, and the choice of some alternatives implies the surrender of others. We are justly revolted that the cultural achievements of many representatives of this regional civilization should have rested upon inhumanity to people of another race. Had the planters been monolithically devoted to business goals, the amount of inhumanity to living men might well have increased to a far greater extent than did the contribution to humaneness of dead letters.

III

The Dependent Years: II

The Protestant Ethic

We have now to consider the possibility that southern value systems contained to a far lesser degree some element which, fulsomely present in the North, helps explain why "capitalism remained far less developed in . . . colonies [which were to become] the later Southern States of the United States of America." The quoted words are those of Max Weber, the eminent German sociologist, who maintained that there existed an intimate relationship between what he called "The Protestant Ethic and The Spirit of Capitalism." Weber traced the origins of the ethic to the religious writings of the sixteenth-century French theologian John Calvin. The beginning point was Calvin's announcement that God had decided ineluctably the eternal fate of every soul forever to be born and that no man could know whether he was among the gathered or the damned. To the hungrily devout who both then and later listened and believed, no pain was comparable to the uncertainty of election. Life became tolerable only if one assumed himself to be among the chosen. Having made the assumption, the corollary was psychologically natural that moments of success in one's "calling," or life-task set by God, were evidences of election, signs of

divine favor. One therefore sought to multiply these signs by ply-
ing one's calling, however humble it might be, with an unflagging
diligence, soberly following regular ways. Habits of this kind, as
even critic Alan Simpson notes, although formed for religious
purposes, could hardly fail to mold the kind of character most
likely to achieve material success. The same emphasis upon diligence in one's earthly calling, upon frugality and a rational and
orderly conduct of life, also characterized Quakerism, which, while
rejecting the doctrine of predestination, developed in England and
in the Netherlands under the influence of Calvinist asceticism.

Weber's thesis is essentially one that seeks to explain change
in the external world in terms of the kinds of human beings who
confront that world. Honesty, industry, zeal, punctuality, frugality,
and regularity—these were the important elements of the "Protestant ethic." These were the Puritan traits, Weber maintained, that
advanced the growth of "capitalism" by promoting rational, systematic business conduct. They bade a man work hard in his
calling and shun frivolous expenditures for purposes of personal
enjoyment. Their effect, therefore, was to promote the accumulation of capital.

Now Weber's opponents are legion, and this is not the place
to review a literature of criticism that is vast and focused mainly
on the applications of his thesis to the development of "capitalism"
in western Europe. Let it suffice to recall Ralph Barton Perry's
point that fifteenth-century Florence was capitalistic but not puritan, that the Boer republics were puritan but not capitalistic, and
that the Venetians, the Hanseatic League, the Fuggers, the Medici,
and the Rothschilds "contributed to the development of modern
commerce and finance without deriving inspiration from protestantism." Certainly it cannot be maintained that under all circumstances the Protestant ethic was a condition necessary to the growth
of "capitalism." However, Gabriel Kolko has recently reminded
us that Weber not only viewed America as " 'the field of [capital-
ism's] highest devleopment' " but also "continually referred to
colonial American history to sustain his thesis." Did the Protestant

ethic promote rational, systematic business conduct among the Puritan merchants of New England? An effort to answer this question requires, first, an examination of Puritanism in early New England, and second, an inquiry into the relationship between the motivations of merchants and the external conditions of foreign commerce. These conditions were common to foreign traders throughout the colonies and we shall call upon records of mercantile experience in Philadelphia, New York, and Baltimore as well as in New England to illustrate their nature.

"Capitalism," Carl N. Degler well says, "came to America in the first ships." Profits to be won from trade and precious metals induced the financial support essential to colonization, and the business goals and techniques underlying the voyages of settlement reflected European "capitalistic" developments that trace their origins to at least the twelfth century. But this is not to deny the overwhelmingly religious motivations of many of the first settlers. In John Winthrop's celebrated sermon aboard the *Arbella,* in the Plymouth covenant of 1620, and in the opening Article of the New England Confederation of 1643 one hears a clear voice saying, in the words of the latter, " . . . we aime, namly, to advance the kingdom of our Lord Jesus Christ, and to injoye the liberties of the Gospell in puritie with peace." The means was to be the New England Way, a Bible commonwealth in which saints of church and state would govern a community of the elect, a corporation whose members, to cite the Cambridge Platform (1629), would "give themselves unto the Lord, to the observing of the ordinances of Christ together in the same society." But between these holy intents and the disenchantment expressed in the jeremiads of the late seventeenth century there intervened the carnal world of trade.

Acknowledging the contribution of trade to the sustenance of the community, the Fathers sought to subordinate it to the true end of man. As early as 1633 Boston established a "Thursday market." Its purpose was to regulate more effectively the conduct of local commercial transactions, "to place the selling of country

produce," as Weeden puts it, "under more effective control."
Other towns took similar action, as, for example, Bristol did in
1696, forbidding the sale of produce on any but a designated day.
As in the cities of medieval Europe, local authorities outlawed
the tripartite sins of trade: forestalling, regrating, and engrossing.
Early statutes fixed the wages of scarce labor and the prices of
basic commodities. The assize of bread, Richard B. Morris tells
us, "was the most persistent regulatory measure employed in
American towns down through the eighteenth century; but other
price, quantity, and quality regulations included the assizes of
casks, leather, wood, and bricks." In general, he adds, the early
settlers accepted the medieval doctrine of the "just price."

The recent researches of John Baldwin have shown that in
the medieval view a price regarded as "just" was not what generations of earlier scholars have believed it to be. It was no alchemic
mixture of component costs designed somehow to enable the
seller to maintain his customary place in a hierarchical social
order. Rather, it was the market price, the going rate, a value
determined by supply and demand. So it was in colonial America,
as the admonition of the Reverend John Cotton makes plain: "A
man may not sell above the current price, i.e., such a price as is
usual in the time and place, and as another (who knows the worth
of the commodity) would give for it, if he had occasion to use
it." But where scarcity existed, "there men may raise their price; for
now it is the hand of God upon the commodity, and not the
person."

What was deplored, in sum, was private, out-of-the-market
negotiation that took advantage of circumstances of special need.
This is the situation to which Increase Mather referred when he
wrote in 1674: "A poor man cometh amongst you, and he must
have a commodity whatever it cost him, and you will make him
give whatever you please, and put what price you please upon
what he hath to give too, without respecting the just value of
the thing." Two years later, the Reverend Mather also attacked
the "odious sin of usury," but Puritan New England, as had

medieval Europe, pointed its prohibition not at commercial loans involving risk but at interest charged on loans to the poor and needy.

To prevent the possibility of victimization of the ignorant or needy through sales arranged by private agreement or outside of market hours, and also to discourage merchants from giving in to the temptation of placing their material welfare above their spiritual health, the Fathers in 1633 had made the charging of extortionate prices punishable by law. In 1639 merchant Robert Keayne was convicted by both state and church of extortion, that is, of putting his own private price upon designated goods instead of charging what other tradesmen did. His was only the most celebrated of a number of similar cases. Indeed, in a long explanatory will drawn in 1653 Keayne maintained that his own pricing practices had been general in the late 1630's. If so, it is evident how soon after settlement a divergence had appeared between privately defined mercantile interest and the interest of the corporate community as interpreted by church and state.

Now Max Weber was a learned and subtle man who never claimed that the Protestant ethic constituted a brash invitation to employ religious doctrines for ends of self-service. He well knew that "Examples of the condemnation of the pursuit of money and goods may be gathered without end from Puritan writings." And so they almost may be, from Old England to New, from Gabriell Powell's admonition in *Resolved Christian* that "we must be accountable for the least farthing which we have received by God; after what manner we came by it, how and to what use we have bestowed and spent it" to John Cotton's solemn reminder that it was a merchant's duty to combine "diligence in business with deadness to the world." Weber believed that the "real" moral objection to wealth was the temptation to relax in the secure possession of it, to enjoy it in idleness, and thus to invite, "above all . . . [a] distraction from the pursuit of a righteous life."

What I think he did not sufficiently appreciate are the implications for his thesis of the historical experience of early New

England that we have just reviewed. This experience shows that the Protestant ethic had no free field in which it might have worked out those impacts upon business character that inhere in its premises. It reveals not an easy alliance betwen Puritan ideology and economic behavior but rather a conflict between the two, a conflict, as Perry Miller has put it, "at every point." It reveals the existence of numerous restraints imposed upon the merchants by the Fathers in an effort to protect the means of subsistence and the religious ideals of the larger community. Subordination of the part to the whole, to a unity knit by the binding power of Puritan doctrine, lasted, the Puritans themselves believed, only ten years. "Had the alliance between the religious conceptions of the Puritans and the merchant class been as real as Weber assumed it to be," Gabriel Kolko has concluded, "the conflict might not have occurred so quickly."

Calvinist doctrine had framed a fine tension between this world and the next, between material reward and carnal cognizance of it. As even Kolko acknowledges, it "was both a help and a hindrance to systematic economic behavior." In the recent words of Robert A. Davison, the doctrine of the calling "offered substantial reinforcement to the psychological make-up necessary for successful capitalistic endeavor." But within individual merchants themselves as well as within Puritan or Quaker communities the balance between service to God and Mammon was difficult to strike. Isaac Hicks, the New York Quaker merchant of the eighteenth century whose career has recently been studied by Davison, resolved his internal conflict by giving up the life of trade for one of religious good works. Many New England merchants, Kolko makes plain, took the other way out: they turned from Puritanism to some form of heresy or to denominations that were "less restrictive." For many men Puritanism wrecked on the rock of plenty. Yet not, one suspects, without an enduring sense of guilt engraved upon the American character.

By the second generation increasing numbers of merchants were tipping the scales in the world's favor. The insight of Alan

Simpson enables us to see that they were organizers now rather than visionaries, men guided more by habit than by direct experience, latter-day Puritans with fading memories of European persecution. William Penn was a Puritan of this kind as when in the 1670's he wrote of the Reformation: "I am sure, 'twas to *enjoy Property* with Conscience that promoted it: Nor is there any better *Definition of Protestancy,* then [sic] *protesting against Spoiling* Property for Conscience." Thus was *England's Present Interest Discover'd.*

And thus America's, too. The English emigrants of mid-century came largely from the West Country, and they were men with little sympathy for Puritanism. Many were attracted by opportunities for trade; others were artisans and yeoman farmers, from the "middling" orders of English society. The latter came in hunger for land, to regain in the New World a niche out of which they had been washed by the economic and social currents of the old. Between the motivations of these later emigrants and those of Franklin's Poor Richard there is only the difference of a more explicit secularism. In sum, it is necessary to conclude that to a significant extent mercantile success was not so much owing to Puritanism as achieved at its expense.

The Merchants

There exist additional reasons why Weber's thesis must be qualified. Its emphasis upon the contribution of the Protestant ethic underestimates the power of external conditions to thwart mercantile intent. A number of students of the period go so far as to maintain that the colonial merchant was all but helpless in the face of external obstacles. I believe this to be an overstatement of the case, yet one in which there is much truth. The "givens" of technology and economic geography framed narrowly the scope of the merchant's entrepreneurial freedom, but that these and other limitations did not leave the life of trade entirely in the lap of luck is suggested by the following late-eighteenth-century complaint of a Baltimore merchant to his Boston agent: "I can only say this that if we do not pay strict attention in writing & answering our Letters by every post, we had better leave writing at all. [sic] and trust all to Chance.—"

The port cities (see Table II) were the habitat of the merchants, and foreign and coastal commerce their bailiwick. To some extent in Charleston, but very much more so in the ports north of Maryland, native rather than British merchants conducted commerce. These ports were outlets for products in which British capital had little interest. Not only was the hinterland of the northern colonies less productive than that of the South, but many of the region's most important products, especially wheat, cattle, and fish, were as a rule unwanted in England. Natives plied the banks of Newfoundland, the coastal settlements, the West Indies, Africa, and southern Europe to find commodities that would enable them to obtain specie, bills of exchange on London, and other means of paying for imports of English manufactures. English vessels, however, dominated transatlantic commerce, and the area of main interest to American shipping was the coasting and West Indian trades, where the smaller size of colonial vessels and their relative closeness to home ports gave them advantages in operating costs. English ships, moreover, were required to take out bond to return immediately to the mother country. Low relative costs and lack of staples for British markets thus opened a wide commercial area to Yankee ingenuity. And to that of merchants of Philadelphia and Baltimore as well. The latter port began its rise after the mid-eighteenth century, when the growing ascendancy of wheat over tobacco in western Maryland and adjacent parts of Pennsylvania opened the way for a native merchant class to market it.

Seated in his countinghouse in one of the coastal cities and not accompanying his wares to market, the colonial merchant necessarily depended upon others for market information upon which to base his investment decisions and for the means of transacting his business at distant ports. His most important decisions were these: what commodities to ship and in what assortment; where to ship them; to whom to entrust their sale; what terms to sell on; what disposition to make of the proceeds of sale; and what to load for the homeward cargo. The man to whom he entrusted their execution was, as a rule, either his ship's captain or some merchant who resided at the port of destination and who thus served as his commission agent. He himself typically served merchants of other ports, both foreign and home, in the same capacity, so that nearly every merchant now acted as principal, consigning goods on his own account, and now as agent, selling and shipping them in response to distant orders. Throughout the colonial period and well into the nineteenth century resident merchants utilized the services of both captains and agents, and sometimes of supercargoes, with captains tending to predominate in the West Indian trade. Because the basic continuity of conditions and techniques is not interrupted until the advent of improved communications, I shall sometimes draw upon early postcolonial evidence in the following discussion.

The wise selection and management of captains and agents was the most important nonpolitical factor in business success. In the seventeenth century, when the volume of trade was relatively small, personal relationships predominated. Family partnerships were conspicuous, as they had been for centuries in European commerce. The researches of Bernard Bailyn have shown that first commercial contacts were secured to a striking degree by the cement of kinship, with brothers, sons, and "in-laws" very frequently becoming the colonial agents of their European relatives. The eighteenth century by no means entirely transfigured old patterns: family partnerships continued to play an important role in the institutional arrangements by which trade was conducted.

Yet a growing volume of trade brought greater regularity in shipments, an increased familiarity with commodities and markets, and more routine in business—factors that together made for greater impersonality in its conduct. As James B. Hedges points out, by mid-eighteenth century the trade of New England with the

Caribbean was so well standardized that a merchant need not puzzle his brain as to the proper ingredients of a suitable cargo. Within the managerial area subject to his control the most important remaining puzzle was how to obtain and hold the services of reliable men, and to an increasing degree men bound to each other only in mutual interest found that ex post facto criticism furnished a guide to subsequent conduct that was capable of minimizing the costs of poor judgment. The prospect of commissions from future consignments made men wish to serve each other as well as they could. And if after trial and remonstrance an agent continued to prove unsatisfactory, he might be dropped in favor of an alternative house recommended by a returning ship's captain or business associate. Surely W. T. Baxter's conclusion that the eighteenth-century merchant "had perforce to trust his agents blindly" is unduly pessimistic.

This is, of course, not to deny that merchants displayed contrasting degrees of skill in these matters. Robert Oliver & Brothers, highly successful merchants of Baltimore in the late eighteenth and early nineteenth centuries, constantly sought to place their business "in the hands of Men of Stability, good information & undoubted integrity." When they found a correspondent who was "*Solid, Liberal* [in making advances on unsold cargoes] & *Active* [,] qualities we consider absolutely necessary for an agent," they endeavoured to hold on to him. They were highly reluctant to change correspondents, and almost always did so only after long and repeated efforts to accommodate differences. But to a merchant who had sent them "so particular" an order that they preferred not to fill it, the Olivers rather majestically wrote: "We have no desire to do commission business unless we can give perfect satisfaction and if you should hereafter think proper to give us any orders, we advise you to state your views and expectations and leave us to Judge of the propriety of carrying them into effect."

As with the Olivers, so with others. The biographer of the Pepperells of Piscataqua concludes that "an important element" in the success of these late seventeenth- and early eighteenth-century New Hampshire merchants "was their ability to maintain satisfactory relations with their correspondents." On the other hand, James Beekman of mid-eighteenth-century New York, "frequently spelled out in his orders price specifications which bore little relation to the actual state of the British market into which his orders came." In other matters, says Philip L. White, he displayed "a remarkable talent for vagueness and ambiguity." The Nathan Trotters of early nineteenth-century Philadelphia, in the words of Elva Tooker, "often . . . left so little discretion to their agents that the latter were prevented from taking action when opportunities arose quite unforeseen." The examples might be multiplied. The point of them is this: the fact that merchants reacted differently to a common environment somewhat reduces the significance of external obstacles as general explanations of failure.

The evidence available for weighing the question whether individual merchants also differed in their skills in *internal* management is difficult to assess. It takes the form of surviving bookkeeping records, mostly dating from the eighteenth and early nineteenth centuries. In the only substantial study of colonial accounting practices yet made, W. T. Baxter concludes that the overwhelming majority of merchants kept their books by crude single-entry techniques. Baxter finds accounting records to have been little more than lists of debtors and creditors, employed for the primary purpose of facilitating barter exchange. He finds few accounts for cash or merchandise and little evidence that the profit-and-loss account served as anything more than a means of writing off bad debts. While merchants had a "nodding acquaintance" with the standard ledger, they seem generally to have been dilatory in their bookkeeping habits. Baxter explains all this by the tiny scale of operations, the prevalence of barter, the snail-like pace of transport, and a preference for a relaxed tempo in business together with a relish for negotiation on the part of the colonial businessman.

One may cite exceptions to these conclusions; for example, the case of Jonathan Trumbull, who periodically balanced his accounts in the 1730's and 1740's. But pending a thorough canvass of all known survivals, it is difficult to be sure of the significance of such examples. In view of the fact that even at the end of the eighteenth century in England it was mainly wholesale merchants who utilized double-entry bookkeeping—and by no means all of them—the hypothesis may be advanced that as trade increased in volume in the eighteenth century, the larger merchants were the ones most likely to adopt the more efficient housekeeping technique that double entry affords. Virginia Harrington reports that "most" wholesale houses in New York appear to have used double entry on the eve of the Revolution, and she cites the ledger and wastebook of the Livingstons as "models of the double-entry books." Similarly, one may point to the Baltimore records of Oliver & Thompson in the 1780's, of Robert Oliver & Brothers in the 1790's, and of Alexander Brown & Sons after 1800 as excellent examples of full double entry, but all these men were post-Revolution migrants to America who evidently brought their knowledge with them. The extent to which earlier residents responded to such newspaper advertisements as John Miller's offer in the South Carolina *Gazette* of May 1733 to teach "the Italian method of bookkeeping" is yet to be determined. However, when a more complete understanding of colonial practices is possible, I think it will be found that bookkeeping records of past profit or loss weighed very little and fresh market information very much in investment decisions. If so, external management will be seen to have been more important than internal.

Even with the latest and most complete information concerning alternative markets, two factors made for a high degree of risk and uncertainty. One was the slowness of transport in an age of sail, the other the small if constantly growing markets, especially those of the vastly important West Indies. While the irregularity of ships under sail has been overstressed, it must be conceded that arrival times often depended on wind and weather. And supply conditions on arrival frequently proved disappointing. In the West Indies even in the eighteenth century, Richard Pares tells us, "Only three ports —Bridgetown in Barbados, Kingston in Jamaica, and above all the

Dutch island of St. Eustatius—were markets of conspicuous size or wide commercial connections. The capitals of the lesser islands were glutted by a very few cargoes—still more so the smaller towns like Spikestown, Barbados." And with nearly every article of North American produce except lumber and livestock perishable in the tropics, cargoes arriving when prices were low could not be stored for long to await an upturn in the market. These were among the main reasons the merchant usually consigned his West Indian cargoes to his captain, so that the latter might be free to move from port to port to effect the best possible sale.

In view of the many difficulties he faced, it is small wonder that the colonial merchant approached the business of earning his living with many fingers in many small pies. A general shortage of circulating currency cut the fluidity of commercial exchange. Provincial governments pleased him by sometimes issuing paper currency, but not a single commercial bank was to exist till after the Revolution. Commodities turned slowly on cumbersome wheels of barter, and as late as the years 1755–70 Thomas & John Hancock of Boston averaged about three transactions per working day. How few these were may be seen by comparison with the 1940's, when a typical Boston department store averaged better than five thousand per day. Because demand for any one service was too small to afford him an adequate livelihood, he, like most other colonial enterprisers rural and urban, undertook to provide numerous ones. He was not only exporter and importer, wholesaler and retailer, a trader on his own account and a commission man, but moneylender, insurer, owner of shares in vessels, and freighter of space as well. Success, as Hedges has well observed, demanded that he "use continuously every ounce of wit, imagination, patience, and perseverance which he possessed."

"Political Capitalism"

Some men used these and perhaps other qualities as well to obtain special advantages from government. As Gabriel Kolko suggests, the kind of "capitalism" they produced owed little to the Protestant ethic. Indeed, their actions "tended to create a political capitalism in which economic success was determined far more by political and social connections than by any special religious motivations." The origins of a situation that was to prove favorable to political manipulation have been traced by Bernard Bailyn to the determination of the Restoration government to exercise a closer supervision over its mercantile empire. Civilian and military officers dispatched during and after the third quarter of the seventeenth century from Great Britain to the colonies—customs functionaries and lesser bureaucrats—tended to settle in the larger trading centers, where they became nuclei of expanding colonial administrations. Colonial officialdom became a "major social magnet," not only because it represented cosmopolitan fashion and political influence but also because it offered access to those who controlled government contracts and other economic advantages. The British government, to enable its colonial executives and their advisors to enforce its more rigorous policy, made available to them a measure of patronage. Within the gift of the governor were public offices "dealing with matters that profoundly affected the basis of economic life— tax collection, customs regulation, and the bestowal of land grants."

An "inner circle of privilege" arose and in time became a wedge dividing the merchants into those who benefited and those who did not. Thus, when the Massachusetts legislature began the legal distribution of land for primarily speculative purposes in the 1720's, it was the town merchants with influential political connections who acquired it. Thus, Thomas Hancock of Boston, using as his agents in England the influential political agents of Massachusetts Bay, secured the greater part of his fortune through British army contracts and by manipulating British Treasury bills. The wedge swelled and aroused among those who failed to benefit from political favoritism a mounting cynicism concerning the uses of government, a cynicism that was to feed the distrust of the executive that marks the Revolution.

Any evaluation of the force of the Protestant ethic, in sum, must take into account the use made by some men of political means and also the external difficulties that often thwarted the "best laid plans." Admittedly, much in the colonial admixture testifies against the point of rational, systematic business conduct. But not everything does. It is impossible to believe that the success of some men did not owe something to an entrepreneurial efficiency greater than that of other men. For them the Protestant ethic may well have sustained the systematic regularity of their ways. If some men escaped the limiting conditions of the colonial economy via political favoritism, others did so by entrepreneurial ingenuity. Both paths led to success, and after 1750 fine town houses with spacious rooms, elegant appointments, and imported luxuries made their appearance in the leading ports. By mid-century all the coastal towns contained what Carl Bridenbaugh has called a "maritime gentry": the Almys, Browns, Channings, and Collinses of Newport; the Beekmans, Morrises, Rutgers, and Crommelins of New York; the Laurenses, Manigaults, Brewtons, and Gadsdens of Charleston; to name only a few. One of the larger mercantile fortunes was that of Thomas Hancock of Boston, who left an estate estimated at £ 100,000 in Massachusetts currency at his death in 1764.

But the fact that we can name names ought give us pause. Such is the attrition of history that it is usually the prominent and successful whose valued records survive, and in all probability we can never learn in detail the stories of the far more numerous smaller men who eked out bare livings or failed. This is highly regrettable, for an explanation of failure is essential to an explanation of success. Was the prime ingredient in failure smallness of capital resources, inefficiency of entrepreneurship, or lack of the advantages made possible by political connections? We do not know nearly enough to say how many of the more successful owed their fortunes to favoritism, or the extent to which they did. Yet the studies of Bernard Bailyn in particular suggest the importance of this ingredient in success and afford a base for the hypothesis

that had favoritism played a lesser role and entrepreneurial efficiency a larger one, the latter might have exerted an impact upon
the rate of growth. Political favoritism affords a path too narrow
for large numbers to crowd upon, but entrepreneurial efficiency
is imitable. While it is important that the few lead, it is more
important that the many be able to follow. What counts for
economic growth is the spread, the deepening, the permeation of
a population by cost-reducing efficiencies. Imitation is more important than innovation.

Social Structure

Considerations of these kinds raise the broader question whether
the structure of colonial society was favorable to growth. How
rigid were its class lines, how difficult was it to cross them, to
climb the ladder of income and status? It is possible to cite
numerous instances in which individuals rose from humble origins
to high levels of economic success, political power, and social
prestige. George Taylor, a signer of the Declaration of Independence, came to America as an Irish redemptioner. Daniel Dulaney,
one of Maryland's prominent lawyers, began his career as an
indentured servant. So did Charles Thompson, the secretary of the
Continental Congress. Concrete figures for particular men may
be given for both the seventeenth and eighteenth centuries. Robert
Turner, an indentured servant in Boston in 1632, died in 1664 with
an estate of £ 1,600. Samuel Shrimpton set up as a brazier, was
inventoried at £ 1,800 at his death in 1698, and is said, besides,
to have owned most of Beacon Hill. Ten years after leaving England in 1766 with £ 250, Bernard Cory, linen draper, had a wife
and three children, six thousand acres of land in Pennsylvania,
and stock worth £ 2,000. John Henderson, a Scot who arrived
in America in 1746 and was apprenticed in the seafaring trade,
valued his house and stores and other property at £ 927 thirty
years later. To these examples we may add the testimony of

prominent persons from the conservative Thomas Hutchinson, governor of Massachusetts, to Crèvecœur and Benjamin Franklin in support of the thesis "America, land of opportunity." You may depend upon it," says William Allen about the middle of the eighteenth century, "that this is one of the best poor Man's Countrys in the World."

The difficulty with the too familiar historical technique of "proof by example" is that it may quite easily be used to "prove" the opposite. Consider the ledgers of Samuel Holten, Jr.,[1] a physician who lived in Danvers, Massachusetts, near Gloucester. Running consecutively for sixteen and a half years from June 1757 to approximately the end of 1773, with occasional entries as late as 1792, these ledgers record sums owed for a variety of medical services. Time and again the physician was obliged to note alongside the name of some debtor: "Dead and left nothing," "Dead and left no estate," "An insolvent estate," or some variant testimony to poverty. During the years 1757–74 a total of 35 persons are so identified. Of these, 23 were male and 12 female, seven of the latter being widows. A count of the number of patients, however, necessarily rough because the names in the index are lined out and sometimes illegible, reveals that the insolvents formed only between 5 and 10 per cent of the total, probably closer to 5 per cent.

Additional evidence of the existence of poverty may be cited. By 1650, according to Carl Bridenbaugh, care of the poor had become a community function in Boston, Newport, and New Amsterdam. In the 1730's, he adds, all the leading seaport towns except Newport built almshouses, with Newport following in 1746. Nor were rural regions free of poverty. In eighteenth-century Virginia, Charles S. Sydnor tells us, aged paupers looked to the county government for assistance. One of the functions of the Albermarle County Court was to appoint persons to supervise elections of overseers of the poor. To these institutional and other evidences may be added such contemporary voices as that of Urian Oakes,

[1] Library of Congress, Division of Manuscripts.

a New England minister who in 1673 described "the people" as "generally poor and low enough."

It is perfectly clear that colonial society had its poor and also its well-to-do. What we do not yet know is how large either group was in relation to the total population, nor the ease or difficulty typically encountered in moving from one to the other. We cannot know these things, Richard B. Morris has recently reminded us, until such sources as land records, church records, inventories of estates, and immigration lists are systematically mined in all the colonies. What happened to the poor redemptioner and the convict servant after they had completed their terms of service? Did they pick up land? advance politically? What of their children? As yet, Morris concludes, "We lack the kind of basic data needed to make valid generalizations on whether there was in fact a rigid caste system or a considerable degree of mobility within the social structure."

Pending the results of the widespread digging for which Morris calls, one may rest tentative impressions upon a few general considerations and upon researches already done for some of the colonies. While local and occasional exceptions exist, surely settlement needs for land could generally be met with relative ease from its abundance. A broad middle belt of "ample subsistence," to use the phrase by which Crèvecœur characterized the situation of the typical American, must have stretched betwen the extremes of poverty and wealth. It is unlikely that the width of this belt was uniform; it must have covered degrees of plenitude and varied with the facts of economic geography, especially fertility of soil and ease of transportation. Yet probably in few societies in history have the means of subsistence been so widely distributed among the mass of the people as in colonial America. The Reverend Andrew Burnaby's description in 1759 of the German settlements he had visited on the frontier along the Shenandoah River may well prove to characterize a far broader group of colonists: "Their inexperience of the elegancies of life precludes any regret that they possess not the means of enjoying them: but they possess what many princes would give half their dominions for, health, content, and tranquility of mind." They were, he added, "ignorant of want."

The greater the degree of ignorance of want, however, the lower the demand for goods and services. It is not too much to say that economic growth required the conversion of that ignorance to knowledge and the diffusion of this knowledge among the population. Without wants markets cannot exist, and to the extent that families and communities enjoyed a high degree of self-sufficiency, to the extent that transportation obstacles and low incomes per capita limited the size of markets, specialization, and the diversification of the economy, to that extent growth was inhibited. The pertinent question we must now face is this: what was the effect of a slow rate of economic growth upon the degree of social mobility?

It is necessary to proceed gingerly here, for the ground is not well known. It is the thesis of recent work by sociologists Seymour M. Lipset and Reinhard Bendix that "social mobility is an integral and continuing aspect of the processes of urbanization, industrialization and bureaucratization." These are processes which, by increasing the number of occupational rungs in the social ladder, afford a larger opportunity for more people to climb to higher levels of income and status. Surely the presence of these processes, particularly the first two of them, is properly to be associated with opportunity for a higher degree of vertical mobility within society. But it does not follow that these processes alone make for it. Another sociologist, Bernard Barber, has found much historical evidence of vertical mobility in nonindustrial societies; for example, those of early feudal Europe, prerevolutionary France, and seventeenth-century England. Other scholars have similarly disclosed the existence of opportunities for upward movement in China, Indonesia, India, and Pakistan.

The "table of organization" of the Virginia Company certainly made no provision for upward mobility. Indeed, the company's original plans for quick profits from precious metals and trade left no room for the contemplation of a social order, and the people it sent to Virginia between 1607 and 1609 occupied the status of workmen. In order to attract labor, however, the company subsequently had to create the status of landowner, to offer a share of company stock and a grant of land to men willing to work for the company for seven years. Here, as Sigmund Diamond points out, was a "guaranty of social mobility." Almost from the outset of colonial settlement, therefore, the shortage of labor in relation to the abundance of land led to a multiplication of "statuses," thus effecting a transition from a joint-stock company's table of organization to the beginnings of a more complex society.

In Massachusetts the Puritan ideal of a divinely planned society of fixed classes, with each man in his appointed place, held on somewhat longer, although buffeted by the West Country deviants of the mid-seventeenth century. By the closing decades of that century it was clear that men would not "remain forever in the stations to which they were born," nor would "inferiors," as Perry Miller expresses it, "eternally bow to gentlemen and scholars." The children and grandchildren of the first Calvinists tended to be assimilated into a larger mercantile world where status was determined, in Gabriel Kolko's words, "more by accumulated wealth than theological niceties."

Blueprint aristocracy failed to fit an environment in which land was plentiful and labor scarce, and the researches of Robert E. and B. Katherine Brown have shown how considerable was the resulting social mobility that developed not only in Massachusetts but also in Virginia. The entire "institutional structure of society which had supported culture in Europe and effected its transfer from generation to generation," Bernard Bailyn has emphasized, "was severely damaged in the course of transplantation." By the eighteenth century, as we shall see in chapter eight, the family was increasingly losing its control of the processes of education, and with it, Bailyn suggests, its control of "recruitment into trades and professions," a control that had maintained an ordered society

and imposed "a measure of constriction on economic growth."
This development, he further suggests, "released entrepreneurial
energies, propelled forward occupational and hence more generally
social mobility, and further softened the lines of social stratification."

It is true that quitrents, or commutations of feudal services,
were charged upon a vast amount of colonial land and often
served as occasions for serious dissension. But other restrictions
were more nominal than real. Primogeniture and entail proved
more an encumbrance than a benefit, and neither took deep root
in America. Jefferson's celebrated sponsorship of their abolition
in post-Revolution Virginia was far less a substantive reform than
a sweeping up of dead letters. All of the colonies imposed property
qualifications for voting, but so widespread was the distribution
of freehold property that the requirements proved widely permissive rather than restrictive. And in small communities where
neighbors knew each other, even the propertyless were permitted
to cast their ballots without challenge except in closely contested
elections.

These things said, and due acknowledgement paid the tendency
of American realities to scour sharp edges into roundness, to reduce
jell to fluidity and to convert the social staircase into a ramp, it
must also be said that we are not discussing the Garden of Eden.
Sharp against the social landscape are the features of the gentry,
maritime and landed, an elite elegant and mannered, in possession
of the artifact badges of betterfolk, expecting and receiving social
deference, and donning the mantle of political leadership as the
obligation of gentlemen. An elite dominated politics in many parts
of the country, completely so in the Chesapeake society and in
that of the Carolina low country. Sydnor stresses the dependence
of the lesser folk of Virginia upon the leadership of gentlemen,
and Bridenbaugh finds the same phenomenon among small farmers
in the Carolina backcountry. In New York politics, says Morris, a
massive party rift between the great landowning families came to
an end only with the political exile of one of them. But while

elites existed, it is necessary to add, they proved highly changeful in the grinding factionalism of colonial politics, and in no European sense of the word can it be maintained that they formed an aristocracy. This was not, that is to say, the society of George III. But neither was it that of Tocqueville's America.

It is this comparative angle of vision that matters most in any discussion of American social change. If we compare colonial society with that of Europe, its fluidity appears marked indeed; if the comparison is between the seventeenth and eighteenth centuries, the degree of mobility of the latter century appears on the whole much greater, and if the comparison is between the eighteenth century and the first half of the nineteenth century, it is again the latter period in which fluidity appears to excel. While the favorable land-man ratio tended to exercise its influence in favor of vertical mobility throughout this period, lesser degrees of other influences characterized the colonial years. As Rowland Berthoff has suggested, a relatively small amount of horizontal social movement during the colonial period tended to make for a *relatively* lesser degree of vertical mobility. Population gains, he points out, came in the main from natural increase rather than from immigration; westward movement, while constant, did not exert upon the social ways of the older seaboard centers the impact delivered by the much greater volume of that movement after about 1815; urbanization, while present, occurred on a relatively small scale. So too did industrialization.

To these considerations we may add the following: few business corporations, as we shall see, existed; governmental functions were limited; salaried positions in the army and navy were held by British officers; and the church had no colonial hierarchy leading to such posts as canon, dean, and bishop. Surely in any comparative sense—and it is with degrees of difference that economic growth is concerned—colonial society afforded a lesser elaboration of occupational statuses than did a later society marked by a greater amount of horizontal movement, urbanization, industrialization, and bureaucratization. Surely the sound of the busy cities of the eighteenth century, as reproduced by Bridenbaugh, is impressive mainly in relation to the quietness of seventeenth-century villages. Surely the "unstable, highly mobile, and heterogeneous society" that Bailyn finds in eighteenth-century America has a motion that is quick in relation to its more "ordered" predecessor society in the seventeenth century, but sluggish in relation to the one that followed in the nineteenth.

Indeed, by the mid-eighteenth century itself the accumulation of wealth and the solidification of leading families in political and social positions anchored in the power and prestige of British officialdom necessarily made for a lesser degree of vertical mobility than had previously existed. Bailyn believes that society in the New England port towns was "solidifying": "Mobility was slowing down as the successful families tightened their control of trade and politics." In addition, the current researches of Daniel Hovey Calhoun point to an institutionalization of the learned professions during the generation or so following mid-century, a process in which conscious effort was exerted to raise both the intellectual level and practical performance of lawyers, doctors, and other groups. Continued detailed investigations of these various signs of a maturing society may support the hypothesis that its accompanying rigidities were poorly calculated to withstand the added tensions produced by the British tightening of the colonial administrative system following 1763.

At any rate, it is difficult not to believe that the Revolution itself exerted a profound social impact. Not only had the British government supplied what Sydnor called a "stabilizing force," a phrase given new content by the recent researches by Bailyn that we have examined. The number of refugees and the amount of property they lost must also be taken into account. Revolutionary France lost only five emigrants per thousand population, but R. R. Palmer conservatively estimates that the loss to revolutionary America amounted to no less than twenty-four per thousand. And revolutionary France, ten times as large as revolutionary America, "confiscated only twelve times as much property from its emigrés, as measured by subsequent compensations, which in each case fell short of actual losses."

The Role of Government

It remains to discuss the difficult question of the impact of government on the colonial economy. Did the British Acts of Trade and Navigation encourage or restrain economic development? Among modern scholars Oliver M. Dickerson and Lawrence A. Harper would presumably range themselves on opposite sides of the issue. While the thrust of Dickerson's work is forcefully against the thesis that the Navigation Acts belong among the causes of the American Revolution, he goes beyond this to present the pre-1764 development of the policies underlying the Acts as a positive contribution to growth in colonial prosperity and population. Harper, on the other hand, maintains that "the colonists were exploited by English mercantilism" and presents quantitative estimates of the costs to Americans of the Navigation Acts, which range from a low of approximately $2,500,000 to a high of about $7,000,000 a year. Relatively small as are these sums, he points out that the annual burden per capita represented by the smaller figure comes within sixteen cents per person of meeting all the expenses of operating the national government during the last six years of Washington's administration. A brief description of the familiar Acts must precede our examination of the issue.

Enacted from time to time after the mid-seventeenth century, the laws contained shipping, commodity, and restraining clauses. The purpose of the shipping clauses was to confine the trade of the empire to English (including colonial) vessels and seamen. The commodity clauses affected both colonial exports and imports. Export regulations were designed to direct to the mother country the important staples of the southern colonies and British West Indies. While tobacco and other "enumerated" articles might also be shipped to another English colony, the so-called "plantation duties," imposed by the Act of 1673, had the intent, at least, of virtually eliminating the development of New England as a distribution center for staples shipped directly to the continent in New England vessels. The objective of the import provisions was to induce the colonists to buy British-made goods in preference to those manufactured elsewhere, and to this end all European and East Indian commodities were required to pass first through an English port before being sent to the colonies. The purpose of the restraining Acts was to discourage the growth within America of industries the output of which might narrow the colonial market for British-made goods, and to this end the Woolens, Hat, and Iron Acts were passed. Other laws regulated the value of foreign coins in the colonies and limited the issuance of paper money at the behest of British creditor interests. In addition to the foregoing, British law also provided for the payment of bounties to encourage the production of such items as indigo and naval stores and for preferential tariff treatment within the British market. Informing this body of legislation was the mercantilist conception of colonies as sources of raw materials and as markets for the manufactures of the mother country. The American colonies were thus envisaged as subservient to the growth of English commerce and industry.

That some of these provisions stimulated the colonial economy seems incontrovertible. Indigo provides an excellent example: the post-Revolution loss of the bounty previously paid on it, together with the increased profitableness of cotton, caused its cultivation to be virtually abandoned. The case of tobacco is more difficult and well illustrates some of the complexities of the subjunctive mood in historiography. Harper argues that Britain was not the natural market for the crop, which only went there under the compulsion of law. Its ultimate destination was the Continent. In 1773 official British consumption amounted to 3,747,979 pounds, with the remainder of the 100,482,007 pounds imported being transshipped, mainly to Holland and Germany. After the Revolution, despite strenuous efforts on the part of the British government to retain control of the trade, British importations steadily declined from 99.8 per cent in 1773 to 62.2 per cent in 1790, 45.5 per cent in 1799, 31.7 per cent in 1821, and 22.7 per cent in 1840. Would not colonial Americans have gained more by direct shipments to the Continent?

In all probability they would have, although not by as much as might appear. Not all of the English middleman's profits, together with extra freights, handling and insurance charges, would have gone to them. Dickerson points out that the English merchants did far more than merely transship the tobacco in the form in which they had received it from America. They graded, sorted, and repacked it, and they used their superior sources of market information to send the right amounts at the right times to the right places for sale. Had Americans shipped their tobacco directly to the Continent, they rather than the British would have had to perform these middleman services. Dickerson implies that they would not have performed them as well. In the decades following the Revolution, he points out, *total* tobacco exports fell off sharply, and he attributes the decline to the loss of the superior British marketing services.

Other considerations complicate even more an effort at quantitative precision in the estimation of colonial loss from tobacco. Had New England rather than British vessels been free to carry the Southern staple to Continental markets, those vessels would probably have had to be large ones. But the heavier operating costs of larger vessels would have lessened the ability of New Englanders to engage profitably in the coasting trade by which they assembled cargoes for West Indian markets. And if the latter trade be assumed under these changed conditions to be of lesser importance as a means of paying for British imports, the cost of West Indian molasses would have risen by at least the amount of freights paid on some non-New England ships employed to import it, with cost-consequences to the rum distilling business of that section. In sum, a judgment that one of the clauses of the Navigation Acts lessened returns to Americans requires an estimate of what the returns would have been in the absence of the clause. But the very absence of the clause implies change in one or more elements of the historical situation so that the values of the changes must also be brought into account.

Similar considerations must be brought to bear in any assessment of the extra costs borne by Americans because of the requirement that European and East Indian goods be transshipped via England. As Harper notes, the requirements entailed the imposition upon colonial trade of extra mercantile profits, taxes, fees, cooperage, porterage, brokerage, warehouse rent, and commissions, costs which would not have been incurred by direct shipments. But had America-bound cargoes been assembled bit by bit in a number of ports instead of being gathered from a single British depot, additional operating costs (including interest) would almost certainly have had to be met. So far as the colonial shipbuilding industry was concerned, Harper makes the telling point that after the Revolution American ships found foreign markets without the protection afforded by the shipping clauses. How little the industry depended upon the British market may be seen in construction statistics. On the eve of the Revolution the thirteen colonies are said to have been building 28,747 tons per year; by 1790 tonnage built amounted to at least 29,606 tons, and in 1815 the total reached 154,624 tons.

It is evident that an assessment of the economic impact of the Navigation Acts must take into account considerations which preclude the facile firmness of a conclusion, quantitative or otherwise. Indeed, the question ought not be separated from the larger one of the savings afforded Americans by the military and naval protection of the British. Nothing less than a full-scale effort at social cost-accounting will do, and, needless to say, one has not yet been undertaken. Until it is, until the probable ramifications of each subjunctive hypothesis are carefully weighed, historical judgment must be tentative. If and when the returns are finally in, however, I believe they will tend to support Harper's judgment that the earnings of Americans were less than they would have been in the absence of the British connection. But whatever the amount of the "loss," previously noted propensities to consume warn against any easy assumption that the whole of it would have been converted into capital.

So far as colonial manufacturing is concerned, the restraining clauses appear to have exerted far less influence than natural conditions. The administration of the restrictive policy was often less than rigorous, depending as it did largely upon the ability and willingness of governors to enforce it. Some governors were colonials in sympathy with the commercial and manufacturing ambitions of the colonists, and some formed profitable business connections in America. Even governors from England sometimes preferred easy duties and local popularity to a tumultuous and embarrassed administration. Weeden's shrewd observation concerning colonial New Englanders probably applies more widely: "They had grown up doing things they found profitable, whatever the British laws had been." More important than the laws were the underlying economic conditions. The shortage of skilled labor and both the scarcity and preferred allocations of capital funds gave to a country in possession of abundant resources an absolute advantage in the production of raw materials and semiprocessed goods. "Balancing advantage against disadvantage," says the historian of American manufactures, Victor S. Clark, "their manufactures seem not to have been retarded or furthered decidedly by subordination to the British government."

Nevertheless, it seems clear that changes in this underlying situation, especially in the advancing eighteenth century, were creating a progressively sharper division between the interests of mother country and colonists. The proportionality of the factors of production was changing as available supplies of capital and skilled labor increased. In this situation, governmental policies that sought to promote rather than to curb industrialization might well have helped set America on an earlier path to more rapid growth.

Instead, policies that had sometimes been indifferently enforced were defined and applied with new vigor in the general tightening of the administrative machinery of empire following the Seven Years War.

Alarmed lest the promise of more rapid Western settlement after 1763 lead to renewed Indian wars and to a situation wherein, because of the distance from the Atlantic seaboard, inland communities would manufacture for themselves, the British government took measures to check or prohibit Western settlements. Manufacturing, noted a paper relating to Indian affairs laid before the Board of Trade in 1768, was "a consequence which, experience shows, has constantly attended, in a greater or less degree, every inland settlement." On the eve of the Revolution Benjamin Franklin learned at first hand how adamant British policy had become on this point. Just before leaving England in 1775, Franklin was drawn into informal negotiations with men closely connected with the ministry and asked to write out a set of propositions he believed would lead to permanent union. One of his propositions was that all acts restraining manufactures be repealed. This proposition, Franklin relates, "they apprehended would meet with difficulty. They said, that restraining manufacturers in the colonies was a favorite here; and therefore they wish'd that article to be omitted, as the proposing it would alarm and hinder perhaps the considering and granting others of more importance."

It may be wondered why the colonial governments did not themselves enact legislation to encourage the development of manufactures. The answer, of course, is that they did. Especially before 1750 provincial legislatures often gave monopoly rights to individuals in order to encourage the regular and reliable supply of some article of large consumption, such as salt, refined sugar, pitch, paper, or stoneware. Sometimes, too, they enacted tariff laws, as, for example, South Carolina did in 1716, when that province laid a duty on all imports except salt. But in 1724 an order-in-council prohibited any colony from imposing duties on British goods. Laws seeking to encourage specific industries were sometimes disallowed by the British government, as, for example, was an attempt by Virginia in 1680 to aid shipbuilding, and one in 1682 to promote the manufacturing of cloth. Vetoing a Pennsylvania statute of 1706, the Board of Trade remarked: "It cannot be expected that encouragement should be given by law to the making any manufactures made in England in the plantations, it being against the advantage of England." Nevertheless, both provincial and town governments on numerous occasions granted bounties, loans, land grants, tax exemptions, and other aids in efforts to encourage the provision of some facility or service—for example, grist mills, deemed essential to community welfare—and such legislation was seldom disallowed.

Similarly, not British opposition but the relatively undeveloped nature of the economy principally explains the paucity of business corporations in the colonial period. As Joseph S. Davis has emphasized, businesses were generally small-scale and local in character. No large supplies of capital or labor were seeking employment, at least before approximately the mid-eighteenth century. Those which were found outlets in unincorporated joint stock companies, legally partnerships, which sometimes reached surprising size in mining, land speculation, and other areas of late colonial enterprise. Had capitalists sought incorporation they would generally have found few legal obstacles in the way. Not only Parliament and Crown, but colonial proprietors, governors, and legislatures as well, possessed, "within limits which were not always clear but which were for the most part wide, the right to erect corporations for operation in America".

While it must be concluded that neither interference by the Crown nor Parliamentary restrictions, not even the extension of the Bubble Act to America in 1741, appreciably hampered the development of corporations in the colonies, it does not follow that the mushroom growth of corporations in the early national period was unrelated to political change. During the entire colonial period only a half-dozen business corporations have been traced, two in the seventeenth century and four in the eighteenth.

In contrast, more than 300 business corporations received charters from state governments during the eleven year period between 1789–1800. To ascribe this startling growth, as Davis does, to a greater degree of economic and social maturity in the post-Revolutionary period, seems insufficient. A distinct political element is present and deserves recognition.

Most colonial corporations were erected by charters granted by royal governors in the name of the Crown, although usually with the consent of the provincial councils. That is to say, the sovereign was recognized as the source of legal authority, with Parliamentary approval required after 1688 in the case of a grant of exclusive or monopoly privilege. In both royal and proprietary colonies the legal right of the assembly to incorporate was subject to the negative of the governor or of higher English authority. The Revolution brought an important change in this situation. Because of the fiction that the Revolution was fought to free the colonists from the exactions of the Crown, a revulsion against executive authority became manifest in the early state constitutions, as well as in the Articles of confederation. The power to incorporate, in a word, shifted from the executive to the legislative arm, where it was more sensitively responsive to community pressures upon government to aid in the provision of community sevices. As we shall see, most of the corporations erected before 1800 were quasi-public in nature, and the community purposes they served continued to dominate the objectives of incorporation well into the nineteenth century.

In the growth of the American economy the Revolution forms a watershed. It does so for a number of reasons we shall later explore. As Alexander Hamilton remarked in 1781, it had been a "narrow colonial sphere" in which Americans "had been accustomed to move" rather than "that enlarged kind suited to the government of an independent nation". But prominent among the contributions of the Revolution is the one we have just discussed. The transfer of full political authority to the legislative arm of governments close to hand and more amenable to popular pressures made it far easier for communities to use the device of the business corporation to obtain the roads, bridges, and other "social overhead capital" necessary to growth.

But the conditions of growth are multiple, not singular, and the contribution made by each of them can more readily be perceived if first we discuss the growth of the economy itself between 1790 and the outbreak of the Civil War.

IV

Economic Growth, 1790–1861

In the years following the Revolution the American economy continued the process of expansion in which it had been engaged since early colonial times. By 1860 the number of people was nearly eight times larger than the approximately four million recorded by the first census in 1790. Table III shows the increases by decades for both whites and Negroes, most of the latter being slaves. Despite a falling white birth rate, which declined steadily

TABLE III

ESTIMATED POPULATION OF THE UNITED STATES, 1790–1860
(in thousands)

Year	Total	White	Non-White
1860	31,443	26,923	4,521
1850	23,192	19,553	3,639
1840	17,070	14,196	2,874
1830	12,866	10,537	2,329
1820	9,639	7,867	1,772
1810	7,240	5,862	1,378
1800	5,309	4,306	1,002
1790	3,929	3,172	757

Source: *Historical Statistics of the United States, Colonial Times to 1957* (Washington, D.C., 1960), pp. 8, 9.

each decade from 55.0 per thousand in 1800 to 41.4 in 1860, the excess of births over deaths was the main source of population growth. Immigration contributed far fewer persons than did natural increase. From the close of the Revolutionary War to 1819 an estimated 250,000 persons migrated to the United States. Immigration statistics compiled by the Department of State after 1819 provide the figures displayed for selected years in Table IV. Simon

TABLE IV

TOTAL IMMIGRATION TO THE UNITED STATES,
SELECTED YEARS, 1820–1860

1860	153,640
1855	200,877
1850	369,980
1845	114,371
1840	84,066
1835	45,374
1830	23,322
1825	10,199
1820	8,385

Source: *Historical Statistics of the United States,, Colonial Times to 1957* (Washington, D.C., 1960), p. 57.

Kuznets and Ernest Rubin estimate net immigration to have amounted to 700,000 persons between 1820 and 1840, and 4,200,-000 between 1840 and 1860. The bulk of the arrivals concentrated in the decade 1846–55, a circumstance reflecting both the "push" of hard times, especially in Ireland, and the "pull" of a burgeoning American economy.

If the number of people increased, so too did the size of the United States. Through purchase, war, and the peaceful settlement of boundary disputes, the nation's landed area more than tripled, rising in square miles from 864,746 to 2,969,640 between 1790 and 1860. In consequence, a population "pressure" of 4.5 persons per square mile in 1790 had risen to only 10.6 per square mile by 1860. The "pressure" was greatest in urban areas, and Table V shows the growth in the number of cities of various sizes, while

Table VI displays the total population in urban and rural territory by size of place. Both rural settlement and urbanization
became to an increasing extent western phenomena, especially
following the War of 1812, when great numbers of people pressed
into the area beyond the Appalachians. In 1790 the population
center of the United States was located twenty-three miles east of
Baltimore, Maryland, but by 1860 it had moved to a point twenty
miles southeast of Chillicothe, Ohio. By 1859 all the area east

TABLE V

NUMBERS OF URBAN PLACES OF VARYING SIZES, 1790–1860

Size of Population	1790	1800	1810	1820	1830	1840	1850	1860
500,000 to 1,000,000	—	—	—	—	—	—	1	2
250,000 to 500,000	—	—	—	—	—	1	—	1
100,000 to 250,000	—	—	—	1	1	2	5	6
50,000 to 100,000	—	1	2	2	3	2	4	7
25,000 to 50,000	2	2	2	2	3	7	16	19
10,000 to 25,000	3	3	7	8	16	25	36	58
5,000 to 10,000	7	15	17	22	33	48	85	136
2,500 to 5,000	12	12	18	26	34	46	89	163

Source: *Historical Statistics of the United States, Colonial Times to 1957* (Washington,
D.C., 1960), p. 14.

of the Mississippi River had been carved into states, and west of
the river Louisiana, Missouri, Arkansas, Iowa, Minnesota, Texas,
California, and Oregon had also achieved statehood. While each
of the nation's three main regions increased in population, Table
VII shows that both the South and the Northeast gathered declining portions of the total every decade after 1810. That of the
West uninterruptedly advanced.

Precisely when the economy began to grow at a *more rapid
rate* is a question on which scholars disagree. The only continuous
estimates of pre-1869 national income in constant prices are those
compiled in the 1930's by Robert F. Martin. According to Martin,
"very little actual economic advance per capita appeared in the

Table VI

Population in Urban and Rural Territory, by Size of Place 1790–1860
(in thousands)

	1790	1800	1810	1820	1830	1840	1850	1860
URBAN TERRITORY	202	322	525	693	1,127	1,845	3,544	6,217
Places of 500,000 to 1,000,000	—	—	—	—	—	—	516	1,379
Places of 250,000 to 500,000	—	—	—	—	—	313	—	267
Places of 100,000 to 250,000	—	—	—	124	203	205	659	993
Places of 50,000 to 100,000	—	61	150	127	222	187	284	452
Places of 25,000 to 50,000	62	68	80	70	105	235	611	670
Places of 10,000 to 25,000	48	54	109	122	240	405	561	884
Places of 5,000 to 10,000	48	94	116	115	231	329	596	976
Places of 2,500 to 5,000	44	45	70	96	126	172	316	595
RURAL TERRITORY	3,728	4,986	6,714	8,945	11,739	15,224	19,648	25,227

Source: *Historical Statistics of the United States, Colonial Times to 1957* (Washington, D.C., 1960), p. 14.

TABLE VII

DISTRIBUTION OF POPULATION BY REGIONS, 1810–1860

YEAR	SOUTH[1]		WEST[2]		NORTHEAST[3]		TOTAL U.S.
	Population	% of total pop.	Population	% of total pop.	Population	% of total pop.	(territories excluded)
1810	2,314,556	32.1	961,407	13.3	3,939,895	54.6	7,215,858
1820	2,918,198	30.4	1,845,863	19.2	4,836,722	50.4	9,600,783
1830	3,774,405	29.4	2,980,294	23.2	6,066,169	47.3	12,820,868
1840	4,749,875	27.9	4,960,580	29.1	7,309,186	42.9	17,019,641
1850	6,271,237	27.2	7,494,608	32.5	9,301,417	40.3	23,067,262
1860	7,993,531	25.6	11,796,680	37.8	11,393,533	36.5	31,183,744

1. South: Alabama, Arkansas, Florida, Georgia, Louisiana, Mississippi, North Carolina, South Carolina, Texas, and Virginia.
2. West: Illinois, Indiana, Iowa, Kansas, Kentucky, Michigan, Minnesota, Missouri, Nebraska, Ohio, Tennessee, Wisconsin, California, Nevada, and Oregon.
3. Northeast: Connecticut, Delaware, Maine, Maryland, Massachusetts, New Hampshire, New Jersey, New York, Pennsylvania, Rhode Island, and Vermont.

Source: Douglass C. North, *The Economic Growth of the United States, 1790–1860* (Englewood Cliffs, N.J., 1961), p. 257.

first half of the 19th century," a failure which he attributed to "general pioneering turmoil, punctuated by controversies, first with European countries, culminating in the War of 1812 with the British, and then the series of Black Hawk, Seminole and other Indians Wars." His figures for real income per capita show a steady decline each decade from $216 in 1799 to $164 in 1829, a loss of 24 per cent. Not until 1849 did income rise to the level of 1799, and then the gain amounted only to 11 per cent over a period of fifty years. The decade 1849–59 yielded the most substantial increase of the entire period, with income rising from $235 to $296. Perhaps most surprisingly, in tracing this 1849–59 rise in income to the various sectors of the economy responsible for producing it, a calculation made in terms of current rather than constant prices, Martin depicts percentile *declines* from the previous decade in manufacturing, construction, transportation and communication, service, and "miscellaneous" (including finance), as well as agriculture. While mining and quarrying registered a small increase from 0.7 per cent to 1.1 per cent, trade leaped from 8.4 per cent to 12.1 per cent. Implicit in Martin's figures, in short, is the thesis that economic growth was primarily the consequence of a substantial increase in trade in the 1850's.

In recent years Martin's early work has been subjected to vigorous criticism, first by Simon Kuznets and then by William N. Parker and Franklee Whartenby. Focusing both on Martin's sources and statistical methods, this criticism is too technical for review here. Believing Martin's national and per capita income figures to be too low, especially for the years 1800–40, Kuznets suggests they be revised on the basis of two main considerations. The first of these is the increase in "nonagricultural industrial employment" that occurred between 1800 and 1840. Assuming that real income per worker is greater in such employment than in agriculture, Kuznets uses urbanization statistics as an index of movement from the one to the other. Secondly, he makes an upward revision in the estimated ratio of gainfully employed to total population. All other things being equal, an increase in this ratio is assumed to result in an increase in real product per capita. Adding together the results of his re-estimates, Kuznets reaches the conclusion that instead of undergoing the decline suggested by Martin, real product per capita actually rose by 19 per cent during the period 1800–40. This conclusion rests, however, on the assumption that no change took place in the productivity of agriculture or any other pursuit during the period. To Parker and Whartenby the assumption is questionable. It must, they believe, be

TABLE VIII

VALUE ADDED BY SELECTED INDUSTRIES, AND VALUE OF OUTPUT OF
FIXED CAPITAL, IN 1879 PRICES: 1839–1859
(in billions of dollars)

	Total	Agri-culture	Mining	Manu-facturing	Con-struction	Value of Output of Fixed Capital
1859	2.69	1.49	.03	.86	.30	.73
1854	2.32	1.32	.03	.68	.30	—
1849	1.66	.99	.02	.49	.16	.39
1844	1.37	.94	.01	.29	.13	—
1839	1.09	.79	.01	.19	.11	.25

Source: *Historical Statistics of the United States, Colonial Times to 1957* (Washington, D.C., 1960), p. 139.

subjected to the "painful techniques of historical research," and in this undertaking Parker is presently engaged.

Meanwhile, Robert E. Gallman's recent estimates for the period 1839–99 of value added by commodity output in agriculture, mining, manufacturing, and construction—four sectors of the economy that accounted for between 60 and 70 per cent of the national product in the post-Civil War era—supply a firmer basis than do Martin's figures for an impression concerning both the direction of movement and some of the main sources of national income in the last two decades before the Civil War. Gallman finds that between 1839 and 1859 output grew at an average decade rate of

57 per cent. In addition to value added, by which Gallman means "the value of output, at producers' prices, less the value of materials and fuels directly consumed in production at delivered prices," Table VIII displays estimates of the value of output of fixed reproducible capital. This Gallman defines as producers' manufactured durables, construction, and the improvements to farm land.

TABLE IX

COMMODITY OUTPUT, POPULATION, AND GAINFUL WORKERS IN COMMODITY
PRODUCTION, QUINQUENNIAL, 1839–1859

				ABSOLUTE FIGURES	
Year	Output	Population	Output per Capita	Gainful Workers	Output
	(millions of $)	(thousands)		(thousands)	per worker
1839	1,094	17,120	$64	4,484	$244
1844	1,374	20,182	68	—	—
1849	1,657	23,261	71	6,190	268
1854	2,317	27,386	85	—	—
1859	2,686	31,513	85	8,140	330
Decennial Rates of Change (per cent)					
1849	52	36	11	38	10
1854	69	36	24	—	—
1859	62	36	20	32	23
1869	23	27	–4	19	2

Source. Robert E. Gallman, "Commodity Output, 1839–1899," in William N. Parker, ed., *Trends in the American Economy in the Nineteenth Century* (Princeton, N.J., 1960), p. 16.

Since a high ratio of capital to output is associated with the process of industrialization, it is noteworthy that the share of fixed capital in commodity output increased from less than 23 per cent in 1839 to about 27 per cent in 1859.

Table IX gives evidence of an acceleration in the rate of change in output per capita during the two decades, and Table X shows the shares of each of the four sectors in commodity output. Most notable in the latter table is the changing division of output between agriculture and nonagriculture, especially manufacturing.

The share of manufacturing in commodity output, less than 20 per cent in 1839, rose to 33 per cent by 1859. On the other hand, despite the fact that the period saw substantial gains in real income per head, the real value added by agriculture (about 47 per cent) was not much larger than the rate of increase in population (45 per cent). In part, the explanation of the shift, as Gallman notes, is the differing income elasticities of demand for agricultural and nonagricultural products. "As income per capita rises, per capita

TABLE X

SECTOR SHARES IN COMMODITY OUTPUT, QUINQUENNIAL, 1839–1859
(per cent)

Year	Agri-culture	Mining	Manu-facturing	Construction Variant A	Construction Variant B
1839	72	1	17	10	8
1844	69	1	21	9	8
1849	60	1	30	10	9
1854	57	1	29	13	11
1859	56	1	32	11	10

Source: Robert E. Gallman, "Commodity Output, 1839–1899," in William N. Parker, ed., *Trends in the American Economy in the Nineteenth Century* (Princeton, N.J., 1960), p. 26.

consumption of agricultural products tends, after a time, to rise relatively little. Thus the share of income devoted to agricultural products is reduced, while that devoted to non-agricultural products is increased." This situation not being alleviated by an export surplus of agricultural products, factors of production were shifted to nonagricultural sectors to meet the requirements of the changing pattern of demand.

It remains to note Gallman's view that during the sixty-year period 1839–99 "the number of gainful workers in commodity production increased at about the same rate as population." This is a significant point. For if Gallman is right in his belief that about 64 per cent of the rise in commodity output over this period is attributable to the increasing number of workers, it is apparent how important was the part played by population growth in the expansion of national output. Productivity gains appear to account for the remainder of the rise, and Gallman sees these increases in output per worker as deriving in part from shifts of workers from less productive to more productive sectors of the economy, and in part to such changes *within* particular sectors as "increased supplies of other factors, improved technology, a better disposition of workers within each sector, improved workers, etc." "In 1839 income per worker in mining and manufacturing [taken together] was much higher than income per worker in the other sectors," and in consequence workers shifted relatively rapidly from agriculture to these more remunerative sectors.

Whereas Martin had emphasized the importance of trade in the 1850's, Gallman places the beginnings of an accelerated rate of economic growth "in or before" the 1840's and associates it with "the early stages of industrialization or slightly before." He expresses surprise that high rates of growth in product per head should appear so soon: the records of other countries (Great Britain is a much-debated exception) usually suggest that rapid increases *follow* rather than accompany early industrialization. But his surprise arises from his acceptance of the view of some scholars that the late 1840's marked "the beginning of U.S. industrialization." There might well be less room for surprise if it were possible to extend into the period before 1839 the kind of investigation carried out by Gallman for the years following 1839. And if the investigation revealed significant beginnings of industrialization before that year, certainly part of the explanation would be at hand for his conclusion that "U.S. product per capita must have been high from the beginning" (i.e., from 1839). Probably the favorable land-man ratio and an expanding foreign and domestic commerce also contributed to this high early product per capita.

A statistical assessment of the sources of national income before 1839 would be extremely difficult to make, however, because of the fragmentary nature of surviving data. Although federal censuses began in 1790, only in 1810, 1820, and 1840 was any attempt made to include in them either agriculture or manufactures. Census data before 1840, concludes Douglass C. North, are "so poor that they are almost worthless." Raymond W. Goldsmith agrees that our "usable" statistical record does not reach beyond that date. Although the contemporary testimony of Ezra Seaman, George Tucker, and others has yet to be evaluated in the light of modern concepts, the strong possibility is that Samuel Rezneck will prove justified in his doubt "whether there is ever likely to be enough material available for any more reliable measure" than what we now have. Shall, then, the beginnings of accelerated growth be equated with the availability of data on national output per capita that may be statistically measured or inferred?

Gallman has made a substantial contribution to our knowledge of the 1840's and 1850's, but the element of uncertainty that remains about even these decades cannot be overlooked. For one thing, he has omitted trade, transport, finance, and other industries from his estimates. For another, while census data after 1840 are fuller than for earlier decades, they are inadequate, and this has sometimes compelled Gallman to resort to assumptions and extrapolations rather than historical evidence. As Neal Potter has pointed out, only 52 per cent of Gallman's estimate of manufacturing output in 1839 are from census data on value of products: *and this 52 per cent is itself an estimate* that is derived from the 1840 census figures on value of product multiplied by the 1850 census ratios of value added to value of product. Gallman's reply to Potter is a reasonable one, but the possibility remains that the use of similar techniques on the sparser data before 1840 would produce results even more questionable. While, therefore, we may reasonably conclude that growth was accelerating in the forties and fifties, it is at least doubtful that the techniques which give us some idea of the dimensions of that growth would be equally successful if applied to earlier data. So long as measurable national output (income) is employed as the criterion of growth, the possibility must be faced that the years before 1840 will form a medieval period in American economic history.

For many historians this would be an intolerable situation. While the kinds of evidence that historians have traditionally used support the notion that the inter-Panic period 1843–57 indeed witnessed an acceleration in the rate of industrialization and economic growth, there exist good reasons for believing both processes were under way before then. The difficult problem is estimating their significance in relation to the later period. Some approaches to the available evidence tend to minimize the earlier years; others suggest it may be wrong to do so. In the first category is a recent essay by Alfred Conrad, who uses data on real wages as an index to national income. Finding only relatively minor wage gains before 1843, Conrad suggests that these years of a "surprisingly low rate of per capita income growth" were ones of industrial preparation, with high proportions of disposable income presumably being channeled into investment. Douglass C. North arrives at a different conclusion. After unusual statistical labors devoted to numerous aspects of American economic change but not to the measurement of aggregate output or income, North concludes: "If one were to date the beginning of acceleration in the economy's growth and the years when industrialization began, it would be during this period" from 1823 to 1843. Within this time span he places special emphasis upon the "accelerated growth of manufacturing throughout the Northeast" during the decade of the 1830's.

Robert W. Fogel, on the other hand, assembles a striking array of evidence in support of the thesis that the 1820's witnessed a rapid rise in the maufacturing share of commodity output.[1] The purpose of the assemblage, it is proper to observe, is to counter Walt W. Rostow's overly dramatic view that during the years following 1843 the American economy "took-off" upon a self-sustained course of accelerated growth. The first piece of evidence is Rolla M. Tryon's conclusion that while household manufactur-

[1] I am much indebted to Professor Fogel and to the Johns Hopkins Press for their kind permission to make use of data from Fogel's forthcoming publication. "Railroads in American Economic Growth: Essays in Econometric History."

ing apparently reached a peak about 1815, "the transfer from home- to shop- and factory-made goods was rather generally completed before the close of the third decade of the nineteenth century." The decade of the 1820's was also one of rapid urbanization, with the rate of increase of city population doubling that of population as a whole. Fogel also points to the rapid growth of a number of leading manufacturing industries during the twenties, most of which "grew at decade rates which exceeded by far the 35 percent increase in population." Cotton textiles was one of the most important. In 1807 the fifteen or twenty mills in existence employed a total of approximately eight thousand spindles. By 1811, according to Albert Gallatin's report to Congress of the preceeding year, an estimated eighty-seven firms were expected to have ten times this number of spindles in operation. By 1820, the spindle total had risen from 80,000 to 191,000. These increases pale before those of the 1820's: in 1831 spindles in use numbered nearly a million and a quarter, and cotton textiles had become "a very substantial industry."

As in cotton textiles, so also in iron making and in the production of woolen goods, carpets, paper, flint glass, lead, sugar and molasses, salt, and steam engines. Arthur H. Cole estimates that factory consumption of wool rose from four hundred thousand pounds in 1810 to fifteen million in 1830, with "fully half" of the increase falling between 1816 and 1830. Carpet production grew from an output of 9,984 yards in 1810 to 1,147,500 in 1834, with most of the increase taking place during a four- or five-year period beginning in 1827. While the steam engine was not produced commercially in the United States until 1805, production was stimulated, especially after 1815, by the development of steamboats. During the 1820's 359 engines were required for this purpose alone. In 1830 Pittsburgh alone produced one hundred engines, and Cincinnati one hundred fifty.

We may summarize this brief survey of scholarly viewpoints concerning industrialization and economic growth in the pre-Civil War period by pointing out that Martin would emphasize the

1850's, Gallman the 1840's, North the 1830's, and Fogel the 1820's! But why stop here? It is true, as North points out, that census returns reveal a "drastic decline" in manufacturing output in every state of the Northeast between 1810 and 1820. But this decline, as North notes, is "much magnified by the incomplete nature of the returns for 1820 and the inclusion of household manufactures in the 1810 figure." The importance of manufactures at the earlier date is emphasized by Secretary of the Treasury Albert Gallatin's 1810 Report on Manufactures: "It may, with certainty, be inferred that . . . annual production exceeds one hundred and twenty millions of dollars. And it is not improbable that the raw materials used, and the provisions and other articles consumed by the manufacturers, create a home market for agricultural products not very inferior to that which arises from foreign demand." Historians have long noted the stimulus given manufactures by the embargo and nonimportation laws following 1807. They had received an even earlier stimulus during the Revolution period from an interruption to imports and other circumstances to be discussed in the next chapter. In 1789 George Washington observed that more "substantial improvements to manufactures" had recently been made "than were ever before known in America." As we shall see, manufactures were of sufficient importance by that year to induce interests in several cities to petition Congress in their favor, and among the stated objectives of the Tariff Act of 1789 was "the encouragement and protection of manufactures."

Still the question will not down: why stop here? Why 1820? Why 1789? Why 1776? We have only to examine the first volume of Victor S. Clark's *History of Manufactures in the United States*[2] to see that ironmaking, shipbuilding, and the manufacture of clothing, nails, utensils, furniture, and numerous other products is to be found almost throughout the colonial period of American history. Would the colonial historian be justified in arguing that manufacturing and economic growth have been constants in our history from some time near its beginnings, and that the notion

[2] New York, 1949.

of acceleration is a myth? Does there exist a parallel between this notion and an earlier and better-known version of the doctrine that economic change may come with unexpected suddenness?

Lecturing at Oxford in 1880–81 on "The Industrial Revolution of the Eighteenth Century," the English historian Arnold Toynbee popularized a concept of sudden change that soon became imbedded in historical literature. Toynbee depicted an England which, prior to 1760, had been a quiet and contented world of "scarcely perceptible movement." Upon this green and joyous landscape had burst a series of inventions in spinning and weaving and in the production of power, and within a span of about twenty years machinery and steam had overrun industry, ushered in the factory system, dislocated population, blackened the air, and blighted the lives of exploited women and children. Eric E. Lampard has compiled an instructive account of the subsequent history of Toynbee's drama. By the early twentieth century it had begun to be critically examined. A. P. Usher's researches in technology revealed an almost unbroken continuity of mechanical change since the late Middle Ages. Alongside Toynbee's half-dozen or so inventors now appeared numerous skilled craftsmen, nameless and unsung, authors of small but indispensable improvements, men whose presence crowded the stage on which the drama of invention was enacted, converting it from a record of individual achievement to a social process. In Toynbee's day, however, as Herbert Heaton reminds us, little was known of sixteenth-century economic life and little of any eighteenth-century industry except textiles. Now we know, thanks to the researches of John U. Nef, that England had undergone an "industrial revolution" between 1540 and 1640 and that Holland, Sweden, and France also contributed to technical progress. Now we know, too, the fundamental relevance to that progress of early modern science. As T. S. Ashton emphasizes, this "stream of English scientific thought, issuing from the teaching of Francis Bacon, and enlarged by the genius of Boyle and Newton, was one of the main tributaries of the industrial revolution." Lengthened perspectives thus enable us to see the wisdom of Thomas C. Cochran's observation that "massive changes in physical environment such as those accompanying the rise of trade at the close of the Middle Ages or the gradual growth of industrialization from the seventeenth century on do not lend themselves to exact or brief periodization."

But Clio, it has often been observed, is a fickle Muse. In recent years scholars have in varying degrees reaffirmed Toynbee's central idea of suddenly rapid economic change. As early as 1937 Usher suggested that "important aspects of the economic history of England . . . seem to warrant the qualified use of the term 'revolution'" He thought the pace of technological change in particular to have been "unprecedented if not revolutionary." In 1948 Ashton, the leading authority on English economic history of the eighteenth century, entitled his masterful study *The Industrial Revolution, 1760–1830*.[8] Two years later, J. H. Plumb boldly returned to the classical point of view: ". . . compared with the centuries which had gone before, the changes . . . of the second half of the eighteenth century were both violent and revolutionary." In 1955 Heaton concluded that the "industrial revolution still stands provided you will scrap 1760 as D day and 1832 as VE day, give greater emphasis to the heavy industries, wring some of the emotion and melodrama out of the story, and develop a sense of . . . proportion."

The moral of the story seems clear. Although manufacturing had been a familiar element in the economic history of Europe for centuries, although England itself had passed through an earlier period of accelerated development between 1540 and 1640, the rapidity of technological change in the later eighteenth and early nineteenth centuries was unprecedented. As we shall see in chapter seven, much the same point concerning the rapidity of technological change seems applicable to American experience. Manufactures occupy a familiar place in colonial economic history, but for the most part market and transport limitations dictated that they be what Clark called "neighborhood manufactures," widely dispersed

[8] London, 1948.

rather than geographically concentrated, local manufactures protected by high transport costs from the competition of distant producers. They were "homespun industries," utilizing the tools belonging to age-old handicraft traditions rather than machinery, and in general they were small in scale. Futhermore, they were technologically "backward." Water power was employed in the mill and furnace industries, but most of the wheels were undershot and utilized only a fraction of the water power applied to them. Power transmission was "so little understood that a separate wheel was generally necessary for each article of machinery." These characteristics endured until shortly before the Revolution, when "considerable improvements were made in the application of power to milling machinery and processes." Even in England, of course, the great inventions that gave that nation her industrial eminence "were not successfully applied to manufactures until about the time of the American Revolution." Clark believed that about 1790 "manufacturing everywhere broke away from ancient technical precedents, [and that] processes of production were revolutionized."

It is clear that the availablity of improved techniques formed one of the necessary conditions to a more rapid pace of growth than was possible in the colonial period. But without an expansion in the size of the domestic market in conjunction, as we shall see, with scarcity in the supply of labor, there would have been no incentive to adopt these techniques. The size of the domestic market increased throughout the nineteenth century to a far greater extent than was possible under the conditions of the eighteenth, and this consideration justifies the conclusion that American industrialization and economic growth characterize the nineteenth century far more than they do the earlier years. If, therefore, contemporary and recent scholars have called attention to developments in each of the pre-Civil War decades from the 1820's on, their emphases only italicize the significance of each of these decades.

Manufactures might have been begun to expand somewhat earlier and more largely had it not been for the high profits to be won in foreign commerce following the outbreak of the Anglo-French wars in 1793. In a day when the entire country boasted fewer than a half-dozen millionaires, the trading firm of Robert Oliver & Brothers of Baltimore made in the course of eighteen months during 1806–07 a *net* profit of $775,000. As Adam Seybert observed shortly after the end of the wars ". . . our catalogue of merchants was swelled much beyond what it was entitled to be from the state of our population. Many persons, who had secured moderate capitals, from mechanical pursuits, soon became the most adventurous . . . The brilliant prospects held out by commerce, caused our citizens to neglect the mechanical and manufacturing branches of industry." This relative neglect came to an end with the period of embargo, nonintercourse, and war, and after industrial beginnings thereby substantially enlarged had recovered in the 1820's from the setbacks sustained from renewed British competition following the War of 1812, the more rapid although not uninterrupted growth of manufactures proceeded apace.

Increasingly after about the middle of that decade and fully by the end of the following one (that is, by 1840) it is possible to speak of a domestic market truly national in its dimensions. The national market, as we shall see, made possible a territorial specialization which, as Douglass C. North has observed, raised the productivity of the economy as a whole. Its importance for American economic growth was very great. In the nineteenth century the American common market was to the United States what the European Common Market is to twentieth-century Europe. But neither market could have arisen out of economic change alone. Both were in part products of deliberate political action requiring the creation of a larger sovereignty. For this and many other reasons that we shall examine in the next chapter it would be difficult to overemphasize the importance of government to economic growth.

V

Federal Government and Community Will

Central versus Local Control

Into the era of national independence from the colonial period moved two strong traditions of government in relation to the economy. One was the tradition of regulation, the other the promotion of economic activity. Both stemmed from the same basic concern for the welfare of the community and were less a reflection of European mercantilist principles than of needs for group survival. Numerous price, wage, and commodity regulations combined with bounties and other grants of special privilege to make for a high degree of community participation in economic life. British legislation, however, while also regulatory and promotive, ran along the periphery of community life, being every largely confined to matters of trade and other external relations. Control over local affairs, including taxation, had long been left in the hands of the colonists. For them, therefore, it was psychologically easy to convert custom into a sense of constitutional propriety: local governments were more intimately aware than any distant administration could be of needed services and of property values capable of sustaining them via their tax yields. This understanding of where the line properly lay between the powers of external and internal governments was explicitly achieved only when the crisis in imperial relations after 1763 made it necessary for some of the colonists to reflect upon the nature of the unwritten constitution governing the British empire. Because the deep problem crystallized by that crisis was to persist within America long after it had been resolved imperially by the Revolution, it will be worthwhile to formulate it here more precisely.

We can best understand the nature of the Revolution if we compare it with the Civil War. What was fundamentally involved in both cases was disagreement between central government and local governments as to the nature of the union. In both cases local governments believed the central government to be violating a constitutional division of powers between them. Parliament of course represented the central government of the British Empire, the local governments being those of the colonies. Colonies together with mother country formed in a constitutional sense a greater British nation. All belonged to the same whole. This view of the nature of the empire, interestingly enough, is given by a contemporary American patriot, James Otis. In 1764 Otis described Parliament as the "grand legislature of the nation." The real problem of the revolutionary crisis was to find a satisfactory dividing line between the powers of the "grand legislature" and those of the colonial legislatures. This was a problem of federalism, of the distribution of powers between different levels of government within the framework of the same organized society. The controversy between Parliament and the American legislatures failed of solution by peaceful means. So too did the later controversy between central government in Washington and the states of the South. In both cases failure led to secession, civil war, and the disruption of the union.

The Declaration of Independence transferred the problem of federalism from London and Whitehall to Philadelphia, where it almost immediately became clear that centers of authority long autonomous, alienated not only by British legislation after 1763 but also by late colonial manipulations of the state for private advantage, would continue to resist the surrender of the substance of power to a remote and uncontrollable government, notwithstanding its American character. It is true that the familiar powers granted Congress by the Articles of Confederation are numerous, and it is also true that we are used to looking upon the Articles backwards from the perspective of the Constitution rather than from within the context of their own present. The result is that often we do not appreciate what a long step towards centralization was taken by the adoption of that document. It nevertheless remains true that the Articles did not grant the indispensable power of taxation nor that of control over interstate and foreign commerce. And Article II made entirely clear that "each state retains its sovereignty, freedom, and independence." The first federal constitution assigned to Congress many powers but withheld the power to enforce them. As David Ramsay pointed out in his almost contemporaneous *History of the American Revolution* (1789): "No coercive power was given to the general government, nor was it invested with any legislative power over individuals, but only over states in their corporate capacity."

So old and so strong was the tradition of local self-government, and so well did it fit a land of magnificent distances and slow communications, that it is remarkable nationalist supporters of stronger government won their way in 1788. Four years later Alexander Hamilton observed to Washington that the "new government was opposed in its first establishment by a large proportion of its citizens. . . ." As late as the 1830's Tocqueville could describe the United States as a country "in which every village forms a sort of republic, accustomed to govern itself." By then, the principle of decentralization had been successfully reasserted mainly by men in the main whose interests it served, and it was to dominate the nineteenth century, with sporadic exceptions. While it would be inappropriate to assess here the recent controversial literature concerning the forces behind the Constitution, few historians have balanced many of the active considerations as well as did David Ramsay in 1789:

The prospects of increased employment for shipping, and the enlarge-
ment of Commerce, weighed with those States which abounded in
sailors and ships, and also with seaport towns, to advocate the adoption
of the new system; but those States or parts of States, which depended
chiefly on agriculture, were afraid that zeal for encouraging an American marine, by narrowing the grounds of competition among foreigners for purchasing and carrying their produce, would lessen their
profits. Some of this description therefore conceived that they had a
local interest in refusing the new system. Individuals who had great
influence in state legislatures, or who held profitable places under
them, were unwilling to adopt a government which, by diminishing the
power of the states, would eventually diminish their own importance:
others who looked forward to seats in the general government, or for
offices under its authority, had the same interested reason for supporting its adoption. Some from jealousy of liberty, were afraid of
giving too much power to their rulers; others, from an honest ambition
to aggrandize their country, were for paving the way to national greatness by melting down the separate States into a national mass. The
former feared the New Constitution: the latter gloried in it. Almost
every passion which could agitate the human breast, interested States
and individuals for and against the adoption of the proposed plan of
government. Some whole classes of people were in its favor. The mass
of public creditors expected payment of their debts from the establishment of an efficient government, and were therefore decidedly for its
adoption. Such as lived on salaries, and those who, being clear of debt,
wished for a fixed medium of circulation and the free course of law,
were the friends of a constitution which prohibited the issuing of paper
money and all interference between debtor and creditor. In addition
to these, the great body of independent men, who saw the necessity
of an energetic government, and who, from the jarring interests of the
different States, could not foresee any probability of getting a better
one than was proposed, gave their support to what the federal convention had projected, and their influence effected its establishment.[1]

Men's motives varied and were often in mutual conflict, as Forrest McDonald has shown, and the interests of states largely depended on how well they had managed their affairs as sovereign
entities during the 1780's. It is improbable the uncertainty can
ever be resolved concerning the relative degrees to which private

[1] *History of the American Revolution* (Philadelphia, 1789), II, 342-43.

and public interests supplied the motive power of men and states favoring a more effective government than was possible under the Articles. Certainly it is true that for some men public was private writ large, but Ramsay supplies grounds for believing that others had "an honest ambition to aggrandize their country" and favored "paving the way to national greatness." Nor do I see any reason for ignoring the supporting role of "the great body of independent men, who saw the necessity of an energetic general government."

Numerous events and circumstances in the 1780's sharpened their vision of this necessity, among them the continued British occupation of the Great Lakes posts, Spain's withdrawal of the right-of-deposit at New Orleans, ineffectual defense against Barbary attacks on American shipping, exclusion of the latter from the British West Indies, and inability of the Confederation government to negotiate important commercial treaties. The well-thumbed catalog of events testifying to disparagement abroad and weakness at home need not be reopened here for a detailed reading. Not least importantly, the demonstrated dependence of an undeveloped country upon foreign loans to win its political independence pointed to the probability of a similar need in the future in the event independence should be challenged. In addition, some men saw clearly that this coin had a reverse side, and that the internal development necessary to a higher degree of economic independence would also require foreign capital. Without the tax power to raise funds in order to discharge interest and principal of outstanding indebtedness, the nation's ability to borrow would be severely limited. As E. James Ferguson, the leading authority on public finance for this period, has said: "Whether the United States could have kept its foreign credit alive without a reorganization of the federal system is dubious."

The Constitution and the National Market

Of the many contributions to growth made possible by the adoption of the Constitution, perhaps the most fundamental was that it laid the legal foundations for a national market. The grant to Congress of authority over interstate commerce deprived the states of the power to interpose obstacles to the free movement of people, products, and productive factors throughout the nation. Had the Constitution failed of adoption, the economic interests of the individual states might well, as in the case of Europe, have divided the continental territory into a number of smaller market areas separated from each other by tariff walls. The ensuing limitations upon demand would have abridged the possibility, first, of regional specialization, and second, of large-scale production. The economies of production that flowed in turn from each of these developments would have been lost; unit production costs would have been higher, and goods and services would have been sold at higher prices to relatively few consumers. That these developments did not occur cannot be credited to the Constitution alone. The Constitution did not create a national market, but it made it possible for one to emerge. And the grant to Congress of the power to "dispose of and make all needful Rules and Regulations respecting the Territory or other Property belonging to the United States," and to admit new states into the union, placed under the same legal protection against compartmentalization future increases in the geographic size of that market.

The doing of business within the national market was to be eased by several facilitating provisions of the Constitution. Among these were powers given Congress to coin money and to regulate its value, to establish uniform bankruptcy laws and a uniform rule of naturalization, to establish post offices and post roads, and to promote the progress of science and useful arts by granting copyrights to authors and patents to inventors. The provision extending the federal judicial power to all cases between citizens of different states opened the courts of the Union to cases and controversies concerning property and other rights which might arise in widely separated parts of the national trading area. The power to call forth the militia to suppress insurrections afforded a means of insuring domestic peace, while an effective national army promised defense of western settlements against Indian attack or foreign encroachment. Finally, prohibiting the states from coining money, from emitting bills of credit, from making anything but gold and silver coin a tender in payment of debt, and from passing any law impairing the obligation of contracts, gave promise of greater security to property values and business transactions.

The Supreme Court under Chief Justice John Marshall was to redeem some of these promises by preserving the freedom of commerce within the national market area from abridgment by the states (*Gibbons* v. *Ogden,* 1824), and by contributing to the security of land titles (*Fletcher* v. *Peck,* 1810), in a day when transactions in land bulked large in the nation's business. Under Marshall, however, the power of the Court tended to fall on the side of vested property rights. While the protection of property is necessary to growth—and we shall see later that Marshall's decision in the Dartmouth College case (1819) did not exert the influence often ascribed to it—we shall find the conclusion difficult to avoid that key decisions by the Court under Chief Justice Roger B. Taney were more distinctly favorable to economic growth than those of his illustrious predecessor.

The National Debt

A second fundamental requirement for economic growth was that the new nation accept the mandate and be given the means of discharging its debt. The connection of the national debt with changing patterns of political sovereignty as well as with the emergence of public credit indispensable to public borrowing justifies a fuller discussion of its origin and course than would otherwise be necessary in a book like this one. The public debt originated in the Revolutionary War and had both a foreign and domestic component. France supplied the only foreign loans until early in 1782, when John Adams prevailed upon a number of Dutch mercantile banking houses to underwrite a loan of approximately $2,000,000. As of August 1782 the debt to France was said by the Comptroller of the Treasury to be "above five millions." Originally, the domestic part of the debt consisted only of loan-office certificates, the "war bonds of the Revolution," but bit by bit Congress assumed the responsibility for other obligations that added to its amount. In February 1782 Congress enacted a law providing for a systematic inspection of the claims of civilians, most of which had originated in supplies furnished the Quartermaster and Commissary Departments, and in 1783 it added the claims of the Continental army. Finally, for a decade beginning in 1782, Congress settled the accounts of officials who had handled public money or property during the war. This consolidation of the domestic debt brought its total to more than $27,000,000, the sum being represented by securities originally sold to individuals or subsequently issued in settlement of their claims. By far the two largest components were war bonds and army claims, each of which amounted to approximately $11,000,000.

Up to 1783 only subscribers to war bonds received interest on their securities, but after the consolidation of the floating debt that we have just traced, Congress, in the words of Ferguson, "considered itself bound to pay interest" on the entire debt. But just as the holders of war bonds had sometimes been obliged to receive not interest but written acknowledgements of their right to it (indents), so holders of claims for other services rendered had also to look to the future. The familiar difficulty was Congress's lack of authority to levy taxes under the Articles of Confederation. Its system of requisitioning sums upon the states, which the latter then tried with varying degrees of assiduity and success to levy upon their respective citizens, proved a "failure . . . during the war" and was "still unproductive" afterwards. According to Paul Studenski and Herman E. Krooss, collections from the states fell to 25 per cent of the sums levied, providing a total of only $2,000,-000 in specie between 1783 and 1789. "The financial plight of the country that confronted the Constitutional Convention," says Curtis Nettels, "is illustrated by the fact that in 1786 the total income of the central government was less than one third of the annual charges on the national debt." Largely because of the accumulation of unpaid interest, the debt reached an estimated total of $52,788,000 by the beginning of 1790. As Studenski and Krooss baldly phrase it: "The United States was bankrupt and no state seemed to care."

The members of the Continental Congress cared. In February 1781 Congress had urged the states to grant it the power to levy upon imports an ad valorem impost of 5 per cent, committing itself to employ the proceeds "to the discharge of the principal and interest of the debts already contracted, or which may be contracted, on the faith of the United States, for supporting the present war." The policy of funding, which Hamilton succinctly defined as "the pledging of adequate funds or revenues for paying the interest and for the gradual redemption of [the] debt" was clearly one upon which, as Clarence Ver Steeg points out, "there was universal legislative agreement." The only question was how to do it. Would the states provide sufficient revenue under the requisition system, or should national sources of revenue be developed?

Ferguson believes an alternative to funding was available and would have been followed had Congress not been dominated by "Nationalists" under the leadership of Robert Morris, Superintendent of Finance. The debt might have been distributed among the states, and had this been done the bulk of it probably would have been retired by some such "cheap" method as levying taxes payable in securities. Ferguson holds this to have been an old agrarian technique, expressive of the will of the majority. Instead, he maintains, the financier prodded Congress into recognizing as the obligation of the federal government such a large quantity of debt that its early assumption by the states was forestalled. To discharge this debt required revenue from federal taxes, but the power to levy them required the unanimous consent of the states to amend the Articles. The use of the amendment process to extend the powers of Congress, however, was the real goal of Morris and the nationalists. The public debt was a means to that end, one that was "vital to the strategy of centralization." The nationalists were a propertied, aristocratic minority that wanted a strong central government that would foster business enterprise, encourage the growth of "commercial capitalism," and rid the country of paper money, tender laws, price regulations, embargoes, and antimonopoly laws. Thus, as an obligation of Congress rather than of the states, the public debt "preserved an economic interest in an extension of Congressional powers" and in the years after 1783 "kept alive the movement for national government" that culminated in adoption of the Constitution.

Several considerations render questionable the conspiracy thesis of Ferguson. For one thing, Congress had adopted funding as a policy in February 1781, while Morris did not accept the proffered post of Superintendent of Finance till May nor officially take office till July. For another, the great bulk of the consolidated debt, approximately $22,000,000 of the total of about $27,000,000, represented sums due holders of war bonds and the army. Surely these were debts "contracted on the faith of the United States, for supporting the present war," as the funding resolution of February 1781 expressed it. Nor does it seem unreasonable so to regard the $3,700,000 decided upon as due to civilians who had supplied the army, frequently under military compulsion. Finally, Ver Steeg seems to me persuasive in his argument that if the financier had been successful in realizing his "overpowering objective, the restoration of the public credit," this would have "significantly increase[d] the prestige of the Confederation which Morris conceived to be essential to the preservation of the Union." Clearly, Morris was "attempting to provide a financial and economic program for the Confederation as Hamilton later provided one for the new government under the Constitution." It is true that after 1783 Morris's "thoughts turn[ed] seriously to a complete replacement of the constitutional structure," but this took place only after the defeat of the funding program. His motives, therefore, require assessment within contexts preceding that event.

The Development Program of Robert Morris

That Morris savored many of the objectives named by Ferguson cannot be denied. Indeed, it should be emphasized that while Morris's immediate goal was to fund the debts of the Confederation on the basis of permanent revenues, the ultimate objective behind his hopes of reviving public credit was the economic development of the nation. The financier's objectives have not previously been depicted in these terms, so that the evidence sustaining the characterization deserves detailed review. The financier did not draw up a series of state papers in the manner of Hamilton a decade later, but he did address, among numerous briefer communications, one long letter to the Congress that fully warrants Ver Steeg's evaluation of it as a remarkable Report on Public Credit.

In this Report, dated July 29, 1782, Morris made a strong plea for the adoption of tax measures he believed would do far more than merely provide funds against which both domestic and foreign loans might be opened and current expenditures met. Advocating, besides an impost, taxes on land, polls, and spiritous liquors, he observed, in the manner of Hamilton, that "Taxation to a certain limited point is not only proper but useful, because by stimulating the industry of Individuals it increases the Wealth of the Community." Not only would taxes rouse men from "indolence" so that they would be able to "provide the means of payment"; they would also "encourage economy" in purchases so that money would be "in readiness for the Tax-gatherer." Even if persons borrowed to pay part of their tax bill, an investment of the remainder of the loan in "additional improvements" in agriculture or trade would more than repay the cost of both taxes and interest. For, Morris explained, while interest at 6 per cent would have to be paid, "It is at the same time notorious that the profits made by Husbandmen on funds which they borrowed were very considerable." He thought it no exaggeration to estimate farm profits at 12 per cent, and "the profits made by other professions are equal to those of the Husbandmen." Assuming therefore "that every person in the community made such a loan a similar advantage would arise to the community." Finally, if government were to contract a loan and be permitted by its receipts to ask so much less in taxes, the same advantage would accrue. Hence, Morris was able to conclude that "in a society where the average profits of stock [i.e., capital] are double to the Interest at which money can be obtained, every public loan for necessary expenditures provides a fund in the aggregate of national wealth equal to the discharge of its own interest."

In every society there must be taxes, Morris insisted, "because the necessity of supporting Government and defending the State always exist." But the level of taxation should be sufficiently high not only to meet these needs but also to provide "works of public utility, such as the opening of roads and navigation." Morris envisaged a special usefulness for his proposed tax on land at the rate of $1 per one hundred acres. He divided into two groups the proprietors of the "land of America." The "most numerous and most valuable part" consisted of those "industrious cultivator[s] who owned and occupied their own lands: the free husbandman is the natural Guardian of his Country's freedom." To men cultivating from one to five hundred acres the tax would be "a trifling object." But not to the "great Landholder." For him Morris had no sympathy, and the reason is clear: "a large proportion of America is the property of great landholders, they monopolize it without cultivation, they are (for the most part) at no expence either of money or personal service to defend it, and keeping the price higher by monopoly than otherwise it would be they impede the settlement and culture of the Country." To meet the high aggregate tax bill on their vast acreages would require them to lower their "monopoly" price and sell to men who would place the land under cultivation. The tax would thus "relieve the indigent and aggrandize the State by bringing property into the hands of those who would use it for the Benefit of Society." Every government should seek to repress land monopoly for the purpose of "encouraging settlements and population."

Morris conceded that his poll tax of $1 on all freemen and, with stated exceptions, on all male slaves between 16 and 60 years of age, might be onerous if levied in Europe. "In some parts of Europe where nine-tenths of the people are exhausted by continual labor to procure bad cloathing and worse food, this tax would be extremely oppressive." But the situation of America differed in this regard so much from that of Europe "that hardly any maxim which applies to one will be alike applicable to the other." Not only was labor "in such demand among us, that the Tax will fall on the consumer"; but "in America where three days of labor produce sustenance for a week, it is not unreasonable to ask two days out of a year as a contribution to the payment of public Debts."

So far as the excise tax on spiritous liquors was concerned, ardent spirits "have always been equally prejudicial to the constitutions and morals of the people. The Tax will be a means of compelling vice to support the cause of virtue, and like the Poll Tax draw from the idle and dissolute that contribution to the public revenue which they will not otherwise make."

One final service of taxation is to be noted. Congress had recommended an ad valorem impost in its appeal to the states in February 1781. Morris believed "it would have been well to have stipulated the precise sum payable on different species of commodities." He saw two advantages in specific duties: "First that coarse and bulky commodities *could* not be smuggled to evade the *heavy* duty, and that fine commodities *would* not be smuggled to evade the *light* duty." In the second place, and here is a point deserving special emphasis in view of a common impression that Morris lacked interest in native manufactures, the heavy duty on coarse commodities "would operate [as] an encouragement to produce them at home."

In the light of this evidence it is clear that Morris framed his financial program with broad objectives of national economic development in mind. In a word, he would encourage westward migration by having government open the way with internal improvements and by compelling holders of idle land to sell it to men who would place it under cultivation. He apparently wished to encourage population growth, and twice in this letter he referred to the convenience of government's possessing population statistics. Finally, he wished to promote domestic manufactures via import duties, to encourage borrowing for the purpose of capital investment in agriculture and industry, to squeeze socially useful labor out of indolence, and to discourage the injurious effects of strong drink.

This concern with the size and efficiency of the labor force, and with increasing the supply of capital, has a very modern ring, as does the almost puritanical emphasis on frugality and civic responsibility. By these emphases underdeveloped nations in the twentieth century often try to initiate a more rapid process of growth. To facilitate this end these nations also seek to attract foreign capital funds to compensate for insufficient domestic supplies. Morris, too, wished to do so: "money lent by the City of Amsterdam to clear the forests of America would be beneficial to both. Draining marshes and bringing forests under culture are beneficial to the whole human race; but most so to the Proprietor." But as he disarmingly noted: "It may seem superfluous to add that credit is necessary to the obtaining of loans." And "this must be done at home before it can be extended abroad." To expect that foreigners would trust a government that had no credit with its own citizens, he had written to the President of Congress in February 1782, "would be madness."

Morris had an additional reason for emphasizing the importance of domestic credit: "It is however an advantage peculiar to domestic loans, that they give stability to Government by combining together the interests of moneyed men for its support, and consequently in this Country a domestic debt, would greatly contribute to that Union, which seems not to have been sufficiently attended to, or provided for, in forming the national compact." "A Government torn by intestine commotions is not likely to acquire or maintain credit at home or abroad." Furthermore, the provision of "solid funds for the national debt" would resurrect debts "which are in a manner dead." And by "distributing property into those hands which could render it most productive" not only would revenue be increased, but the restoration of public credit would revivify private credit: the "secret hoards would be unlocked."

Other Early Interest in Internal Improvements

The similarity between Morris's objectives and those of Hamilton is remarkable and points to the essential continuity between the Federalist program for economic development in the 1790's and that of the nationalists a decade earlier. Did these programs represent the interests and express the wishes of a mere wealthy minority? I shall have more to say on this important question after describing the legislation of the nineties, but it is pertinent to note here that both programs originated in a wider public demand for development than is commonly appreciated. Indeed, both were later and more comprehensive definitions of what Samuel Rezneck once called a "widely prevalent and pervasive zeal for useful improvements" that can be traced back at least as far as the mid-eighteenth century.

Useful knowledge and improvements come close to defining the "philosophical" interests of Benjamin Franklin and his intercolonial circle of *"virtuosi* or ingenious men," as he termed them. His original circular letter of May 13, 1743, suggesting the establishment of the American Philosophical Society, bore the title: "A Proposal for Promoting Useful Knowledge among the British Plantations in America." Among numerous items of useful knowledge Franklin included "new mechanical inventions for saving labour, as mills and carriages, and for raising and conveying of water, draining of meadows, etc.; all new arts, trades, and manufactures, that may be proposed or thought of; . . . [and] new improvements in planting, gardening and clearing land." Fused in

1769 with the American Society Held at Philadelphia for Promoting Useful Knowledge, the American Philosophical Society displayed a keen interest in many forms of "useful improvements" and established a standing Committee on American Improvements. Among the objects engaging the pragmatic attention of the Committee was the importation of silkworms for the encouragement of manufactures and the study of the prospects of a canal to connect the Chesapeake and the Delaware. The Committee members conducting the latter study were later praised as men "whose views, extending beyond themselves, [were] employed upon objects of general benefit and utility." Similarly, the American Academy of Arts and Sciences, incorporated in Boston in May 1780 following the efforts of John Adams in its behalf, included within its objectives the promotion and encouragement of "improvements in agriculture, arts, manufactures and commerce" and a determination of "the uses to which the various natural productions of the country may be applied."

The early interest of the American Philosophical Society in internal improvements received added impulse from the political misunderstandings preceding the Revolution. "After the troubles caused by the Stamp Act [1765]," says Weeden, "we note a growing desire for American goods, with a constant social pressure to encourage the use of them, and the manufacture on a larger scale." Towns in Massachusetts offered premiums to encourage the growth of raw materials and their manufacture while the New York Society for the Promotion of the Arts, Agriculture and Œconomy offered premiums for local manufactures, established a spinning school, and conducted a fortnightly market for the sale of New York manufactures. In February 1776 Congress adopted a resolution proposing the formation of societies for the promotion of manufactures in all the colonies. Already at this early date, as Rezneck points out, Alexander Hamilton had a vision of America's "grandeur and glory" that would follow upon the development of manufactures. Nor was he alone. Among the patrons and managers of the United Company of Philadelphia, a public enterprise that flourished between the years 1775–78, were such men as Tench Coxe, Samuel Wetherill, and Christopher Marshall, all of whom became "persistent and devoted advocates of American manufactures."

During the depression years of the 1780's "patriotism provided the impetus" for a renewal of manufacturing zeal. Beginning in 1785, the mechanics, tradesmen, and manufacturers formed societies and committees in New York, Boston, Baltimore, and Providence for the purpose of promoting public encouragement of their interests. Urging union and cooperation upon similar societies in other towns, the Boston Association of Tradesmen and Manufacturers declared in a circular letter of 1788: "These States are so extensive in their boundaries, so various in their climate, and so connected in their national interests, that if a plan could be adopted throughout the confederation for the exchange of the produce and manufactures of each State, we conceive it would serve to cement a general union." In February 1789 Washington wrote to Jefferson that "the greatest and most important objects of internal concern, which at present occupy the public mind, are manufactures and inland navigation." It is clear that by the first years of the federal government, "Manufactures, like the Constitution, were expected to strengthen the country and help it achieve true independence." Reflecting these concerns of the "public mind," Congress invited Hamilton to draw up his well-known series of economic reports. Taken together, as Joseph Dorfman observes, the reports "constitute a theoretical plan which is just beginning to be appreciated."

Hamilton's Program

Alexander Hamilton's values are too well known for detailed description, informing as they do his celebrated Reports on Public Credit (January 1790 and January 1795), a National Bank (December 1790), and Manufactures (December 1791), as well as his private correspondence and other writings. Like Morris, the Secretary of the Treasury (1789–95) emphasized the need for an alliance between government and men of wealth in order to cement the union, bolster public credit, provide increased capital funds for development from both foreign and domestic sources, and provide the setting of stability in which those funds would flow with confidence. Envisaging a wide promotional role for government he wished it to encourage the development of a balanced and self-sufficient economy, and held that the "improvement of the communications between the different parts of our country is an object well worthy of the national purse." Like Morris he regarded taxation as "a spur to industry": "We labor less now than any civilized nation of Europe; and a habit of labor in the people is as essential to the health and vigor of their minds and bodies, as it is conducive to the welfare of the state." He also wished to discourage the "consumption of ardent spirits," which he found regrettable "as well in regard to the health and morals as to the economy of the community." Like Morris once again, Hamilton stressed the need to increase "the active or productive capital of a country" and scorned "dead stock."

The parallelism cannot be extended too far, not because of many significant differences between the views and objectives of the two men but because differences in historical context and opportunity permitted Hamilton a fuller exposition and also because, as I believe, Hamilton was the more farseeing of the two. He advocated, for example, government aid to institutions supporting agriculture and the arts, and he favored the founding of a national university. One significant contrast should be noted: Morris wished to encourage western settlement by destroying large-scale ownership of land, whereas Hamilton saw migration as injurious to the progress of manufactures and preferred using the public lands as a source of revenue.

The development programs of the two financiers differed less in their content than in their legislative fate. Fundamental change in the political structure permitted most of Hamilton's to be enacted into law, although it is true that the revenue objectives of the tariff legislation before 1816 were more pronounced than their protective aspects. The Constitution gave Congress the power to tax, naming first among the objectives of that power: "to pay the debts . . . of the United States" (Art. I, sec. 8). Article VI made explicitly clear that "all debts contracted and engagements entered into, before the adoption of this Constitution, shall be as valid against the United States under this Constitution, as under the Confederation." Then in August 1790 Congress enacted the well-known Hamiltonian measures for funding not only the Revolutionary War debts of the Confederation but also those of the states. In 1789 Congress had already provided a source of national revenue by levying duties on imports; in 1791, yielding to Hamilton's fears that income from duties might not prove sufficient for both the needs of current expenditures and the servicing of the debt, it enacted the first of three excise tax bills to be passed during the 1790's. These measures, together with deliberate open-market purchases of securities by the Secretary of the Treasury, soon raised the credit of the United States.

The restoration of public credit had effects important for economic growth. In the first place, eroded capital values were restored. Paper claims, which appear to have fallen as low as 15 cents on the dollar in early 1788, rose above par by August 1791. In the second place, foreign capital seeking investment in government funds began to flow in increasing volume into the United States. Foreign holdings of American public debt amounted to $2,746,840 on November 13, 1788, and on August 16, 1790 the sum was $5,477,042. Purchased at par and above, these holdings continued to rise, reaching $20,288,637 by May 1795 and $33,041,-135 on September 30, 1801. Finally and most importantly, there occurred a result that to my knowledge has never been better described than by historian Richard Hildreth more than one hundred years ago:

The great secret of the beneficial operation of the funding system was the reestablishment of confidence; for commercial confidence, though political economists may have omitted to enumerate it among the elements of production, is just as much one of those elements as labor, land, or capital—a due infusion of it increasing in a most remarkable degree the productive activity of those other elements, and the want of it paralyzing their power to a corresponding extent. By the restoration of confidence in the nation, confidence in the states, and confidence in individuals, the funding system actually added to the labor, land, and capital of the country a much greater value than the amount of the debt thereby charged upon them.[2]

It is indeed possible that the resurgence of public credit, by lowering the interest rate on government debt, led in turn to a reduction in the market rate of interest and thus cheapened the capital costs of investment. Certainly this was one of the objectives which the brilliant William Bingham, merchant-banker of Philadelphia, had in mind when he urged Hamilton in November 1789 to do everything possible to resuscitate the public credit. Other nations, he reminded the Secretary of the Treasury, were "in the practice of mortgaging their revenue to their Creditors."

If we offer a less Substantial Security, we must Submit to a consequent Depreciation in the Value of our Funds,—This will essentially tend to raise the Market rate of Interest, of which the public Funds are generally the Index.—Now, a great object of Government should be to lower the Interest of Money, which, independent of other Advantages (as connected with the flourishing State of Agriculture, Manufactures, & Commerce) would enable the Public to borrow on Such Terms, as would admit of extinguishing part of the Capital of the Debt, if its Creditors would not assent to a reduction of their Interest,—A Government should therefore pledge every security it can offer, to engage the Confidence of the public Creditors, which, if once impaired, the pernicious Effects will be felt in all its future Dealings.[3]

"Our public credit," a jubilant Washington wrote in July 1791, "stands on that ground, which three years ago it would have been considered as a species of madness to have foretold."

Looking back upon funding Hamilton was expansive. "What have been the effects of this system?" he asked. His answer was:

[2] *The History of the United States of America* (New York, 1856), IV, 276.
[3] Quoted by James O. Wettereau, "Letters from Two Business Men to Alexander Hamilton on Federal Fiscal Policy, November, 1789", *Journal of Economic and Business History*, III, August 1931, p. 673.

An extension of commerce and manufactures, the rapid growth of our cities and towns, the consequent prosperity of agriculture, and the advancement of the farming interest. All this was effected by giving life and activity to a capital in the public obligations, which was before dead, and by converting it into a powerful instrument of mercantile and other industrious enterprise.[4]

Hamilton's unicausal explanation is insufficient, but it does underscore my general point that the contribution of these fundamental measures of government to growth cannot be ignored. What government had done was to tax one group of people (chiefly, buyers of imported goods and grain farmers who converted their crops into whiskey) for the immediate benefit of a smaller group of people (securities holders) in order to achieve a later and larger benefit for the American community as a whole. It had adopted a program of forced savings as a technique for increasing the supply of capital funds in an underdeveloped country. And while part of that increase was direct and immediate, much the greater increment came as a by-product of restored public and private confidence. Blending inseparably with profit opportunities created by growing markets and expanding population, the improved security framework of investment played an important part in the nation's subsequent ability to attract needed funds from abroad.

The Legislation of the 1790's

"In matters of industry," Hamilton wrote in 1801, "human enterprise ought, doubtless, to be left free in the main; not fettered by too much regulation; but practical politicians know that it may be beneficially stimulated by prudent aids and encouragements on the part of the government." During the dozen years of Federalist rule from 1789 to 1801, enterprise received from government a number of "prudent aids and encouragements" in addition to the measures taken in behalf of the nation's credit. To nascent manu-

[4] Richard B. Morris, ed. *Alexander Hamilton and the Founding of the Nation* (New York, 1957), p. 317.

factures Congress in 1789 gave a tariff which, while mild in comparison with later ones, F. W. Taussig calls "protective in intention and spirit." Some two years later, in December 1791, Hamilton submitted his Report on Manufactures, calling for payments of bounties, premiums, and awards, and recommending twenty-one increases in existing tariff rates and five reductions in the rates on raw materials. The House pigeonholed the report, but in March 1792 a new tariff law incorporated eighteen of his twenty-one increases and three of his five reductions. The shipbuilding industry benefited from a multipronged effort to develop a native merchant marine. The fisheries and coastal trade were closed to vessels not built and owned by Americans, while discriminatory tonnage and import duties favored native construction and ownership over foreign vessels in international trade. The subsequent expansion of shipping tonnage under American registry from 972,000 tons in 1800 to 5,354,000 tons in 1860 owed much to this encouragement. To encourage trade with the Far East, duties on Oriental products imported in foreign vessels were made higher than those carried in American ships. Finally, the mercantile community generally and the interests of national credit as well were served by the chartering of the Bank of the United States in 1791. Besides providing short-term loans to government and business, the Bank augmented the scarce currency supply and performed numerous other services. Not least of these was its widening of the market for government securities through the requirement that three-fourths the amount of each subscription to the Bank's stock be paid for in those securities. Foreign holders of Bank stock, as James O. Wettereau pointed out, were extensive, amounting to thirteen thousand shares in January 1798 and to eighteen thousand shares in March 1809.

Federal Legislation and Community Will

To what extent did this strongly promotive legislation represent the wishes of the American community? In view of the emphasis I have placed upon the importance to economic growth of a people's desire for growth, the question is a significant one, and it is extremely difficult to answer. As is so often the case in history, the great mass remains inarticulate. The complexities of the present case are compounded not only by the attrition of direct historical evidence, but by the existence of obstacles to the formation and expression of public opinion. Some of these are implied in Jefferson's emphasis upon the importance of public education, in the dispersion of settlement, the problems of transportation, and the relative paucity of organs of information, especially in the rural areas where most people lived. Legal limitations upon the suffrage remained significant until about 1810. All of these considerations make more difficult the problem of deciding what program spoke for the interests of the majority. We know the majority were farmers but the extent to which the legislation of the nineties was contrary to their interests and opposed by them is far from certain.

Some historians have characterized this legislation as "capitalistic" and contrasted it with the agrarian persuasion of Jefferson. A familiar tradition makes Hamilton spokesman for the interests of an elite in commerce, finance, and manufacturing, and associates him with intervention by central government in behalf of these interests. Jefferson is depicted as the champion of a rural America in which the rights of the states are viewed as the bulwarks of republicanism. Occasionally substantive parts of this tradition are challenged, as occurred some three decades ago with the publication of a distinguished study of Jefferson by Gilbert Chinard. The most recent and most vigorous statement of an opposing point of view is that of E. A. J. Johnson, who is convinced that "great national policy decisions concerning economic development must be based on agreement not on discord, variance, or uncompromising truculence," and that "it is only meretricious to contrast Hamiltonian with Jeffersonian policy or solemnly to attribute intervention to one party and libertarianism to another." We may determine which of these views lies closer to the truth by tracing the rise of opposition to the Hamiltonian program and then comparing Jefferson's presidential principles to the measures he proposed for enactment by the federal government.

Unquestionably, much of the early legislation enjoyed widespread support. As Ferguson says, the "remarkable ease" with which the transfer of the substance of political power to the central government was accomplished testifies to the "growth in national feeling." It would be a mistake, he adds, to assume that Hamilton's proposals regarding the public debt "seriously divided either the people or their delegates in Congress." Madison's suggestion that the government discriminate between original and present holders of securities was rejected by the great majority of Congress. Ethically attractive, it appears to have arisen out of Madison's desire to restore his declining political prestige in Virginia, and while it might have been possible to identify "a great many" original holders, discrimination, as Hamilton forcefully argued, would have jeopardized the security of future transfers and damaged public credit. The proposal to assume the debts of the states encountered far more opposition, especially on the part of the South, where "to a relatively greater extent than elsewhere" the costs of the war had already been absorbed by the states. The circumstances in which Jefferson put aside his initial hostility and entered into his famous "bargain" with Hamilton are familiar.

It proved otherwise with Hamilton's proposal in December 1790 that the government charter a national bank. Jefferson feared that the resort by the Secretary of the Treasury to loose constructionism to justify the constitutionality of the bank would prove a foot in the door that would enable him to move increasingly in the direction of the more consolidated government he was known to favor. Jefferson attributed to motives of personal profit the support given Hamilton by a number of Congressmen who owned securities. "Are the people in your quarter as well contented with the proceedings of our government as their representatives say they are?" he asked New York's Robert R. Livingston on February 4, 1791. Affirming the existence of "a vast mass of discontent gathered in the South,"

Jefferson sought to reverse the trend in government by increasing the weight in the "republican scale" in Congress. His letter of the same date to George Mason of Virginia shows how he hoped to accomplish this: the "only corrective of what is corrupt in our present form of government will be the augmentation of the numbers in the lower house, so as to get a more agricultural representation, which may put that interest above that of stockjobbers."

Parties began to form in Congress in 1792, and such was the success of Jefferson, Madison, and other leaders of the opposition that it is perhaps possible to speak of a Democratic-Republican majority in the House in the Third Congress (1793–95). Certainly by the end of that Congress in 1795 differences in reactions to the Hamiltonian program and to issues growing out of the behavior of revolutionary France had produced two apparently rigidly formed parties. Thereafter the electorate returned Federalist majorities to the Congresses of the 1790's, but with the election of Jefferson in 1800 a Democratic-Republican majority appeared in both House and Senate. And in both chambers the size of that majority increased steadily during Jefferson's two administrations.

Now Jefferson occasionally remarked that political opposition served the useful purpose of criticism, but fundamentally he did not believe in the party system. Both during his presidency and later he was convinced that "the mass of our countrymen, even of those who call themselves Federalists, are republicans." This did not apply to the Federalist leaders, whom he considered irredeemable monarchists, a mere faction he wished to sink into an abyss so deep as to make its resurrection impossible, as he once put it. "I will not say our *party,* the term is false and degrading, but our *nation,*" he wrote in 1811. "For the republicans are the *nation.* Their opponents are but a faction, weak in numbers, but powerful and profuse in the command of money, and backed by England." The bulk of the membership he believed to have been "decoyed into the net of the monarchists by the X. Y. Z. contrivance" and he made it a cardinal point of his Presidency to win it back to republicanism. "The greatest good we can do our country is to heal it's party divisions & make them one people," he wrote in July 1801. Both during his presidency and afterwards he rejoiced in the electoral evidence of mounting republican ascendancy, and in 1825, the year before his death, it pained him to observe that "the parties exist as heretofore." It is clear Jefferson believed that republicans composed, as he expressed it in the fall of 1801, "a very great majority of the nation."

As spokesman for that majority Jefferson subordinated his own private views to those he believed were held by his fellow citizens. "However, their will, not mine, be done." In November 1801 he spoke of "a sense of obligation imposed on me by the public will." "My idea is that where two measures are equally right, it is a duty to the people to adopt that one which is most agreeable to them," he wrote earlier in that same year. "What is practicable must often controul what is pure theory," he said in 1802, "and the habits of the governed determine in a great degree what is practicable."

The historical tradition which emphasizes Jefferson's "Vergilian vision," his hostility to banks of issue, speculation, and the fluctuant values of a "paper system," to great cities, to manufactures other than those made in households, and to commerce other than that necessary for the carrying off of the agricultural surplus, calls attention to the private, not the public, values of the President. Indeed, despite undoubted change in his opinions, as for example may be seen in his famous letters to John Jay in April 1809 and to Benjamin Austin in January 1816, I am convinced that the weight of his private preference from the writing of *Notes on Virginia* to the last years of his life falls on the side of agrarian simplicity. The nation's experience before and during the War of 1812 does not mark, as it is sometimes implied, his permanent shift to the cause of industrialism. He reacted angrily to the Tariff of 1824, and six months before his death deplored, in a letter to Madison, that "the general prostration of the farming business, under levies for the support of manufacturers, etc. with the calamitous fluctuations of value in our paper medium, have kept agriculture in a state of abject depression."

But Jefferson's agrarian preferences, as Chinard has said, "remained largely theoretical, sentimental, and personal." They do not help us understand why John Randolph, John Taylor of Caroline, Nathaniel Macon, and other "Old Republicans" among his contemporaries and many historians since have believed, as Joseph Dorfman expresses it, that Jefferson, "anti-Hamiltonian out of supreme office, became in good part Hamiltonian as President." His behavior in office becomes clear when we realize that he sought to give expression not to his private values but to the majority will. As Chinard has noted, "one may find a flagrant contradiction between his public utterances and the private letters he wrote to his friends." These contradictions attest neither to hypocrisy nor insincerity but rather to Jefferson's feeling that he had no "right to attempt to shape the destinies of his country according to his own preferences."

In both his public pronouncements and official acts we see a President desirous of furthering the nation's economic development. Believing a large territory necessary for the preservation of a republic, he instructed government agents to "familiarize . . . [the Indians] to the idea that it is for their interest to cede lands at times to the U.S." If the Indians gave up hunting and adopted agriculture and household manufactures, and Jefferson was "disposed to aid and encourage it liberally," they would be enabled "to live on smaller portions of land. . . . While they are learning to do better on less land, our increasing numbers will be calling for more land." By purchasing the Louisiana Territory he more than doubled the land area of the United States. Protection of the western trade via New Orleans prompted the original negotiations, and his desire to expand that trade to the Pacific induced him to dispatch Lewis and Clark on their famed expedition of 1803. "The object of your mission," he informed Captain Meriwether Lewis in April 1803, "is to explore the Missouri river, & such principal streams of it, as, by it's course & communication with the water of the Pacific Ocean may offer the most direct & practicable water communication across this continent, for the purposes of commerce." Wishing to encourage population growth as well as trade and increases in the size of the national domain, he recommended to Congress in 1801 a liberalization of the naturalization laws. And in 1802 he suggested to Congress the probable expediency of encouraging western settlement in areas to which Indian titles had been extinguished.

An expanding population, territory, and domestic trade required improved communications with the interior, and in both his sixth and eighth Annual Messages Jefferson invited Congress to consider the application of surplus revenues "to the improvement of roads, canals, rivers, education, and other great foundations of prosperity and union, under the powers which Congress may already possess, or such amendment of the constitution as may be approved by the states." The federal government had already taken steps which would culminate in its construction of the National Road. In April 1802 Congress admitted Ohio to the Union by an enabling act which also provided that five per cent of the net proceeds of sale of public lands within that state should constitute a fund for the building of roads. In this act lay the origins of the National Road, and in 1806 Congress adopted "An Act to Regulate the Laying Out and Making of a Road from Cumberland, in the State of Maryland."

Following the President's Annual Message of that year, the Senate directed Secretary of the Treasury Albert Gallatin to draw up "a plan for the application of such means as are within the power of Congress, to the purposes of opening roads and making canals, together with a statement of the undertakings of that nature, which, as objects of public improvement, may require and deserve the aid of Government." Gallatin's resultant Report on Roads and Canals, which Carter Goodrich characterizes as "a notable ten-year plan of national action," was predicated on "the maintenance of peace, the continuation of substantial revenues from customs, and the absence of great military expenditure." Since none of these conditions obtained, it proved impossible to implement the report. Its existence, as well as the passage of the Ohio Enabling Act, nevertheless reveals the willingness of a Democratic-Republican President and Congress to employ the resources of the national government for purposes of development.

President Jefferson also revealed this willingness on other occasions and in relation to other areas of economic expansion and national development. In 1802 he invited Congress to "protect the manufactures adapted to our circumstances" and to "foster our fisheries and nurseries of navigation." "On my part," his message concluded, "you may count on a cordial concurrence in every measure for the public good." Two years later he called attention to an even broader array of "great interests," all of which he had identified in his First Annual Message:

Agriculture, manufactures, commerce, and navigation, the four pillars of our prosperity, are the most thriving when left most free to individual enterprise. Protection from casual embarrassments, however, may sometimes be interposed. If in the course of your observations or inquiries they should appear to need any aid within the limits of our constitutional power, your sense of their importance is a sufficient assurance they will occupy your attention.[5]

As Chinard observes, this last sentence "could only mean one thing, that the President was not ready to depart entirely and radically from Hamilton's policy of giving encouragement to manufactures." "If it is true," Chinard adds, "that during Jefferson's administration industrial and agricultural interests clashed for the first time in America, I fail to see that the President made any effort to favor agriculture at the expense of industry."

If the Hamiltonians stood for a protective tariff, so too did the Jeffersonians. Reporting on various petitions for protection addressed to Congress, the House Committee of Commerce and Manufactures observed in February 1803 that "sound policy" justified "granting governmental aid for the protection of such manufactures as are obviously capable of affording to the United States an adequate supply" of the numerous products specified in

[5] *The Works of Thomas Jefferson,* ed. Paul L. Ford (New York, 1905), IX, 339. The date is December 8, 1801.

the petitions. Facing a prospect of government surplus in 1806, Jefferson did not recommend abandoning protective duties: "Shall we suppress the impost and give that advantage to foreign over domestic manufactures?" he asked rhetorically. It would be preferable, he said, to continue the impost and apply its proceeds to "the great purposes of the public." "People generally have more feeling for canals and roads than education," he confessed to Joel Barlow at the end of 1807. "However, I hope we can advance them with equal pace." Noting at the end of 1808 the increasing application "of our industry and capital to internal manufactures and improvements" as a result of the suspension of foreign commerce, Jefferson commented: "little doubt remains that the establishments formed and forming will—under the auspices of cheaper materials and subsistence, the freedom of labor from taxation with us, and of protecting duties and prohibitions— become permanent."

Anyone remembering Jefferson's four-year tenure as Secretary of State could hardly have been surprised by the direction taken by his policies as President. In 1793, as Taussig says, he had "advocated vigorous measures of protection directed against England." In that year, says Jefferson's biographer Dumas Malone, the future president "was more concerned with the total economic life and development of the country" than was Hamilton!

As President, he was only less so. Jefferson's essential economic difference with Hamilton concerned fiscal matters, and his larger difference he believed to be a moral one. He deplored a system he believed contrived for deluging the states with paper money instead of specie, "for withdrawing our citizens from the pursuits of commerce, manufactures, buildings, and other branches of useful industry, to occupy themselves and their capitals in a species of gambling, destructive of morality, and which has introduced its poison in the government itself." He set his face against note-issuing banks, with no more understanding of their economic function than Jackson or Benton were later to display. Yet precisely as the Jackson administration was to do following the Bank War, he favored a policy of depositing public monies in banks that were politically friendly: "I am decidedly in favor of making all the banks Republican, by sharing deposits among them in proportion to the dispositions they show," he informed Gallatin in July 1803. "It is material to the safety of Republicanism to detach the mercantile interests from its enemies and incorporate them into the body of its friends. A merchant is naturally a Republican, and can be otherwise only from a vitiated state of things."

In fine, I do not argue that Jefferson advocated industrialization to the extent that Hamilton had. But he did advocate it, and the development of other sectors of the economy as well. He did so despite private preferences to the contrary, believing that this was what "a very great majority of the nation" wanted. If he was right in his judgment, and his constantly increasing support by the electorate suggests he was, does it not become difficult to maintain that whereas Jefferson served majority interests, Hamilton served those of a minority? Both employed the resource of government to promote development; both wished to employ it even more than either was allowed to do. And if these things are true, does it not follow that E. A. J. Johnson is right in maintaining that there is no essential difference between the economic objectives and political means of the groups represented respectively by Hamiltonianism and Jeffersonianism? Both bespoke the interests and wishes of a nation anxious to root its political independence in the soil of economic development.

Later Federal Aids to Development

The three Republican presidents who followed Jefferson in the White House virtually complete the identification of Hamiltonianism and Jeffersonianism. Madison approved bills establishing the Second Bank of the United States and the Tariff of 1816; Monroe signed a General Survey Bill that looked forward to a broad system of internal improvements, approved a measure authorizing Congress to subscribe $300,000 to the stock of the Chesapeake and

Delaware Canal Company, and signed into law the Tariff of 1824; John Quincy Adams won Congressional authority to survey the Florida canal route, clear the Ohio River, grant lands to Illinois and Indiana for canals to be built by those states, make stock subscriptions to the Louisville and Portland Canal, the Dismal Swamp Canal, and the Chesapeake and Ohio Canal, and push the ever rising level of the tariff to a new high in 1828.

We may add to this list of federal aids to enterprise during the pre-Civil War years: the use of the public domain to make land grants to the states for internal improvements, the adoption of increasingly liberal laws governing its alienation to the public, the employment of Army Engineers to survey railway routes, the granting of rebates on imports of railroad iron, construction of military roads on the frontier, and the improvement of rivers and harbors. In addition, the distribution of the treasury surplus in 1837 provided funds which a number of states applied to purposes of internal improvements. The fiscal activities of the Treasury Department and occasionally the policies of the Second Bank contributed to monetary and credit stability, although these may have had adverse effects on growth. Government also provided subsidies for steamships, subsidies and bounties to the codfishery, money for the first magnetic telegraph line, and interest-free advances on government contracts with the manufacturers of small-arms. Not least, it used the public domain to promote the cause of education, granting lands to the states for common schools and, in the 1860's, for state universities.

VI

The Shift from Federal Aid

Grants of land to aid in the development of educational institutions and improved transportation constitute the main exception to a general tendency on the part of the federal government to play a declining promotional role as we approach the Civil War. During Jackson's administrations government took a definitive stand against the use of federal funds for new internal improvements projects, turned over the completed portions of the National Road to the four states in which they lay, refused to extend the life of the Second Bank, and moved in the direction of lower tariffs. In the main, advances to the makers of small-arms ceased after 1830. The Treasury Department was formally separated from the banking system under Van Buren; in 1846 and again in 1857 tariff rates were substantially lowered; and in 1858 the program of subsidies for steamships came to an end.

Democratic administrations predominated after 1829, and in this later period if not during the first quarter of the century Democrats adhered somewhat more closely to the Jeffersonian ideal of limited government. With respect to river and harbor improvements, Presidents Van Buren, Tyler, Polk, Pierce, and Buchanan were more strict constructionists than even Jackson had been. While it would be a mistake to discount the force of Old Republican values,

[124

especially in the case of Jackson, it is not primarily a growth in political idealism that explains this phenomenon. The most fundamental explanation is the maturation of conflicting sectional, state, and occupational interests. The sharpness of these differences made it difficult to reach agreements covering any wide area of national life. Once again, therefore, as in the years preceding the Revolution and in those of the Confederation period, the constitutional question of the nature of the Union thrust itself increasingly into the forefront of American public life. As in those earlier years, a diversity of local interests militated against decisive action on the part of the central government.

Two other strands also enter into this developing centrifugal pattern. For one, with the increasing accumulation of stocks of private capital, men and groups lacking the advantages given by law to older corporate groups turned in the name of egalitarian opportunity against privilege sanctioned by the political process. Secondly, as slavery edged ever closer to the center of the national stage, southern leaders determined to contain federal authority within narrow bounds. As John Randolph observed during a debate on internal improvements during the 1820's: "If Congress possesses the power to do what is proposed by this bill they may emancipate every slave in the United States." In a basic sense, therefore, those leading public issues which involved the constitutional power of the federal government also involved slavery. But questions concerning land policy, the tariff, internal improvements, and the Bank also possess an independent importance. The fear of emancipation cannot explain all presidential vetoes of internal improvements bills or public pronouncements concerning the unconstitutionality of direct federal action in this area. Opposition to logrolling, waste, local bickering, and corrupt uses of patronage also played a part.

In the area of public land disposal policy, New England businessmen until the mid-forties supported southern opposition to more liberal terms, although for different reasons. The increasingly industrializing Northeast feared a loss of labor, and the consequence of higher wages. Southerners feared both the consequences of loss of revenue from land sales and a possible peopling of the Southwest by newcoming small farmers who might prove less deeply committed to the defense of slavery than older residents. In addition, many new territories were unsuited to the plantation slave system. Increased immigration in the forties and fifties, together with increased investment opportunities in the West, changed the viewpoint of many New Englanders, and thereafter the South represented the main obstacle to the enactment of homestead legislation.

Vital differences over the tariff were also sectional and occupational in nature. Calhoun, Hayne, and other political spokesmen of the southern planters pointed out that a region which consumed a large quantity of manufactured goods would have to pay higher prices because of the tariff: if it were so high as to be prohibitive, the absence of competing foreign imports might enable domestic producers the more easily to agree on price increases; if the level were lower, some part of the duty on imports would be added to the price. Already paying commissions, interest, and shipping charges to New York and other merchants engaged in marketing and financing the sales of their cotton, a tariff would squeeze them at the other end and push the real terms of trade—the amount of manufactured goods a given quantity of cotton would buy—further in their disfavor. After 1816, following a brief flirtation with the possibility of developing a more balanced regional economy, the predominantly Democratic South, with the support of important Whig elements, threw its weight against protection. Aided by northern commercial and railroad interests, as Thomas C. Cochran points out, southern spokesmen managed to obtain lowered tariffs after 1833 and to prevent or modify subsequent increases prior to 1861.

Internal improvements at federal expense, too, were nearly always opposed by the South. Not only was the region well supplied with rivers for carrying western produce to the South and southern cotton to sea, but the construction costs would reduce federal funds and make necessary an increase in the tariff level to replenish them. In the earlier years of the century, furthermore, the "greatest of the improvements," as Carter Goodrich observes, were those designed to overcome the barrier of the Appalachian Mountains. But improved trade connections between East and West "brought little benefit to the southern states and to the Lower South, none at all." Henry Clay's "American System," which called for tariff protection for the East and internal improvements for the West, posed the possibility of an East-West alliance that would threaten the political position of the South. Presiding over the Memphis Convention in 1845, however, John C. Calhoun bespoke southern anxiety over the effects upon southern wealth of the great rise in direct shipments of western produce to the East, and called upon the federal government to improve the navigation of the western rivers. The West favored rapid settlement not only for its effects on land values, general business, and access to eastern markets but also because growing population provided a greater degree of security against Indian attack. For the same reasons the region's spokesmen in Congress generally approved liberal land policies.

Finally, we may determine sectional attitudes toward the Second Bank of the United States by examining the vote in the Senate on the 1832 bill to recharter that institution. New England fell short of unanimous support by the single opposing vote of Hill of New Hampshire; the middle states cast only three votes against the bill, two from New York and one from New Jersey; the South and Southwest, on the other hand, cast only three votes in its favor, those being the Louisiana senators and one from Mississippi; the West favored the institution except for the divided votes of Kentucky, Illinois, and Missouri. As Ralph C. H. Catterall, the historian of the Second Bank, summarizes the vote: "The determined opposition was from the South and the Southwest."

State Aid to Development

Even within the individual states distinct geographic and other interests made state-wide agreements difficult, and they were often achieved only by the grant of costly or wasteful concessions to disaffected areas or groups. Intrastate conflicts were nevertheless more easily harmonized than differences between national regions, and, in consequence, the promotional activities of state and local governments exceeded by far those of the federal government. Public encouragement of enterprises essential to community welfare had long been practiced, and the forms assumed by some of these activities after independence would have been familiar to the colonial period. Such, for example, were Vermont's grant of tax exemption to local manufacturing establishments between 1812 and 1830 or New York's offer in 1817 of freedom from jury duty and militia service to employees of textile mills. Other states held out land grants and bounties as attractions or sponsored agricultural and industrial fairs. But it is not these traditional types of public encouragement that make memorable the years after independence.

The Quasi-Public Corporation

More than sixty years ago Guy S. Callender pointed to the United States as one of the first countries to exhibit the "modern tendency to extend the activity of the State into industry," but only in the last two decades have studies of Massachusetts, Pennsylvania, Georgia, Missouri, and Virginia, together with some of the municipalities, given us a clear appreciation of the political ingenuity displayed by democratic communities eager to advance their economic well-being. Perhaps the most ingenious technique was that of using the business corporation as an agency of the state to accomplish public purposes. Incorporation had long existed as a device for giving legal life to public or quasi-public associations, and during the colonial period it had been used to establish towns, boroughs, and cities as well as organizations devoted to charitable, educational, and ecclesiastical purposes. But in all those years it had been employed only a half-dozen times for business organizations. In contrast, state governments created more than three hundred business corporations between the end of the Revolution and 1801. A brief examination will disclose their semipublic character.

Fully two-thirds of them were established to provide inland navigation, turnpikes, and toll bridges. Thirty-two were empowered to underwrite insurance policies, a need deriving from expansion of the geographic area and the volume of foreign commerce, especially after the outbreak of European war in 1793 opened the commercial world to American neutral vessels, increasing their risks of loss. At the same time, the increased volume of trade gave rise to a need for the short-term credit facilities of commercial banks, with the result that no less than 34 were incorporated between 1781 and 1801 (27 of them between 1790 and 1801). Commercial expansion, by increasing the size of urban populations, also increased their needs for other services, so that 32 corporations for the supply of water and 4 for the erection of docks were created in the six-year interval between 1795 and 1801. The greater need of urban communities for protection against fire losses was reflected in the organization of nearly a dozen mutual companies between 1786 and 1800. Most insurance companies, however, were permitted to underwrite both fire and marine risks.

The experience of Pennsylvania suggests that these early objectives of incorporation continued to predominate in the antebellum period. Of 2,333 business corporations chartered by special act between 1790 and 1860, 64.17 per cent were in the field of transport, 11.14 per cent in insurance, 7.72 per cent for manufacturing, 7.2 per cent in banking, 3.21 per cent for gas, 2.79 per cent for water, and 3.77 per cent for miscellaneous categories. It is not difficult to visualize the semipublic character of early manufacturing corporations. Certainly in the troubled years preceding and during the War of 1812 some state governments appear to have adopted the view that the chartering of domestic manufacturing concerns was required by patriotism. Between 1808 and 1815 New York issued more charters (165) to joint-stock companies engaged in manufacturing than to all public utilities combined (164), a phenomenon that appears not to have reoccurred in any other period before the Civil War. But the larger truth is that, given the strength of the American desire for economic development, the scarcities of capital funds in the early years following independence, and the sharpness of competition from foreign suppliers, manufacturing was endowed with a quasi-public and not a private character, and given numerous encouragements by the state.

It is not only the functions of the corporations but the language of the laws creating them, the powers of government in which they were sometimes clothed, and their subsequent relation to the state that reveals their unmistakable semipublic nature. "Be it enacted by the Senate and House of Representatives in General Court assembled," reads a Massachusetts statute of 1818, that the following named individuals "hereby are constituted a corporation and body politic" for the purpose of erecting a flour mill. As bodies politic, corporations were accorded certain exclusive privileges to encourage the devotion of scarce private capital to public ends. Among these privileges were monopoly rights of way, tax exemption, the right of eminent domain, and the right granted to many nonbanking corporations to engage in banking and to hold lotteries in order to raise needed capital more easily. Many states established state-owned banks or invested in bank stock to provide funds or sources of credit for public enterprises. Between 1824 and 1840 the western and southwestern states issued more than $165,-000,000 in bonds to provide banking capital to corporations. In Pennsylvania it was legislative practice to include in bank charters a requirement that specified transportation companies be given financial assistance. The charter granted in 1835 to the Second Bank, for example, called for subscriptions totalling $675,000 to the stocks of ten named companies and for grants of financial assistance in the amount of $139,000 to eleven others.

Corporate charters also provided for strict regulation by the state, including, for example, detailed specifications relative to the size and power of boards of directors, the liability of officers and stockholders, the nature of capital structures, and operations to be undertaken. In addition, bank charters specified maximum interest rates, dividends were controlled by law, and public utilities were subjected to rate regulation. In this connection it should be noted that the significance of Marshall's decision in the Dartmouth College case (1819) is sometimes misapprehended. That decision, holding a corporate charter to be a contract, did not place such charters beyond the control of the state issuing them. As Louis Hartz has pointed out, the decision did not alter the established practice of including elaborate regulations in original charter acts, and even so far as subsequent regulations were concerned, "the inclusion of reservation clauses in charters and the pursuit of a strict construction policy by the state judiciary severely limited the effect of the anti-state barrier erected by Marshall."

Before approximately the 1840's and 1850's one general condition provides much of the explanation for the endowing of particular groups with a privileged status before the law. This was a shortage of private stocks of capital, together with a natural disinclination on the part of holders of such supplies as did exist to venture them in enterprises of high risk. Capital scarcities particularly affected needs for transport, where returns on investment were apt to be not only long deferred but to take the diffused form of enhanced land values, increased employment and business opportunities, and other external gains. Most of the canals and railroads, as Carter Goodrich has emphasized, were not projected as links between settled points. They could not exploit opportunities for gain already in existence but had themselves to create those opportunities by affording ease of movement at reduced costs for people and products. They were "developmental" rather than "exploitative" in character. Public assistance, by lessening risks of loss, helped attract private funds to ventures they might not otherwise have supported.

In addition to their grants of corporate privileges the states both invested public monies in the securities of corporations and themselves constructed and managed numerous works. Indeed, as George Rogers Taylor expresses it, "in no other period of American history has the government been so active in financing and actually promoting, owning, and controlling banks and public works including turnpikes, bridges, canals, and railroads." Pennsylvania, for example, not only invested more than $6,000,000 in some 150 "mixed" corporations, but spent over $100,000,000 on the construction and operation of the Main Line canal and railroad system. By 1860, Massachusetts had invested more than $8,000,000 in eight railroads; by the same date Missouri had pledged some $23,-000,000 for a number of internal improvements. According to the calculations of Carter Goodrich, Julius Rubin, H. Jerome Cranmer, and Harvey H. Segal, no less than 73.4 per cent of a total investment of about $188,000,000 in canal construction in New York, Pennsylvania, Ohio, Indiana, Illinois, and Virginia between 1815 and 1860 was financed by state and municipal governments. The states raised most of these sums by borrowing, with foreign lenders providing a large proportion of them. State governments could sell their bonds to foreign investors because of the great prestige and strength given American public credit by the rapid payment of the national debt and its final extinction in 1832. As Guy S. Callender has pointed out, "No other country had ever paid off a national debt, and it was felt that there could be little risk in lending money to a people whose resources were so great and whose disposition so frugal."

Besides direct financial assistance the states frequently guaranteed corporation bonds, thus making them easier to market. In essence, the guarantee meant that interest payments on bonded indebtedness would be secured by the taxing power of the state rather than by distant and uncertain revenues from corporation projects in process of construction. It is scarcely surprising that corporations wanted what was often described as "the loan of the state's credit." In his study *Foreign Bondholders and American State Debts*[1] Reginald McGrane quotes an English banker as saying it was the guaranty of the state "which alone made these stocks 'palatable to European capitalists.'" The "same statement," McGrane adds, "is found constantly recurring in the correspondence of bankers and in the columns of the press."

Foreign Investment in the United States

It is impossible to ascertain accurately the amount of foreign capital that found its way into this country in the antebellum period. Taking into account a variety of contemporary estimates of English capital invested in the securities of both states and corporations and extended to American merchants through the medium of commercial credit, Guy S. Callender concluded some sixty years ago that it was "safe to say that nearly three hundred million dollars of foreign capital was lent to this country between 1815 and 1840." A more recent method of estimating capital imports is to analyze the composition of the international balance of payments, making separate calculations of receipts and payments on account of merchandise trade, transportation, travel, interest, dividends, and remittances, and then assuming that "the net residual indicates capital flows." The result of such a method necessarily reflects the errors and omissions inherent in the inadequate data from which the calculations are made, but the technique is the best one available. Employing it, Douglass C. North, the leading contemporary authority on the application of the method to this period, has presented figures on capital imports and exports for each year between 1790 and 1861. If we deduct the latter from the former the result is a total capital inflow of more than $500,000,000. This inflow was relatively modest until after the War of 1812, with peak years occurring in 1816, 1836, and 1853.

[1] New York, 1935.

Certainly these huge imports played a prominent part in economic growth. As North emphasizes, they directed resources into transportation facilities and cotton expansion, and they financed import surpluses essential both to consumer well-being and to the release of inflationary pressures. Without good public credit, capital imports on anything like this scale would have been impossible. After 1830, as Callender points out, "the whole country looked to England for capital to carry out its system of internal improvements." Once the market for American securities in London failed, "work on public improvements in most of the states was checked, and ceased altogether in some of the Western States."

This failure came two years after the beginning of the Panic of 1837. Overextension, corruption, maladministration, and other factors accentuated a crisis in which five states temporarily defaulted on their interest payments and one partially repudiated the principal of its debt. A wave of revulsion against state participation in internal improvements swept over the Old Northwest, and between 1842 and 1851 all six of its states bound themselves constitutionally not to make loans to improvement enterprises. In addition, Michigan, Indiana, Ohio, and Iowa also prohibited stock ownership, Maryland, Michigan and Wisconsin prohibited state works, and Ohio, Michigan, and Illinois abandoned their extensive programs of state construction. Pennsylvania sold part of its state stock in 1843, Tennessee virtually abandoned her improvements program, and in the early 1840's Virginia somewhat checked hers. The check to state enterprise was to prove only a temporary one, with a second wave of revulsion following in the 1870's, but it was sufficient to induce promoters of improvements projects to turn increasingly to local governments for aid. Their efforts were extraordinarily successful.

Local Aid to Development

Municipal governments participated in improvements projects to an even greater extent than did the states, especially in the decade following the Civil War. No fewer than 2,200 laws passed by 36 states between 1830 and 1890 authorized the giving of local aid. In New York, Harry H. Pierce finds that 315 municipalities pledged approximately $37,000,000 towards the construction of the state's roads between 1827 and 1875. Large as were the pre-Civil War commitments of Pennsylvania, Louis Hartz concludes that state investment at its height was "of minor significance compared with investments by cities and counties." James Neal Primm finds that in Missouri during the 1850's it was the cities and counties along the routes of the railroads that bought most of the stocks of the state-aided railroads. In the antebellum South, according to the calculations of Milton Heath, cities and counties contributed $45,625,512.05 out of total southern aids of $144,148,684.92. Baltimore, Cincinnati, Milwaukee, and other cities also made generous contributions, subscribing to stock, purchasing railroad bonds, guaranteeing the credit of railroad companies, and even making donations. By 1879 outright gifts totalled nearly $30,000,000!

Robert A. Lively has recently observed that "a persistent theme in the nation's economic development" has been "the incorrigible willingness of American public officials to seek the public good through private negotiations." One need add to this rich suggestion only its obverse: the equally incorrigible insistence of private citizens that government encourage or entirely provide those services and utilities either too costly or too risky to attract unaided private capital. It was especially on the undeveloped frontiers of the nation that capital needs and development needs conjoined most pressingly. Social overhead capital, especially in transport, was a frontier need and a prerequisite for economic development. As these frontiers receded, private investment could flow in larger relative proportions into areas properly scoured of risk by community action. Government, therefore, typically played the role of pioneer. Because of wide popular demand that it do so, the roles of political man and private citizen are difficult to distinguish. If, therefore, waste and lack of scruple, political and private, sometimes appeared on stage, and if one also finds such subordinate elements as "glib promoters reaching eagerly for public funds" or hopeful administrators seeking state investments so profitable that taxes could be reduced, the play itself was in large part written by community consensus.

In the closing decades of the antebellum period there is a noticeable rise in hostility to the state, only part of which is explicable in terms of reaction to economic depression and governmental defalcation. Perhaps basically the new attitude reflects the fact that as supplies of capital accumulated through profits won in internal and foreign commerce and in manufacturing, new groups rose to challenge the privileged positions of vested corporations. As we shall see in chapter eight, the note of egalitarianism is struck again and again in the political discourse of the time, and there is little reason to doubt that an increasingly active electorate and a professionalization of politics contributed importantly to a newly forming system of values. Some historians have attributed to this egalitarian impulse the general incorporation movement that marks the thirties. Studies of that movement in Massachusetts, New Jersey, Pennsylvania, and Missouri, however, as Lively points out, "reveal it to be something other than a Jacksonian extension of privileges to all comers." In these states general laws were "rigid and unwelcome rules written by men who wanted to restrict corporate power and growth." Enterprisers sought to avoid them, and their success in doing so may be measured by the fact that incorporation by the traditional means of special legislation remained dominant until 1875.

Corporate Expansion

The future, however, was to belong not to hostility to incorporation per se but rather to the privileged corporation possessing exclusive rights entrenched in law. It was to belong to the corporate values of Roger B. Taney, who deserves appreciation as the jurist of what Lee Benson has well called the "Egalitarian Age." Taney took his stand on the premise that the interests of the community override all special interests. To promote those interests the state chartered corporations and gave them "peculiar privileges." But the gift must be carefully scrutinized when made to make sure that public interest really justified the privileges. And they must be narrowly construed thereafter to prevent vested property rights from interfering with the right of the state to create additional corporations in the public interest. Corporate egalitarianism is the phrase which appears best to describe Taney's ideal of publicly sponsored free competition in the interest of community welfare. His essential contribution was so to adjust constitutional law to the needs of the corporation as greatly to stimulate its use in business.

Taney gave clear expression to his corporate egalitarianism even before his appointment as Chief Justice of the Supreme Court in 1836. A former director on the boards of Maryland banks, he spoke from knowledge when he declared: "There is perhaps no business which yields a profit so certain and liberal as the business of banking and exchange; and it is proper that it should be open, as far as practicable, to the most free competition and its advantages shared by all classes of Society." Believing that Nicholas Biddle's Bank of the United States restrained free enterprise in banking, he played, as Jackson's Secretary of the Treasury, a well-known key role in the "war" against that institution. While it is impossible to impute the subsequent increase in the number of state-chartered banks alone to the Jacksonian victory over the Second Bank, that event does help explain why the number of banks rose from 506 in 1834 (the year in which federal deposits ceased to be made in the Bank) to 901 in 1840.

In one of his first statements as Chief Justice, an analysis written in June 1836 of an act providing for the rechartering of the banks in the District of Columbia, Taney vigorously stated his conviction that the power of the state must not be used to grant special privileges to any corporate group except for the purpose of promoting the public interest:

Every charter granted by a state or by the United States, to a bank or to any other company for the purpose of trade or manufacture, is a grant of peculiar privileges, and gives to the individuals who compose the corporation, rights and privileges which are not possessed by other members of the community. It would be against the spirit of our free institutions, by which equal rights are intended to be secured to all, to grant peculiar franchises and privileges to a body of individuals merely for the purpose of enabling them more conveniently and effectually to advance their own private interests. No charter could rightfully be granted on that ground. The consideration upon which alone, such peculiar privileges can be granted is the expectation and prospect of promoting thereby some public interest, and it follows from these principles that in every case where it is proposed to grant or to renew a charter the interests or wishes of the individuals who desire to be incorporated, ought not to influence the decision of the government. The only inquiry which the constituted authorities can properly make on such an application, is whether the charter applied for is likely to produce any real benefit to the community, and whether that benefit is sufficient to justify the grant.[2]

These principles inform Taney's decision in the Charles River Bridge case (1837), wherein he refused to uphold the claim that the bridge company's charter of incorporation gave it exclusive, monopolistic business rights by implication. Were this precedent established, modern improvements would be at the mercy of old corporations. The country would "be thrown back to the improvements of the last century, and obliged to stand still, until the claims of the old turnpike corporations shall be satisfied; and they shall consent to permit these states to avail themselves of the lights of modern science, and to partake of the benefit of those improvements which are now adding to the wealth and prosperity, and the convenience and comfort, of every other part of the civilized world." The effect of Taney's decision was to free new businesses from the fear of monopolistic claims on the part of older corporations with ambiguously worded charters. In 1851 he applied the same principle to railroads in *Richmond Railroad* v. *Louisa Railroad* and served the public interest by opening another area of enterprise to free competition.

Other decisions of the Taney Court also stimulated corporate

[2] Quoted in Carl Brent Swisher, *Roger B. Taney* (Hamden, Conn., 1961), p. 367.

development. In *Bank of Augusta* v. *Earle* (1839) he held that a corporation might do business via its agents in states other than the one from which it had received its charter, provided those states permitted it to do so. In *Louisville, Cincinnati, and Charleston R.R. Co.* v. *Letson* (1844) the Taney Court extended to corporations the legal fiction of citizenship, thus assuring them the protection of federal judicial review of assaults upon them by the states. In *Briscoe* v. *The Bank of the Commonwealth of Kentucky* (1837) the Court upheld the constitutionality of banknotes. Finally, to abbreviate the list of instances that might be cited, in *Woodruff* v. *Trapnell* (1850), *Planters' Bank of Mississippi* v. *Sharp* (1848), and *Curran* v. *Arkansas* (1853) Taney opposed attempts of banks or states to circumvent their legal obligations, thus increasing men's sense of security in transactions involving corporations and their instrumentalities.

The extent to which the pre-Civil War rise of the business corporation can be attributed to the encouragement given by the Taney Court is difficult to estimate, but it seems likely the new jurisprudence was influential. At any rate, the fifties saw a phenomenal increase in incorporation, with nearly half of all corporations chartered between 1800 and 1860 appearing in that decade.

One would be mistaken, however, in placing too great an emphasis upon corporations in the antebellum years. The fifties heralded the dawn of the "Corporate Age," but it was only the dawn. Industrial techniques that required large capital sums were of recent origin in important fields and made their way but slowly among constituent firms. Not until after 1835 did expensive metallic textile machinery come into general use. Not until 1839 were the first successful coke-smelting furnaces built in the United States. As late as 1869 nearly half the mechanical power used in manufacturing came from water wheels and turbines rather than from steam engines. Once again, it is not so much the first appearance of new techniques as their spread that matters in economic growth. Imitation is more important than innovation. Among the important explanations of imitative lag must be set not only the inertia of traditional and less costly methods. Ignorance also counted for much, as did the scarcity of technical journals, trained engineers, and cost-accounting techniques. The gradual overcoming of these obstacles contributed in the post-Civil War years to a wider dissemination of mechanized production methods. But on the eve of that conflict individual proprietorships and partnerships rather than corporations were able to amass the capital funds required for the control of most of the resources devoted to manufacturing.

It is thus apparent that the contribution of government and law to economic growth was not a sufficient one. Difficult and in some respects artificial as it is to draw a sharp distinction between "public" and "private," what may be usefully regarded as the "private sector" of the economy also made vitally necessary contributions to growth. The nature of these contributions we shall examine in the next chapter.

VII

The Private Sector

For the purposes of this analysis we may conveniently comprehend within the term "private sector" a discussion of private sources of capital funds, the formation of the national market, and the origins of technological change in industry and agriculture. It will be evident how difficult it often is to lay down a clean line between what is public and what is private. As the individual does with society, they interpenetrate in numerous ways. In civilized communities private property itself consists of legal rights; it is law and government alone that secure it. We have just seen the nature of the many-sided contributions made by government at many levels to the formation of the national market. The loan and investment policies of commercial banks, even when made in pursuance of private judgment rather than in conformity with legal requirements, were yet made by institutions receiving their legal life and other privileges from government. The same thing is true for such other funds-providing institutions as insurance companies. So far as invention is concerned, it will be obvious that patent and copyright laws provided a hospitable climate within which economic and other factors might function. Interdependencies of these kinds are indissoluble.

Private Sources of Capital Funds

Savings are the only source of capital funds, although savers may be foreign as well as domestic. Domestic savings may be voluntary or forced. Taxation is a form of forced savings, and, as we have seen, it was state taxation which, by securing the interest due on both state and corporate bonds, made it possible to sell them abroad and thus tap foreign savings. Americans also earned foreign exchange by selling goods and services abroad, and while these earnings financed the importation of some capital equipment, one main contribution to domestic capital formation was indirect. During three periods in the antebellum years, namely 1793–1807, 1815–18, and 1832–39, the terms of trade on which American exports were exchanged for imports of consumer goods were favorable to the United States. That is to say, a greater rise in export than in import prices permitted a given quantity of American goods to command a larger quantity of foreign goods. By buying abroad instead of at home Americans thus saved money, and the savings could be released for purposes of domestic capital formation.

Douglass C. North attaches a high importance to favorable terms of trade in initiating inflows of capital. Rising prices of American exports made investments in America look promising to foreigners. North emphasizes that up until 1845, and to a lesser degree thereafter, almost every favorable movement in the terms of trade was paralleled by an inflow of foreign capital; unfavorable movements either reduced the inflow or brought an actual outflow.

Shipping earnings and sums brought in by immigrants contributed to the foreign exchange earnings which financed imports, but exports of agricultural surpluses, particularly cotton, provided the great bulk of them. The value of cotton exports rose from $17,529,000 in 1815 to $191,806,555 in 1860. As North points out, cotton "constituted 39 per cent of the value of exports from 1816 to 1820, and increased to 63 per cent of total export values from 1836 to 1840." While it declined somewhat thereafter, it amounted to more than half the value of exports during all the remaining years before the Civil War.

Voluntary domestic savings contributed directly to the capital accumulation out of which came not only public works but also industrial capital formation. The relative importance of the domestic and foreign contributions cannot be estimated, however, because of insufficient knowledge of the investment and loan experience of the domestic institutions which made accumulation possible. These institutions were several, and all had their rise in the antebellum period. Some of them, namely, savings banks, lotteries, and life insurance companies, served as means by which the small savings of large numbers of people were collected into sizable pools of capital.

Originating at the end of 1816 as philanthropic institutions designed to encourage thrift in the poor, savings banks spread rapidly in the northern and middle Atlantic states. Their number increased from 10 in 1820 to 61 in 1840, and to 278 in 1860; at the same interims, total depositors rose from 8,635 to 78,701, and to 693,870, while deposits themselves increased from $1,138,576 to $14,051,520, and to $149,277,504. It is the uses to which these deposits were put that make the savings banks pertinent to capital formation and economic growth. In the first place, many of them came to be capital suppliers to commercial banks, not only by redepositing their own deposits in those institutions but also by investing in their stock. Their trustees often formed interlocking directorates with the officials of commercial banks. In New England, to employ Paul B. Trescott's phrase, many were "virtually savings departments of the commercial banks." Mortgage loans were common, but many also made loans on the security of bank stock, or themselves invested in bank stock and in such other corporate securities as railroad and canal stock.

Savings banks also made direct loans to transportation companies and industrialists. The outstanding loans of the Provident Institution for Savings in the Town of Boston to railroad companies were never less than $250,000 between 1840 and 1860 and at one time reached $700,000. In their recent careful study of the Savings Bank of Baltimore, 1818–66, Peter L. Payne and Lance E. Davis have shown that direct loans to industrialists "played a significant, if minor, role in providing capital for the early industrial development of Baltimore." The technique used was the familiar one of converting short-term loans into long-term ones by frequent renewals.

On the basis of his re-examination of the sources of finance for nine large, integrated textile mills in Massachusetts from 1827 to 1860, Davis concludes that while previous historians had "correctly assessed the importance of equity capital in industrial finance . . . they may have overemphasized the role of retained earnings . . . and have failed to acknowledge the contribution that was made by loan capital—particularly the long-term credit granted by the credit intermediaries." These intermediaries included life insurance companies and savings banks, with the latter appearing to have been especially important. Between 1839 and 1859 the number of savings banks in Boston increased from 31 to 86, and their deposits from $5,608,158 to $39,424,418. This influx of new funds to the investment market induced the institutions to search for new outlets, and the textile industry became the major industrial beneficiary. The usual device utilized was the three-signature loan, with no collateral required, and the typical loan was made for two years or longer "and renewed almost as a matter of course." During the forties and fifties the proportion of loans to the total assets of the nine firms increased. So far as an individual firm was concerned, its age was a crucial factor in its capital structure. In its early years it might have some trouble obtaining loans, but as it became established, loans became more plentiful. The more successful it became with the passing years, the greater its ability to finance expansion out of retained earnings and the less its need for loan capital.

The heyday of lotteries was a brief one, but before their rapid decline after about 1830, they served as significant institutions for the collection of capital from small investors. Fractional parts of tickets might be purchased for as little as 12.5 cents, but George R. Taylor points out that persons of considerable economic standing as well as the poorest laborers participated as purchasers. Apparently expanding rapidly after the War of 1812, states employed lotteries to raise sums for road and river improvement, support of education, and other purposes. The value of lottery tickets authorized in nine eastern states is reported to have exceeded $53,000,000 in 1832. Perhaps victims to some extent of the moral crusade against gambling that was part of the great reform movement of the period, lotteries also owed their decline to the rise of other financial institutions, particularly of opportunities to invest in stocks and bonds.

Life insurance developed much less rapidly than fire and marine insurance. While some life policies and annuities had been written by the early marine and fire insurance companies, the first company to specialize in life insurance was not incorporated until 1812. Rapid development came after 1843. While the total amount of insurance in force was apparently less than $10,000,000 in 1840, and, according to Taylor, "possibly not equal to even half that figure," the total exceeded $160,000,000 in 1860. Alfred H. Conrad illustrates by the case of the Massachusetts Hospital Life Insurance Company the way in which the funds of life insurance companies might aid the process of industrialization. Before 1830 this company concentrated its investments in farm mortgages in western Massachusetts. In the thirties, "securities and business loans became more important in the portfolio, and the locus shifted to the neighborhood of Boston and to the textile industry." In the forties, the company was of "singular importance" in the textile capital market as a source of term loans.

The role of commercial banks was more important in capital formation than is commonly appreciated. We have seen that banks in some states were required by their charters to subscribe to the stock of internal improvement companies or make loans to them. The historian of American banking, Fritz Redlich, states that "the idea that banks should loan their credit only and should invest their capital permanently in mortgages and stock as a security for the noteholders" triumphed in America with its embodiment in the Free Banking Acts of the 1830's, 1840's, and 1850's. Some banks extended both loans and investments voluntarily. David M. Cole reports that "most" of those in Washington, D.C., did so, although this was not required by their charters. He cites, for example, a statement of the Bank of Columbia dated January 1, 1822, which shows "Loans to road and canal companies $84,430.54," and one of the Bank of Potomac showing that on April 29, 1834 more than $40,000 was invested in the shares of various turnpike companies. In addition, there existed numerous so-called "improvement banks": banks that were tied to canal, railroad, gas light, industrial, and other enterprises. The Dry Dock and Chemical Banks of New York, the Morris Cannal and Banking Company of New Jersey, the Georgia Railroad and Banking Company are examples of improvement banks which, in the words of Redlich, "created capital for the desired enterprise by the issue of purchasing power in the form of bank notes."

Commercial banks also contributed significantly to the formation of industrial capital. As Cole well says, the "banks of the United States have never followed the British theory of confining their loans to short-term, self-liquidating paper. There were many demands for loans for compartively long terms, and the necessary volume of short-term paper was not always available." Redlich cites a description given in 1837 by a British author which clarifies the difference between American and British practice:

Their rule is our exception, our rule is their exception. They [the Americans] prefer accommodation paper, resting on personal security and fixed wealth, to real bills of exchange, resting on wealth in transition from merchants and manufacturers to consumers. . . . [Thus], ships and steamers [are built in America] with the proceeds of three months accommodation paper, [and] manufactories, mills, breweries, [and] distilleries erected; the borrower thinking himself sure of a renewal of the bill [i.e., promissory note] when it falls due.[1]

[1] Fritz Redlich, *The Molding of American Banking: Men and Ideas* (New York, 1951), II, 47.

Redlich reports that this practice of making and renewing accommodation loans had become so common by 1840 that when Connecticut banks attempted to discount exclusively business paper "subject to no renewal," it was deemed "a great innovation." The practice, in short, was not the exception but the "rule," commercial banks "thereby financing the long-term needs of agriculture and capitalistic industry."

Because of their evident, although quantitatively indefinable, role in the provision of investment credit, the increase in the number of commercial banks and in their issues and deposits becomes a primary datum in economic growth. Commercial banks were completely absent from the colonial scene. As Guy Callender explains, "Goods were sold on long credits of a year or more by English merchants, and the bills either carried by them until collected or else discounted by bankers in England. There was thus no basis for commercial banking in the colonies." There could be none, Margaret Myers points out, till the Revolutionary War had "cut off the credit upon which the trade of the colonies had been wont to depend, and at the same time undermined the paper money which the Colonial governments had issued. The new states relinquished the right to emit bills of credit, and the vacuum which was thus created brought about a demand for bank facilities."

Their subsequent growth was rapid, and Table XI depicts increases in their number, and in the amount of bank notes and deposits for selected years between 1815 and 1860. The first available estimates of deposits date only from 1834. This is unfortunate. The notion persists that the extension of bank credit in the form of deposits subject to check was unimportant before the emergence of clearing houses not long before the Civil War. In fact, the creation of bank deposits was an important practice in the larger mercantile cities by 1800. In all probability the leading merchants maintained accounts in the relatively few extant banks, permitting the banks themselves to act as their own clearing houses by the simple device of crediting an incoming check to the account of one depositor and debiting it to that of another. As Taylor says,

Mathew Carey "pointed out as early as 1816 that deposits rather than bank notes or specie furnished the chief medium of payment in the great commercial cities."

The total money supply included coins as well as banknotes and deposits, and John G. Gurley and E. S. Shaw have compiled estimates of both nominal and real totals for selected antebellum years. By "real" money they mean nominal money corrected for

TABLE XI

BANKING STATISTICS, SELECTED YEARS, 1815–60

Year	Number of State Banks	Bank Notes (in millions of dollars)	Deposits (in millions of dollars)
1815	208	45	
1820	307	45	
1830	330	61	
1834	506	95	76
1835	704	104	83
1840	901	107	76
1845	707	90	88
1850	824	131	110
1855	1,307	187	190
1860	1,562	207	254

Source: William M. Gouge, *A Short History of Paper-Money and Banking* (N.Y.: B. & S. Collins, 1835), p. 61; and Members on the Staff, Board of Governors of the Federal Reserve System, *Banking Studies* (Washington: Board of Governors, 1941), pp. 417–18.

changes in commodity prices, a correction which discloses the purchasing power of nominal money. In Table XII "Demand deposits" together with "Currency outside banks" (coin and banknotes) equals "Nominal money supply." The explanation of the fact that the supply of "real" money exceeded that of "nominal" money at each of the given intervals from 1819 on is to be found in the behavior of prices. It is not easy to measure long-run change in the price level, but the trend of prices appears to have been definitely downward in the period 1815–60. While wholesale prices moved upwards during the thirties and fifties, Taylor concludes after careful analysis that most of the upward pressure came from agricultural prices. He believes the unmistakable downward trend in industrial prices "may well have been the result of the techno-logical improvements of the age." Gurley and Shaw conclude that the overall commodity price level fell nearly fifty per cent in the period 1800–60.

TABLE XII

THE NOMINAL AND REAL MONEY SUPPLY, 1799–1859
(in billions of dollars)

June	Nominal Money Supply	Demand Deposits	Currency Outside Banks	Real Money Supply	Real Money Supply per Capita (dollars and cents)
1799	.03	—	—	.03	$ 5.80
1819	.08	—	—	.09	9.60
1839	.24	.09	.15	.29	17.40
1849	.27	.09	.18	.45	19.90
1859	.58	.26	.32	.95	31.00

Source: J. G. Gurley and E. S. Shaw, "Money," in Seymour E. Harris, ed., *American Economic History* (New York: McGraw-Hill, 1961), p. 105.

The fact that prices fell during a period in which the nominal supply of money rose points unmistakably to the real need on the part of a growing population and expanding economy for increased means of transacting a swelling volume of business. Indeed, the growth of the money supply fell short of that need.

These considerations afford a better perspective in which to evaluate the commercial banks of the period than do the two lead-ing points of view from which historians have traditionally done so. One has fixed upon such undeniable attributes as the lack of uniformity in banknotes and the colorful excesses of fraudulent "wildcats." But it is doubtful the former caused much more than inconvenience and certain the latter was not typical, least of all, as

Bray Hammond has shown, in the West, where historians have almost always placed them. The other point of view has reflected the concern of the mid-twentieth century with the danger of inflation and the role of a central banking system in preventing it. But it is at least doubtful whether the First Bank of the United States (1791–1811) and its successor institution (1816–36) exercised the control functions of modern central banks in any regular and continuing way, even under their most enlightened administrations.

Bray Hammond and Thomas P. Govan believe that the Second Bank of the United States under President Nicholas Biddle typically restrained credit expansion on the part of the state banks in the interests of monetary stability. If it did, the considerations we have adduced concerning the volume of money and the behavior of prices would make it difficult to avoid the judgment that it was the wrong thing to have done. The commercial banks helped meet the crying need of the antebellum period for capital, but neither they nor any other institutional or other source proved capable of doing so fully. To be sure, there was much ignorance of banking, numerous failures, and also a consequent waste of resources. Undoubtedly the need of the times was not only for more banks but better managed ones. Yet the informed judgment of Fritz Redlich deserves emphasis: "It can hardly be doubted that the American national economy through unsound, inflationary banking was developed more quickly than would otherwise have been the case." Waste was a premium paid for savings that were anticipated rather than earned, for means of development that otherwise would have had to wait upon a more patient accumulation.

In addition to the commercial banks, unincorporated "private" banks rose to a position of importance during the period. Their number was especially marked in the West, many states of which prohibited incorporated banking, but their general rise was swift after the demise of the Second Bank opened fields of business, especially those of domestic and foreign exchange, which that institution had dominated during most of its life. Private banks generally did not issue notes, but they did carry on a deposit and loan business. In the early 1860's about five hundred of them were in existence, and they accounted for about 20 per cent of all bank deposits. Many operated on a very small scale, and some were mercantile firms in which banking was only a sideline. Some were large, however. Trescott points out that in 1863 three held over a million dollars each in deposits, including Jay Cooke's firm in Philadelphia. Stephen Girard and Alexander Brown & Sons had achieved early prominence, the latter developing from foreign trader to investment banker, a course following by other leading houses of the period. It was of course in the marketing of securities that investment bankers discharged their essential function.

Securities, like banks, provided a means of collecting savings and making them available for long-term investment. In virtually every section of the country, however, there existed local scarcities of capital funds. For this reason, Alfred D. Chandler, Jr. points out, promoters of railroads and canals had to look to the largest eastern commercial centers and especially to the money markets of Europe for funds to complete their projects. And because "distant investors preferred bonds with their appearance of secure principal and guaranteed income," promoters had to rely on bonds rather than stocks as the major instruments for raising capital. So important was the London money market that both state governments and promoters issued their bonds in sterling denominations and made interest and principal payable in London.

Sales of bonds to distant investors required the services of middlemen. Before the 1840's and 1850's, however, the progress of incorporations and the quantity of securities to be marketed were insufficient to justify the services of full-time investment bankers, so that security sales were handled by commercial banks, unincorporated banks, brokerage houses, merchants, or special agents. In marketing their sterling bonds, state governments relied heavily on the agents of British mercantile houses operating in New York and Boston. During the 1830's, railroad and canal builders either went directly to the London money market, where specialized investment bankers already existed, or reached this market through the merchants and bankers of Philadelphia, especially Thomas Biddle & Company, and Nicholas Biddle, the latter America's pioneer investment banker.

Only for a brief period in New England during the 1840's was the investor willing to buy the common stocks of railroads rather than bonds. The manufacturing and mercantile community of Boston was then the nation's most important money market, and this community was sufficiently close knit that railroad promoters often succeeded in reaching investors without the services of a middleman. After 1850, however, the investment market was increasingly centralized and institutionalized in New York City, and railroad builders depended largely on the bankers and brokers of Wall Street to sell their mortgage bonds, with principal and interest made payable in New York, other eastern cities, Great Britain, and on the Continent.

The New York Stock Exchange listed few industrial securities prior to the Civil War. No shares of industrial corporations appeared on the Exchange until 1831. Even in Boston, which was then closer to the manufacturing center of the country than New York, no industrials appeared on the Exchange until 1827, and in 1830 there were only six. The forties and fifties saw a lengthening of the list, since, as we have seen, equity financing was the main reliance of the Massachusetts textile firms studied by Lance E. Davis. By 1835 the New York list included eight coal and mining companies, three gas lighting companies, and four others, but its length was insignificant in comparison with that of the rails. The antebellum manufacturing corporations, as Margaret Myers pointed out some thirty years ago, seldom found it necessary to turn to the investment market for funds. "Many had been organized originally as small concerns, and had grown by a process of accretion. Owners ploughed their profits back into the business, and employees invested their small savings in the factories with whose management they were well acquainted." To these considerations it is now necessary to add the greater reliance upon loan capital that the more recent studies of Davis have disclosed.

Undoubtedly, the main sources of "ploughed back profits" were two: the reduced unit costs of production deriving from technological innovation, and the expansion of sales with the widening of markets. To this latter development we now turn.

The Formation of the National Market

The settlement of new territory and the pushing of the frontier further into the interior had been characteristic features of American life since colonial times. At the end of the Revolution perhaps 250,-000 people inhabited the backcountry of Pennsylvania, Virginia and the Carolinas. Following the Revolution these backwoodsmen and many emigrants from Tidewater who had been ruined by the war or by soil exhaustion moved into the region west of the mountains. By the time of the census of 1790, there were 109,000 people living in Kentucky and the region south of it, while those who had settled in western Pennsylvania and Virginia, Callender believed, must have amounted to as many more. The census of 1800 showed 387,183 inhabitants of the Western States and Territories. That of 1810 disclosed 1,337,946, and by 1820, 2,419,369 were living in the Mississippi Valley.

A good deal of near self-sufficiency appears to have obtained in the West, and the essential reason for it was the high cost of transportation. Of course those who lived on or near navigable rivers engaged in commercial agriculture. Such backcountry produce as wheat, flour, butter, pork, and pork products from western Pennsylvania, Ohio, and Indiana, tobacco and hemp from Kentucky, cotton from Tennessee, and lead from Missouri, Illinois, and Wisconsin was loaded on flatboats and sent southward to New Orleans. There it was transferred in the main to coastal vessels destined for ports along the Atlantic seaboard, chiefly New York, Boston, and Philadelphia. But before the invention of the steamboat and its first use on the Mississippi in 1816, trade moved almost entirely in one direction—south, with the current. As Taylor expresses it, upriver shipments were "almost prohibitively expensive even for the most light and valuable merchandise."

To obtain goods in return for their downriver exports Western farmers had to depend upon the land routes across the Appalachian highlands from Philadelphia and Baltimore. Across the overland stretch of three hundred miles wagoners hauled textiles, hats, shoes, hardware, and other products, but transportation over this short distance "cost more than shipment by sea and river all the way from Pittsburgh to Philadelphia." Direct overland shipments to the East were even more costly, except for livestock driven on the hoof. According to Taylor, with costs for teaming at thirty cents per ton-mile, "the mere charge for carting wheat to Philadelphia equalled its whole selling price if it were drawn 218 miles; for corn this was true for a distance of 135 miles."

These high costs of getting goods to and from market exerted profoundly limiting effects upon the commercialization of agriculture. The value of receipts at New Orleans from the interior amounted in 1816 to less than $10,000,000, and by 1820 it had increased by only $3,000,000. It is true that local markets existed, but they were too small to support more than a neighborhood trade and small-scale manufacturing of consumption goods, a manufacturing that was protected by high transport costs from the competition of distant producers. With 24,562 people in 1810 New Orleans was the only town in the entire West of any considerable size. Pittsburgh had 4,768 inhabitants, Lexington 4,326, and Cincinnati 2,540. Louisville, Nashville, Natchez, and St. Louis were villages of about 1,000 inhabitants each.

In a speech in Congress in 1810 Congressman Porter of western New York gave an able analysis of the problem of the West:

The great evil, and it is a serious one indeed, under which the inhabitants of the western country labor, arises from the want of a market. There is no place where the great staple articles for the use of civilized life can be produced in greater abundance or with greater ease, and yet as respects most of the luxuries and many of the conveniences of life the people are poor. They have no vent for their produce at home and, being all agriculturists, they produce alike the same article with the same facility; and such is the present difficulty and expense of transporting their produce to an Atlantic port that little benefit is realized from that quarter. The single circumstance of want of a market is already beginning to produce the most disastrous effect, not only on the industry, but on the morals of the inhabitants. Such is the fertility of their land that one-half their time spent in labor is sufficient to produce every article which their farms are capable of yielding, in sufficient quantities for their own consumption, and there is nothing to incite them to produce more. They are, therefore, naturally led to spend the other part of their time in idleness and dissipation. Their increase in numbers far from encourage them to become manufacturers for themselves, but put to a greater distance the time when, quitting the freedom and independence of masters of the soil, they submit to the labor and confinement of manufacturers.[2]

Porter's observation that "there is nothing to incite them to produce more" deserves special emphasis. Between output per person and incentive to produce, an obvious relationship exists. What is difficult to know in any precise way is how the different elements within a wide area of environmental change affect incentives. In this case it is clear enough that because of "the want of a market" underemployed human and natural resources existed in the West. Until those resources were more fully made available to the East and South, the ability of the economy as a whole to grow more rapidly would be limited. In a word, a fundamental prerequisite to growth was the more complete integration of the West into the national economy, a strengthening of the tenuous bonds linking that region with its sister regions.

In the main, it was a series of familiar technological innovations in transportation that brought increasing strength to those bonds. The steamboat was the first of them. By making possible upriver trade and greatly reducing transport costs both up and down river the steamboat, in the words of Taylor, "gave the first great impetus

[2] Quoted in Guy S. Callender, "The Early Transportation and Banking Enterprises of the States in Relation to the Growth of Corporations," *Quarterly Journal of Economics*, XVII (1902), 123.

to western growth." It shifted the terms of trade sharply to the advantage of the western farmer. It is true that its use for down-river shipments lowered transport costs and somewhat reduced prices received by westerners for their produce when sold at New Orleans and at Atlantic ports. But the greater fall in upriver transport costs reduced still more the costs of imported goods. In a word, the steamboat permitted a given quantity of western produce to command a larger quantity of eastern goods, and greatly encouraged migration into the Ohio Valley and the commercialization of its agriculture.

At the same time an independent influence was achieving similar results in the Southwest. In the years after 1815 cotton planters for the first time began to migrate in considerable numbers into that region. Here fertility of soil, numerous navigable rivers and the fact that cotton, a commodity possessing large value in small weight, could bear the expense of transportation to the rivers over long reaches of land, combined to form a profitable contrast to the situation in older cotton-growing areas. "In the upland areas from Virginia to Georgia," says Lewis C. Gray, "the expansion of cotton and tobacco left behind an ever-widening circle of lands suffering from soil exhaustion. Year after year the old lands were depleted until it was no longer profitable to farm them. By 1850 a large proportion of Virginia and Maryland east of the Blue Ridge was a waste of old fields and abandoned lands covered with under-brush and young cedars."

From the older slave states emigrants poured into the more promising Southwest. Alabama and Mississippi had no more than 75,000 people in 1816, but only four years later their combined population was 200,000, and this doubled during the next decade. Louisiana had 76,000 in 1810, 143,000 in 1820, and 215,000 in 1830. Callender says that certain parts of Tennessee, Arkansas, and Florida, where cotton could be raised, "were settled with equal rapidity." New Orleans, the "great central market to which the cotton product of this region was sent," received only 37,000 bales in 1816. In 1822 the amount was 161,000, in 1830, 428,000, and in 1840, 923,000 bales. At the same time the cultivation of sugar in Louisiana rose from 30,000 hogsheads in 1823 to 186,000 in 1845.

Now it is possible to overstate the extent to which this great staple-producing region depended upon outside sources for its supplies of food and manufactured goods. Callender believed the dependence was pronounced and that the profits to be won from cotton and sugar were so high as to induce planters to employ their capital and other resources "for the most part" in the production of these staples. The consequence was that the planters of the Southwest became the first great market for the farmers of the Northwest, and Callender saw the increase in the number of steamboats on western rivers, in tonnage carried by flatboats, and in the value of receipts at New Orleans as evidence of the growing interdependence of the two regions. There are indeed "no reliable statistics of the trade," but Callender and the more recent scholars who have followed his view, especially Louis B. Schmidt and Douglass C. North, tend to minimize the degree of self-sufficiency achieved by many southern planters and the extent to which the food supplies shipped to New Orleans from the Northwest were bound for markets other than those of the Southwest, namely, those of Europe and the West Indies, and most especially, those of the urban Northeast.

The planter, says Paul Gates, "attempted to make his plantation as self-sufficient as possible," and in the South as a whole, and not merely the Upper South, it was corn rather than cotton that was the most important crop throughout the antebellum period, whether the criterion of importance be value of the crop, acreage devoted to it, or quantity produced. What fed the increasing dependence of the Northeast upon the food supplies of the Northwest was not only the growing urbanization of that area but also the loss of fertility of much of the farm land along the Atlantic coast. Gates reports that the Hessian fly together with the midge, caused the abandonment of wheat as a major crop in many parts of the East by the 1830's. Yields of tobacco, wheat, and other crops were so low that in that decade Maine and Massachusetts offered bounties on wheat production. Claimants under the Massachusetts law averaged only about fifteen bushels per acre in 1839.

While it is therefore necessary to qualify the degree of interdependence existing between southwestern planter and northwestern farmer, Gates makes clear that the Gulf states did "concentrate" on cotton and that the Deep South could not meet its own needs for corn and pork. The alluvial land, or "black prairie," of Alabama and Mississippi did not yield good crops of corn, and millions of bushels were imported each year from the Northwest. In sum, the total market for northwestern farm produce was far wider than that of the Southwest alone, but the demand of the latter must certainly have been an important factor in the prosperity of the northwestern farmer.

The advent of canals and then railroads brought to the developing West stimuli which greatly reinforced those imparted by steamships and the movement of the cotton belt. The impetus given by canals deserves special emphasis. According to Carter Goodrich, "the initial reduction in costs provided by canal transport, as compared with wagon haulage, was more drastic than any subsequent differential between railroads and canals." Taylor reports that the cost per ton-mile of moving freight from Buffalo to New York in 1817, before the opening of the Erie Canal, was 19.12 cents. For the period 1857–60 the average cost over the Erie Canal was 0.81 cents. Especially after approximately the mid-thirties, when the completion of some of the mid-western canals brought the beginnings of a significant shift in the direction of flow of western produce from the circuitousness of the Mississippi-Atlantic Ocean route to the directness of West-East shipment via the Great Lakes, Erie Canal, and Hudson River to New York City, canals exerted a developmental impact upon the countryside, making possible a large *new* production of foodstuffs. New settlers moved into the Northwest with the lowering of transport costs on the overland transappalachian stretch, and older migrants were encouraged to grow larger cash crops for disposition in the East and abroad. According to Abraham H. Sadove, by 1844 the amount of tonnage shipped eastward via Lake Erie and the Erie Canal was already slightly greater than that sent down the Mississippi River. By 1853, the former route accounted for 62.2 per cent and the latter for only 28.9 per cent of the total.

The result of these increases in the extent of commercial farming was a raising of the level of income per capita in the Northwest, permitting the farmers of the region to purchase more and more manufactured goods from the East. The value of merchandise shipped to the western states on the Erie Canal amounted in 1836 to less than $10,000,000, but in 1853 it reached a peak of $94,000,000. This widening of the market for eastern goods, as Harvey H. Segal has suggested, had in turn the effect of inducing a higher level of investment in the East. Finally, the expansion of production facilities raised the level of income in that region and permitted an increasing demand for western commodities.

There thus developed an increasingly high degree of interdependence between the principal regional markets of the nation. The interdependence is revealed in Arthur H. Cole's data on prices. Between the Revolution and the early 1820's, price movements exhibit marked divergencies as between regions, but in the following decades the divergencies sharply decrease. To maintain, however, that there obtained in West, East, or South little diversification in their respective patterns of investment would be erroneous. Yet there did tend to develop a marked degree of regional specialization, with Northwest concentrating its resources on the production of foodstuffs, Southwest on cotton, and Northeast on manufacturing. Income received from exports of cotton, mainly via New York City, played a leading part in making regional interdependence possible. This income enabled the South to pay the Northeast for its various marketing services and for manufactured goods, and it enabled that region also to pay the West for foodstuffs exported to the South; finally, it permitted the West to pay the Northeast for manufactured goods.

The great increase in population, the settlement of the West, the phenomenal improvements in transportation, and increases in incomes per capita had made possible a territorial specialization which raised to new levels of efficiency the interdependent working of the economy as a whole. And while it would be wrong to underestimate the importance of the steamboat, canals appear to have contributed most to the opening of substantial trade between East and West. They supplied the means, Goodrich properly concludes, by which the American people "were for the first time able to make effective use of the great interior and to establish a national market on which industrial development could be based." The spread of the railroads in the Northeast between 1835 and 1850, and between East and West in the 1850's, further contributed to the development of interregional trade and the siting of manufacturing in the northeastern quadrant. Clearly, all forms of improved transportation helped fortify the interdependence of agriculture and manufacturing and helped create the national economy of which Tench Coxe and Alexander Hamilton had dreamed long before its advocacy by Henry Clay. In a word, transport improvements within a national political area defined by the United States Constitution, and confirmed by the Supreme Court, increased the size of the national economy by enlarging and interrelating its regional markets. The external economies and those of scale thereby made increasingly possible accrued to both agricultural and industrial producers, and augmented the profits out of which additional capital could be formed to speed the pace of further growth.

The Origins of Technological Change in Industry and Agriculture

While it is clear that capital formation is a prerequisite of economic growth, it is not alone the size but also the quality of the capital stock that matters. Capital in any form increases the productivity of labor, but some forms are more efficient than others. A forked stick is more efficient than a farmer's bare hands but less so than a hoe; plows, in turn, are more efficient that hoes, and horse-drawn plows than those moved by manpower, at least under "normal" conditions. Subject to the same qualification, tractors are more efficient than horse-drawn plows. As this elementary illustration suggests, an innovation in the form of capital may permit an increase in output per worker, but successive innovations may be increasingly "capital intensive." Yet it is probable that no constant relationship can be said to exist between productivity and capital intensity. H. J. Habakkuk believes that in early nineteenth-century America the more capital-intensive of the available techniques were also the most productive ones; but Edward F. Denison has recently questioned whether that is true today. The precise relationships between innovation, capital intensity, and labor productivity under balances of productive factors that shift over time is a difficult problem requiring much historical research.

During the past decade scholarly effort has tended to concentrate less on innovation than on capital accumulation per se as a source of increase in per capita income. A seminal hypothesis advanced by Walt W. Rostow in 1956 goes far to explain this emphasis upon the quantity of capital. Central to Rostow's conception was the assumption that an economy's "take-off" upon a sustained process of growth required a sharp acceleration in the annual rate of net addition to capital stock. The assumption generated both theoretical interest and historical research, and the consequences of the latter appear to have been devastating. Most notable has been the contribution of Simon Kuznets. In his examination of the growth experiences of a dozen countries Kuznets found no instance in which there occurred a sudden increase in net investment of the magnitude required for "take-off." Perhaps largely because of this negative result, problems concerning the origins and diffusion of qualitative differences in the form of the capital stock appear to be moving once again to the forefront of scholarly interest. "Once again," because it is precisely upon the importance of innovation that the late Joseph Schumpeter concentrated his life work, as is also true in the case of Abbot Payson Usher.

It is easy enough to list the major mechanical innovations appearing in nineteenth-century transport, industry, and agriculture, but the history of American technology has not been sufficiently explored to permit us to know why they were adopted when and where they were by particular firms and industries. Some scholars, for example, Irving H. Siegel, maintain that "It is not sufficient to say that technological change is an 'endogenous variable' and that its direction is 'determined by economic forces.'" Others, for example, Douglass C. North, prefer to emphasize the role of the market in selecting potential innovations from the available fund of knowledge and invention. Jacob Schmookler relates the influence of the market to the process of invention itself. In established industries, at least, Schmookler suggests, "historical shifts in inventive attention appear to reflect the interplay of advancing knowledge, which opens up new inventive opportunities for exploitation, and the unfolding of economic needs and opportunities arising out of a changing social order." Other useful insights, as we shall see, have been provided by H. J. Habakkuk in particular and by W. Paul Strassmann, Nathan Rosenberg, and Harold F. Williamson.

The most careful evaluation of American manufacturing progress prior to the Civil War is contained in the reports of two groups of English technicians who visited the United States in the 1850's. According to these reports, American production methods, more highly mechanized and standardized than those of the English, were employed in the manufacture of products ranging from "doors, furniture, and other woodwork; boots and shoes; ploughs and mowing machines, wood screws, files and nails; biscuits; locks, clocks, small arms, nuts and bolts." In Habakkuk's judgment, the English were still far ahead of the Americans in most fields of technology at this date, yet the "greater degree of American mechanisation in a number of industries and the greater stress on standardisation are unexpected enough to call for an explanation." Why, he asks "should mechanisation, standardisation and mass-production have appeared *before* 1850 and to an extent which surprised reasonably dispassionate English observers?"

Habakkuk's own answer to this question is an essentially simple one. The factor-endowment of the United States imparted a bias in favor of a technology that employed more capital per unit of output than labor. Capital-intensive techniques were often cheaper: labor, especially unskilled labor, was dear and its supply inelastic. Such was the demand for unskilled labor in relation to its supply that the money wage for adults ranged between a third and a half higher than was the case in England. For varying degrees of skilled labor the differential was much less, and during the early decades of the century the "premium on artisan skills" appears to have been even lower in America than in England. After mid-century there developed a much greater scarcity of skilled than of unskilled labor. Until then, an American manufacturer wishing to increase his output of goods therefore found it less costly to do so by methods which emphasized the use of relatively cheaper skilled labor. He often preferred mechanization, that is to say, because the manufacture and use of capital-intensive techniques required a higher proportion of skilled to unskilled labor per unit of output than did alternative labor-intensive techniques.

In addition, the kind of labor that was relatively most dear "performed the simple, unskilled operations which were, from a technical point of view, most easily mechanised." An increased demand for labor, then, raised the wages of skilled labor *less* than the wages of the unskilled. This was particularly true during the boom phase of the business cycle, when a general attempt was being made to expand capacity. It was then that the scarcity and relatively higher wage-cost of unskilled labor was most likely to emerge, such was the demand in a developing country for the use of general labor in road, canal, railroad, and other overhead construction. Boom periods, therefore, witnessed the most rapid progress toward mechanization.

Two main factors account for the scarcity of unskilled labor. Prior to the 1840's immigration contributed relatively small increases to the supply. And the existence of abundant land siphoned off potential increments from sources within the nation. This is not to maintain that industrial workers quit the cities for the countryside, although at one point in his argument Habakkuk does imply they might do so. In general, however, he does not adopt the frontier hypothesis of Frederick Jackson Turner. Instead, he relies upon the modification given that hypothesis by Carter Goodrich and Sol Davison, a modification which holds that "the abundance of western land drew away many thousands of potential wage earners (from the hill towns of New England and from the exhausted farms of New York and Pennsylvania) who might otherwise have crowded into the factories." Not only was land abundant, it was also accessible. What made it so was the national government's increasingly liberal policy of land disposal, together with the fact that, until the 1850's, the costs of farm-making were relatively low. In sum, the resulting movement onto the land of potential wage earners, in combination with the small amount of immigration, provided an important support for the wage levels of the industrially unskilled.

The main support came from the high productivity per capita in agriculture, and it is upon this that Habakkuk places his emphasis. He holds output per man in agriculture to have been high for a number of reasons. Not only was land abundant, accessible, and fertile, but because the cultivator was often the owner and his family supplied the labor, the advantage of the high output accrued to the cultivator. His income included an element of rent, of agricultural profits, and of wages. In addition, numerous frontier farmers enjoyed windfall gains in the form of an unearned increment as population movements raised the value of their lands. Indeed, "For the farmer on the moving frontier the annual income from the farm was probably less important than this deferred return on his capital and effort."

The high returns in agriculture made possible by these various contributions provided a floor for real wages in manufacturing, a minimum beneath which they could not fall. And high real wage costs, in turn, gave manufacturers an incentive to replace labor by machines. Although this raised capital costs per unit of output, Habakkuk points out that subsequent reductions in these costs were made possible by running the machines hard and fast, by incorporating later capital improvements, and possibly by reinvesting large proportions of profits that were maintained at high average rates by imperfections in product and labor markets.

However, the effects on wages and profits of the absence of well-organized labor markets cannot be known with any degree of confidence. "To measure real wage trends in the first half of the nineteenth century," Stanley Lebergott has recently acknowledged, "is probably impossible." Wage data are far too few, scattered, imprecise, and incomparable to warrant regarding estimates as anything more than "careful guesswork." Lebergott's own careful guess is that real nonfarm wages showed hardly any rise in the antebellum period. "Instead of the closely proportional change that exists between wage rates and upward productivity trends in today's more highly organized labor markets these early records do not suggest wages gaining in proportion to productivity." If this is true it would tend to support Habakkuk's emphasis on the contribution of imperfect labor markets to the maintenance of high average profits, for that imperfection meant that, up to a certain point, the manufacturer "could exploit his labour." If so, this squeezing of labor may have contributed to capital formation. But we do not know the fact of the matter. Commenting on Lebergott's tentative conclusion, Albert Rees finds it "hard to believe for a period [1800–1880] that saw the full transition from handicrafts to large-scale industry."

The expansion of production by means of machinery rather than by labor exerted a very important influence on technological progress. It was precisely the more capital-intensive of the existing range of techniques that had the greatest possibilities of technical advance. Once installed, machines permitted an accumulation of experience in their operation and the making of minor modifications and adjustments that enhanced their efficiency. Accumulating knowledge and skill also made it easier to solve technical problems and "sense out the points where the potentialities of further technical progress were brightest." Furthermore, the same considerations that warranted the adoption of such techniques in the first place might also justify a replacement of existing equipment by improved kinds. Old equipment made poor use of scarce labor. Habakkuk also argues that the preoccupation of manufacturers with the problem of labor scarcity, together with their use of accounting methods that were too primitive to inform them concerning the proper components of capital costs, led them to slight the question whether the new equipment might not reduce their return on capital. To these considerations should be added Strassmann's point that machinery in some industries, for example, textiles before 1835, was wooden rather than metallic and hence inexpensive. The notable willingness to scrap extant machinery for new, a willingness that did much to keep manufacturers abreast of the latest techniques, tended to give way to greater caution once the cost of capital goods decisively rose.

Certainly before then, however, and to some extent afterwards, the zeal for the new is impressive. After a stay in America, Friedrich List wrote in the 1820's: "Everything new is quickly introduced here, and all the latest inventions. There is no clinging to old ways, the moment an American hears the word 'invention' he pricks up his ears." Writing in the 1830's about the cotton textile industry, J. Montgomery observed that although the number of inventions originating in the United States was not high compared with those that came from Britain, "the common stock of inventions was very rapidly integrated into the American economy." The attitude of industrial labor toward innovation made it easy not only to introduce new machinery and improve it, but also to adopt administrative methods designed to economize the use of labor. Because of the scarcity of labor, the introduction of new machines and techniques did not threaten the jobs of workers; without displacing anyone, they increased labor productivity and possibly brought some increase in wages. Numerous changes in production methods originated in the ingenuity of working men themselves.

Habakkuk believes the principal effect of labor scarcity in the early decades of the nineteenth century was "probably to induce American manufacturers to adopt labour-saving methods invented in other countries earlier and more extensively than they were adopted in their country of origin." It is true that the English ban on the export of machinery was not raised until 1843, but in practice the prohibition had earlier been relaxed by issuances of special licenses or by smuggling. By the end of the 1820's there was a substantial export from England of machines made by cheaper British labor, and the removal of the prohibition imparted a still greater incentive to adopt capital-intensive techniques. Yet even in the late eighteenth and early nineteenth centuries a number of important inventions by Americans themselves were directly induced by the search for labor-saving methods. For example, Oliver Evans's milling machinery introduced an early form of production line and halved the labor required. A number of nail-making machines were also invented prior to 1800.

By the 1820's and 1830's pressures were developing in a number of fields to invent new techniques. Except for carding and drawing, Americans during the decade 1814–24 radically improved all the processes involved in cotton manufacturing, and the most important of the adaptations and inventions—the ring spindle, the Goulding automatic roving machine, the self-acting temple, and various self-stopping devices in case of breakage—were "in large measure due to the dearness and instability of the available labour." The mechanization of weaving proceeded rapidly after Francis Cabot Lowell designed his power loom in 1813. The power loom was rapidly adapted to the weaving of woolens and worsteds, and in these industries Americans also made important advances in carding and in the finishing processes. Viewing the progress of technology throughout the economy generally, the Commissioner of Patents observed in 1843: "The advancement of the arts, from year to year, taxes our credulity, and seems to presage the arrival of that period when human improvement must end."

Habakkuk emphasizes that the fields in which the effect of labor conditions on technique had "the most important long-term consequences" were those to which it was possible to manufacture goods by the method of interchangeable parts. The independent contributions made to the development of this method by Eli Whitney and Simeon North are well known, as is the importance of the assistance given by government contracts in the small-arms industry, to which field the method was first applied. Before the Civil War the technique was being used for the manufacture of wood-screws, woodworking, nuts, bolts, locks, clocks, watches, agricultural machinery, footwear, typewriters, and sewing machines. According to Williamson, manufacturing by interchangeable parts, together with the use of assembly line techniques, was the principal mark of distinction between American mass-production methods and those of most other countries, including Great Britain. The beginnings of the assembly line date from Oliver Evans's introduction of the principle of a continuous process of production in a flour mill which he built in 1782. The importance of labor scarcity in inducing the principle is clearly to be seen from Evans's statement that he was prompted "to study how I could make the mill exceed all others. I first conceived the grand design of applying the power that drives the millstones to perform all the operations which were hitherto effected by manual labor." By the 1850's Cryus F. McCormick was employing both techniques in his Chicago reaper factory.

The nature of one of the driving forces behind the spreading use of new machines and techniques is clearly visible. Successful application to one field stimulated their adoption elsewhere. "Their success inspired imitators, and shaped entrepreneurial attitudes towards the most likely lines of development." Furthermore, the penalties for not adopting capital-intensive techniques increased as communications improved and as labor and product markets became less imperfect. "If *some* manufacturers expanded output by adopting capital-intensive methods and in so doing raised the labour-costs of their competitors, those who did not expand, and still more those who expanded with inappropriate equipment, became high cost producers and lost their share of the market." To an increasing extent, industrial competition replaced the role that high agricultural earnings had previously played in inducing the adoption of capital-intensive techniques. For in the 1850's, as Clarence H. Danhof has shown, it was less possible than in earlier decades to meet the costs of farm-making on the frontier—and in the Northwest generally—by the labor and sacrifice of the farmer and his family.

Recent work by Nathan Rosenberg makes it clear that one additional stimulus to technological progress is deserving of special emphasis. The more manufacturers mechanized, the wider the market for the machine-making industry. In the early part of the century, makers of machines did not exist as a separate industry. Manufacturers of various end products mainly made their own machines. With increased mechanization, machine-making shops emerged as adjuncts to end-product factories, appearing first in the New England textile industry. These shops also made their own lathes, planers, and other machine tools, although some were imported from England. As the market for machines widened, a machine shop often undertook to produce several different types of machines, but after 1840 there occurred a high degree of specialization in their manufacture. According to Jonathan T. Lincoln, "With the wide extension of the railroads, locomotive-building became an important industry, too big to share quarters with spinning-frames and looms; and gradually the skill acquired in the building of machinery for the early factories was passed on and permeated the manufacture of machinery for many industries, in shops established for these specific purposes." By the 1850's visiting English technicians could observe that "in the adaptation of special apparatus to a single operation in almost all branches of industry, the Americans display an amount of ingenuity, combined with undaunted energy, which as a nation we should do well to imitate." Particularly in woodworking and small-arms, Americans had developed machine tools more specialized than those available in England. And the 1850's and 1860's witnessed the rapid emergence of firms making highly specialized machine tools.

There thus emerged during the forty years before the Civil War an important capital goods sector of the economy which increasingly specialized in the production of producers' durables—machines and machine tools. This new sector not only responded to increasing demand for its products by becoming more and more specialized. It had itself every incentive to widen its market by adopting labor-saving improvements in manufacturing techniques which would enable it to provide machines as cheaply as possible. In consequence, the durable goods industry itself became a main source of technological innovation that permitted capital saving for the economy as a whole. Furthermore, the machine shops became important training schools for numerous machinists. Especially important was the independent machine shop opened in 1810 in Pawtucket, Rhode Island, by David Wilkinson, a brother-in-law of Samuel Slater. According to Lincoln, all the textile-machine companies founded in the first half of the nineteenth century, with "one or two notable exceptions," owed their origins to the skill imparted by Wilkinson.

The insight of Rosenberg enables us to see that the acquisition and diffusion of specialized technical knowledge, a process of vital importance to an industrializing economy, owed much to a phenomenon which he usefully describes as one of "technological convergence." The technical processes involved in the manufacture of machinery were common to many industries rather than unique within each of them. What gave these processes their common character was the basic fact that industrialization in the nineteenth century involved the growing adoption of a metal-using technology employing decentralized sources of power:

The use of machinery in the cutting of metal into precise shapes involves, to begin with, a relatively small number of operations (and therefore machine types): turning, boring, drilling, milling, planing, grinding, polishing, etc. Moreover, all machines performing such operations confront a similar collection of technical problems, dealing with such matters as power transmission (gearing, belting, shafting), control devices, feed mechanisms, friction reduction, and a broad array of problems connected with the properties of metals (such as ability to withstand stresses and heat resistance). It is because these processes and problems became common to the production of a wide range of disparate commodities that industries which were apparently unrelated from the point of view of the nature and uses of the final product became very closely related (technologically convergent) on a technological basis—for example, firearms, sewing machines, and bicycles.[3]

This emphasis on the machine tool industry as "a key transmission center for expertise in the making and use of machinery" (Strassmann) and upon the diffusion of knowledge as a prerequisite of industrialization, adds significantly to our understanding of the basic forces at work in that process.

There is one additional "force," however, that it would be well to include. The foregoing discussion has concentrated on technological progress as a by-product of efforts to check or compensate for high-wage costs in an economy marked by scarce labor and abundant land. It has been concerned with the consequences of the need to "economize," and in this sense it has concerned "economics." It ought also to have concerned business. Habakkuk's analysis insufficiently emphasizes the importance of prospective gains from widening markets. It was not alone the need to cut unit production costs that stimulated the search for labor-saving techniques. It was as well, and perhaps even more importantly, the need to increase output in order to profit from cyclically rising product prices. Granted that labor scarcity dictated the capital-intensive form which the effort to do so would often take. It is yet questionable that the push of costs availed as much as the pull of prospective profits. Both elements were, of course, pertinent, and Habakkuk does not fail to note their presence. What is at question is the distribution of emphasis.

Habakkuk does emphasize an aspect of the market that facilitated mechanization, namely, its homogeneity. "American demand was for uniform standardised types of product," and for relatively low-quality goods. Both of these facets of demand were favorable to mechanization. Broadly speaking, machinery could most easily be devised for products made in large quantities to a single pattern.

[3] Nathan Rosenberg, "Technological Change in the Machine Tool Industry, 1840–1910," *Journal of Economic History,* XXIII (Dec. 1963), 423.

As for quality, Habakkuk notes that many of the new textile methods, when first introduced, were "too clumsy to be suitable for anything except coarse products." Standardization, furthermore, "could be applied not only to final products but to the machines which produced them." This demand for standardized goods is attributed to the income effects of the country's factor-endowment. "The high price of labour, and the abundance of land and the relative equality in its distribution ensured that a higher proportion of income than in England went to the middle-income groups who demanded the type of good which lent themselves to mechanisation." The cheapness of food, Habakkuk adds, "ensured a high *per capita* demand for industrial goods."

An increasing demand for foods and raw materials made possible by the growth of cities and incomes per capita, improved transport, and foreign markets placed agriculture under the same compulsion faced by industry to increase output with limited labor supplies. The farm family with its many children was the first source of labor. Trained early to do the milking, haying, plowing, planting, and hauling, farm children learned care in the handling of equipment and livestock. That hired men, in contrast, should have been a source of almost universal complaint is hardly surprising in view of the impermanency of status of many of them in a country rich in land. Many were Scandinavian and German immigrants working as farm labor or on construction jobs only until they could raise sufficient funds to start farming on their own. Others were drifters moving from one temporary job to another—haying, harvesting, or picking apples and hops—men without ambition, irresponsible, and careless in the use of equipment. The free farmers of the northern states, nevertheless, employed a surprising number of laborers, either for special tasks like butchering, for the summer months, or at most as a rule for six months out of the year. Paul W. Gates estimates that in 1860 there was one farm laborer or tenant for every two farms. But because of the high cost of labor and the uncertainty of retaining it, the farmer was ready to "adopt such laborsaving devices as were available and practicable, provided that in doing so he could reduce his overhead costs and at the same time market a greater volume of goods."

The extent to which in fact he did so is at present uncertain. There appears to be little or no uncertainty about the southern planter, however. "With a plantation system containing great stretches of undeveloped land, a wide and thinly scattered rural population, low land values, and slave labor which had no incentive to use tools and draft animals carefully, the South," according to Gates, "did not feel the same necessity to make labor more productive through the use of machines." Gates believes the planters "were not entirely aware of the cost to them of the labor supply they used so prodigally in the production of staples and in less economic enterprises," and points out that early nineteenth-century improvements in tillage and harvesting machines did not affect in any important way the growing of cotton, tobacco, sugar cane, or rice. But while field work was done with antiquated implements, new machinery did improve techniques for processing and marketing crops. By the 1830's, for example, the great plantations were introducing steam to power large machines used in the ginning of cotton and were using heavy horse- or mule-drawn screw presses for baling it. Mechanization of extractive and manufacturing processes on the great sugar plantations of Louisiana was notable as early as the 1820's.

The uncertainty concerning the progress of agricultural technology is applicable in the main to owner-cultivated farms. On the one hand there is the view of Habakkuk. "That shortage of labour and abundance of land had always provided an incentive to mechanise American agriculture," he writes, "is obvious." It was certainly not obvious to Congressman Porter of New York, whose views concerning the effects of the lack of markets upon the incentives of western farmers in 1810 have been previously noted. But quibble-quoting is the ready refuge of inexact knowledge, and Habakkuk can cite the authority of the English visitor W. Cobbett in support of his view that as early as 1818 the American farmer not only cooperated with superior natural resources but had superior equipment. Certainly in that year Cobbett seems to have suggested that the high productivity of American agricultural labor was "in some measure due to the fact that its operations were more efficiently organised," and in 1835 Richard Cobden commented that the agricultural implements of New England exhibited "remarkable evidence of ingenuity . . . for aiding and abridging human as well as brute labor." Habakkuk explains in the following terms why American agricultural methods should have become more mechanized than those of Great Britain: "With abundant land and scarce labor the marginal product of an agricultural machine was obviously greater on the plains of Ohio than on the fields of the English Midlands; in the U.S.A. the machine enabled land to be cultivated which would otherwise not have been cultivated at all." On the other hand, P. W. Bidwell and J. I. Falconer believe that "The first four decades of the nineteenth century were characterized by important beginnings in agricultural progress, rather than by striking or revolutionary accomplishments. It was a period of preparation both in the technical and in the business side of farming— preparation for subsequent progress and expansion." Which of these views is more probably correct? Is it likely or is it not that technological improvement increased agricultural productivity before mid-century?

Marvin W. Towne and Wayne D. Rasmussen agree with Bidwell and Falconer. "Research, experiment, and education," they write, "precede the benefits of technological innovation. Evidence suggests that an increase in the application of technology to agriculture began in the early part of the nineteenth century but that it did not cause a significant increase in productivity until the middle of the century." While many implements and machines were being developed during this period, for example, Jethro Wood's iron plow (1819), steel plows adapted to tough prairie soils (1830's), harrows and seed drills (1840's) and corn planters (1850's), "relatively few were manufactured and sold commercially." "No substantial rise in demand for grain products had occurred, and farmers generally felt no strong incentive to buy machines that would increase output." Besides, there was a "general resistance to the adoption of new ideas," and this required time and educational effort to overcome.

Presumably, resistance confronted improved techniques for both extensive and intensive farming. Not only did farmers lack a strong incentive to buy machines that would increase labor productivity. Resistance also confronted improved techniques for increasing yields per acre. Towne and Rasmussen do not deny that some men were carrying on agricultural experiments. Such learned farmers as Jefferson, Washington, and Henry Laurens engaged in agricultural research, as did Samuel Deane, Elkanah Watson, John Bordley and other experimental agriculturalists, not to mention such business-men as Robert Oliver of Baltimore and Nicholas Biddle of Philadelphia. Their influence on ordinary farmers, however, as was the case with state and local agricultural societies formed during and after the 1780's, seems to have been slight. The latter, says Russel B. Nye, "were far more successful in gathering scientific material than in disseminating it." Almanacs remained the most effective medium for transmitting the results of research to the average farmer, although almanac makers were not always fully aware of the latest and most accurate information. The first farm journal was published in 1810, local fairs began about the same time, state agencies to promote better agriculture began with the New York Board of Agriculture in 1819, and in 1839, $1,000 was appropriated to the Patent Office for agricultural work. Un-doubtedly, George Washington identified the most important obstacle to the progress of agricultural improvement when he told Arthur Young: "The English farmer ought to have a horrid idea of the state of our agriculture or of the nature of our soil, when he is informed that one acre with us only produced eight or ten bushels. But it must be kept in mind, that where land is cheap and labour dear men are fonder of cultivating much than cultivating well."

Real farm gross output increased considerably during the 1850's, and in the decade 1855–65 the annual rate of real investment in implements and farm machinery rose to $23,000,000 (in 1910–14 dollars), more than double that of the preceding decade. By the

1850's, resistance to innovation had been overcome, foreign and domestic markets had widened and transport improved, and the United States stood on the threshold of what Towne and Rasmussen call our "first agricultural revolution." What made for "revolution" was the rapidity of change from manpower to horsepower. By 1860, for example, every stage in the growing of grain was amenable to the use of horse-drawn machines.

That the technological contribution to increased agricultural productivity was greater after mid-century than before seems clear. Yet while the general question of the extent and sources of pre-Civil War agricultural productivity must await the results of the work currently being done by William N. Parker, there is some reason to believe that Towne and Rasmussen have underemphasized the importance of technological innovation in the earlier decades. For one thing, they not only overlook earlier influences of urbanization and improved transport upon the demand for agricultural products but also underestimate the contribution to rising productivity made by the iron plow (1819). According to Gates, the cast-iron plow with replaceable parts "early became the most widely used plow in the Northeast," and by 1850, 200 different patterns and types were being manufactured. Worcester, Massachusetts was turning out 1,000 plows a year as early as 1830 and Pittsburgh in that year could boast a steam factory with a capacity of 100 per day. The iron plow, Clarence H. Danhof points out, "reduced the labor required in plowing by about half with a consequent tendency toward increased acreage tilled per man." Similar changes occurred in the methods employed in cultivating cotton and corn, he adds, "while the displacement of the scythe by the cradle in harvesting small grain was similarly important."

One might also mention the somewhat earlier importance of such other agricultural implements as John Deere's plows, which, with their highly polished wrought-iron moldboards and steel shares, made possible the great grain farms of the Middle West by "scouring" cleanly the sticky prairie soil of that region. At work on the plow in 1837, Deere was turning out 10,000 a year by 1857. By

1851, Cyrus McCormick was making 1,000 mechanical reapers a year in his Chicago factory. The contribution of the reaper to labor productivity may be seen in the following estimate by Leo Rogin: a man with a sickle could cut one half to three-quarters of an acre of wheat in a day, with a cradle he could cut two to three acres a day, and with a self-rake reaper he could cut ten to twelve acres a day. Gates judges the effect of the adoption of the reaper upon the agriculture of the Northwest to have been "tremendous." Farmers turned from corn to wheat, and wheat acreage more than doubled. "A major wheat-producing center came into existence in northern Illinois and southern Wisconsin." In the years 1849–57, eleven counties in northern Illinois purchased approximately one-fourth of the total number of McCormick reapers sold.

Factory-made implements like plows, mowers, harrows, threshers, and reapers found new and wider markets when the extension of canals and railroads made it possible to ship them into regions previously cut off from main lines of communication. But even if the complete statistical record of production and shipment were available, it would miss what may be an important part of the story of agricultural technology in the pre-Civil War years. Not only did farmers themselves rough-hew plows, cultivators, harrows, and wooden implements of many other kinds, but local blacksmiths were available to put a piece of iron on their plow shares, iron tines on their forks, and iron spikes on their harrows. Although surviving records are too few for quantitative estimates, crossroads ingenuity may have made a considerable contribution to agricultural productivity.

VIII

The Social and Cultural Dimension

Education

Capital consists of current resources that are devoted to future output instead of present consumption, and it is apparent on the face of it that the formation of capital, and constant improvement in its quality, are requisite to higher levels of future growth. But capital is not only physical in character but human as well, and the constant improvement in its quality by means of education and training, and often by measures to improve motivation and health, is also requisite to growth. Throughout most of human history the available body of knowledge has been the preserve of the few. In the modern world it is seen with increasing clarity that economic growth requires the widest possible diffusion of knowledge among the people. For example, a United Nations group recently concluded that "most underdeveloped countries are in a situation that investment in people is likely to prove as productive, in the purely material sense, as any investment in material resources." Investment in education and training can increase both geographical and occupational mobility by enabling labor to move from unskilled to more skilled work, and can also facilitate innovation and raise productivity. In his recent study of the sources of economic growth in the United States in the twentieth century, Edward F. Denison suggests that after 1929 a rising level of education contributed more than any other source to the rise in output per person employed.

One difficult problem in estimating the influence of education in earlier American growth is that of determining the meaning of the term. Should "education'" be conceived narrowly in terms of technical knowledge and vocational training? Should it be confined to formal institutions for its dissemination, together with their academic programs? For several reasons I believe that either narrow recourse would miss the essence of the matter.

In the first place, it seems clear that an increase in the general level of literacy, the extension of a basic general education, both now and in the past, did much to facilitate the training of skilled workers. Alfred Marshall certainly believed that the influence of nontechnical education on industrial efficiency "is greater than it appears." Early nineteenth-century opinion would have agreed with Marshall's assessment. In his *Science and Mechanics,* published in 1829, Zachariah Allen observes: "From the habits of early life and the diffusion of knowledge by free schools there exists generally among the mechanics of New England a vivacity in inquiring into the first principles of the science to which they are practically devoted." And the informed visitors Whitworth and Wallis, dispatched from England to study and report upon American industrial techniques, commented in the 1850's: "The compulsory educational clauses adopted in the laws of most of the States, and especially those of New England, by which some three months of every year must be spent at school by the young operative under 14 or 15 years of age, secure every child from the cupidity of the parent, or the neglect of the manufacturer. . . . This lays the foundation for that wide-spread intelligence which prevails amongst the factory operatives of the United States. . . . The skill of hand which comes of experience, is, notwithstanding present defects, rapidly following the perceptive power so keenly awakened by early intellectual training."

A sufficient reason for not confining to formal institutions of education the search for educational influences on growth is that the pace of American growth accelerated during a period when, as we shall see, those institutions were relatively few in number. But it would be shortsighted to conclude from this that education bore no relevance to technological innovation. As Abbot Payson Usher points out, not only innovation—the application of invention to processes of production—but invention itself, is a process, the character of which has often been misconceived. Usher warns against "an identification of invention with an act of genius. It leads toward an undue emphasis upon a relatively small number of acts which are presented without due regard to the conditions which make them possible, and to a concept of change at infrequent intervals in units of great magnitude, although the simplest effort of analysis makes it clear that acts of insight are numerous, pervasive, and of very small magnitudes." He believes that the study of technical change in the economy "has been hindered by the failure of students to treat effectively the kinds of novelty that are a normal and continuous consequence of the skilled activity of engineers and technicians." Based on a lifelong study of European technology, Usher's general admonition bears specific relevance to American history in the pre-Civil War period.

During these years, H. J. Habakkuk points out, technological progress was still more empirical than scientific, it "depended more on the response to particular and immediate problems of industrial practice than on the autonomous development of scientific knowledge." Technical development, therefore, was "likely to take the form of slow modifications of detail, as opposed to spectacular leaps to a new technique decisively superior from the start to its predecessors." Most of the "great inventions" of the period, he adds in the words of J. C. Gilfillan, resolve themselves on close inspection into a "perpetual accretion of little details probably having neither beginning, completion nor definable limits."

If technical change, then, was a record written, not by a handful of garret-bound heroes, but by engineers who had obtained their knowledge through practical experience in canal construction and by innumerable workers in shops, mills, factories, and fields, it follows that the school of daily labor must have furnished a highly significant part of "education." "New ideas," says Habakkuk, "were often the least important part of invention or at least the part which was most easily borrowed. What determined whether and where the ideas bore fruit was the practical capacity brought to bear on them." Probably most Americans learned most by doing. Experience on the job or in the use of a tool or machine suggested ways in which operations might be improved and tools made more useful. This is what Habakkuk means by the observation that American inventive ingenuity was to a considerable extent a result rather than a cause of mechanization.

There is much reason to believe American ingenuity also preceded mechanization and that it received a considerable stimulus from what Tench Coxe called "the peculiar value of labour-saving machinery to a nation of moderate numbers dwelling in a country of redundant soil." Their dwellings were also frequently dispersed over a wide area, so that ingenuity received an additional stimulus from the necessity of a high degree of self-reliance. Relatively little mechanization existed at the opening of the nineteenth century, yet this was a time when, in the words of George S. Gibb, "varied and dextrous mechanical abilities were all but universal." And Hamilton notes in his Report on Manufactures that "a remark often to be met with" was that "there is, in the genius of the people of this country, a peculiar aptitude for mechanic improvements." "The American working boy," a distinguished English inventor of machine tools, James Nasmyth, observed in the mid-nineteenth century, "develops rapidly into a skilled artisan"; "there is not a working boy of average ability in the New England states. . . ," he added, "who has not an idea of some mechanical invention or improvement in manufactures, by which, in good times, he hopes to better his position, or rise to fortune and social distinction."

It is clear that nineteenth-century Americans were receptive to labor-saving ideas, whether originating abroad or at home, and that they learned from experience how to convert those ideas into productive forms and improve upon them. It is no less clear that their economic and physical environments enlarged their capacity for learning from experience. So too did some of the institutions within their social environment, especially the family, apprenticeship, and those providing more formal channels of education. An unobstructed view of the manner in which they did so can most easily be obtained from the vantage point of their colonial origins, for more formal institutions appeared in response to the declining influence of less formal ones, without entirely replacing them.

Conceiving education largely as "the entire process by which a culture transmits itself across the generations," Bernard Bailyn in a thoughtful recent essay emphasizes the role of the family as the most important of the agencies of transfer. Initially a "patrilineal group of extended kinship gathered into a single household," the colonial family shouldered most of the burden not only of shaping the child to civilized patterns of living but also of providing at least elementary lessons in vocational training. In a great many cases, it gave "all the vocational instruction necessary for mature life." Apprenticeship represented an extension and formalization of the family role in vocational training. It was a "contractual exchange of vocational training in an atmosphere of family nurture," a combination, as Paul H. Douglas expresses it, of education and industry which made possible learning by doing. But it was also a vehicle for moral indoctrination, Christian training, and instruction in literacy.

Among numerous influences tending to disrupt the family, perhaps none was more important than what Bailyn calls the failure of the "ultimate sanction of a restrictive economy": "where land was abundant and labor at a premium it took little more to create a household than to maintain one. Material independence was sooner or later available to every energetic adult white male, and few failed to break away when they could." Remarkably soon after the beginnings of settlement the family, yielding to "intractable circumstances of material life" which lowered the prestige of parents while invigorating the more adaptable and less conservative young, began to fail in the discharge of its traditional educational functions. It did not, it must be said, surrender until much later the training in useful arts provided by the household system of manu-facture. It would require the progressive rise of a market economy for girls to begin to forget how to spin, weave, embroider, knit, darn, crochet, and make butter, cheese, and candles, and for boys no longer to learn how to fashion plows, harrows, sleds, wagons, carts, shovels, and flails, as well as kitchen and table utensils. Look-ing back upon his New England childhood in the 1840's and 1850's, the pioneer psychologist G. Stanley Hall remembered the house-hold system as one which "at its best appears to me to have con-stituted the best educational environment for boys at a certain stage of their development ever realized in history." It was in its responsi-bility as the renewer of broader human values that the family began to fail, and in Puritan New England, New York, and the South communities sought by more formal means to cope with the resulting threat to civilization.

In New England "a high cultural level, an intense Biblicism, concentrated settlements, and thriving town institutions led to a rapid enhancement of the role of formal schooling." After 1647 a series of laws passed in Massachusetts and Connecticut ordered all towns to maintain teaching institutions. During the seventeenth century, at least, these attempts at public-supported and public-controlled education appear to have produced a high level of literacy. At the turn of the century, however, Weeden characterizes New England as having entered upon a "dark age," with general culture at a lower level than at any time before or since, and with few Massachusetts towns escaping fines for neglecting their schools.

In the South, efforts were made to establish parish or other local schools, but "scattered plantations," as Timothy Dwight was later to explain, were "subject to many serious disadvantages. Neither schools, nor churches, can without difficulty be either built by the planters, or supported. The children must be too remote from school." The wealthier planters in the seventeenth and eighteenth centuries sometimes imported indentured servants to act as tutors, or hired men trained in the North. What tutors taught might range from Latin and Greek grammar and literature, some English literature, and arithmetic and spelling, which Princeton-trained Philip Fithian taught the children of Robert Carter of Nomini Hall, to the learning implied by the following entry in the diary of John Harrower, who also taught in eighteenth-century Virginia: "This morning about 8 AM the Colonel delivered his three sons to my Charge to teach them to read write and figure." While numerous southern wills contained bequests for the education of surviving children, the fate of large numbers of them may not unfairly be encapsulated in the Duc de la Rochefoucauld-Liancourt's description of Winchester, Virginia, in the mid-1790's: a town of some 21,000 souls, more than thirty "well-stocked stores and shops," and "Two or three pitiful schools."

Involved as it was with the fortunes of the family, apprenticeship also underwent a significant alteration by the eighteenth century. While remaining an important institution for the transmission of skills, its broader educational functions tended increasingly to be taken over by evening schools, the number of which enjoyed a remarkable growth during the course of that century. The schools ministered not alone to the needs of apprentices but also to those of persons occupied by daytime concerns. Their original purpose, Carl Bridenbaugh explains, was "to instruct apprentices whose indentures stipulated a certain amount of reading, writing, and ciphering." The "real destroyer" of apprenticeship, as Douglas makes clear, was the division of labor made possible by the factory sysem of production. With the rise of the factory in the nineteenth century, there was "no longer the need for as large a proportion of skilled workers in industry as formerly." The development of machinery and the specialization of labor "rendered it unnecessary for the vast majority of factory operatives to know more than one, or at most a few, processes." Only a few needed "the all-round knowledge formerly required and which apprenticeship was designed to give."

The elementary schools which emerged out of the inability of the family to maintain its traditional role in the New World were, of course, not the only formal institutions of learning to appear in the colonial period. If in New England the "main business" of elementary education was, in the language of Edmund S. Morgan, "to prepare children for conversion," the objective of Harvard College was to make available to future ministers the best learning of the day, while that of the early secondary schools, the first of which was the Boston Latin School (1635), was to prepare boys for entrance into college. American higher education in particular owed much to religion. By the time of the Revolution eight colleges in addition to Harvard had been founded, all save one of them under the auspices of a church. Indeed, nine out of every ten of the 182 "permanent" colleges established by 1860 had some connection with a religious society. According to Russel B. Nye, "No educational leader before the Civil War would have placed intellectual above religious values."

Nevertheless, as Richard Hofstadter and C. DeWitt Hardy emphasize, among the oldest and longest sustained tendencies observable in American higher education is its drift toward secularism. It is perhaps not too much to find its germ in the early curriculum of Harvard itself, which was dominated by the Latin and Greek writers of antiquity. Despite the revivalism of the Great Awakening, a distinct change in the tone of American society was evident by the middle of the eighteenth century. Educated men were responding to the intellectual influence of the European Enlightenment, and "the American concern with the useful, the practical, and the mundane was growing."

Secular studies, however, may vary considerably in the degree to which they confront the problems and interests of the "practical" world. In his *Proposals Relating to the Education of Youth in Pennsylvania* (1749) Benjamin Franklin expounded, "although without substantial effect," the need for a practical element in studies. Advertising the opening of a course of studies five years later, Samuel Johnson of King's College (the present-day Columbia

University) listed the availability of mathematics, surveying and navigation, commerce and husbandry, geography, geology, and history, among other subjects. And in 1772 President Witherspoon of the College of New Jersey (Princeton) observed that education promoted arts and industry as well as "virtue and happiness," dwelling with some pride upon the scientific offerings of the college.

Efforts to instill a more "practical" element in learning were to continue in the antebellum period. About 1815, for example, the Reverend Robert Finley asked: "Might we not adopt with some prudent modifications in our literary institutions, that part of the ancient Jewish system of education, in which they trained their pupils to an acquaintance with mechanical pursuits, in connexion with letters and science, and while they strengthened and enriched the minds of their scholars with literary culture, established them in the practical knowledge of the useful arts and mechanical employments of life?" That such considerations exerted little influence upon most colleges is indicated by the nature of their curricula. Hofstadter and Hardy describe the American college curriculum before the Civil War as consisting chiefly of studies in Latin, Greek, mathematics, logic, and moral philosophy, "with occasional smatterings of Hebrew and rather elementary physics and astronomy." It was assumed, they add, that education was "for gentlemen."

However, the period was not devoid of institutions of a more utilitarian bent. In 1823 there opened in Gardiner, Maine, a full-time scientific and technical school known as the Gardiner Lyceum, and in the next year the Rensselaer School was founded in Troy, New York. In a Review of the Announcements of the Lyceum that was published in 1825 in the *United States Literary Gazette* may be seen the purposes of its founders:

It had its origin in the wants of the community, . . . and in the desire of useful, practical knowledge, which is more and more felt through all parts of the country, in proportion as it becomes more free. The eminent practical sagacity for which they are distinguished must often be exhausted in the discovery of methods, which would be deduced with perfect ease from simple principles in geometry and natural philosophy. But these sciences, together with chemistry and other analogous branches of knowledge, have been rarely taught, except at college, and as a part of a course of studies for persons intended for the learned professions. The academies and high schools are almost universally preparatory and subordinate to the college. . . . In the secondary schools, little else is taught but reading, writing, grammar, arithmetic and geography. The Gardiner Lyceum was intended to supply this deficiency, for a portion of our country, and to furnish that kind of instruction which is not furnished elsewhere, and which is most necessary to many important classes in the community.[1]

The Gardiner Lyceum, supported by gifts, tuition fees, and in part by the state legislature, offered a three-year program of short-term courses taught at the college level. From algebra, geometry, linear drawing, bookkeeping, geography and mensuration during the first year, the student proceeded in his second to trigonometry, surveying, navigation, "application of Algebra and Geometry," differential and integral calculus, mechanics, perspective, chemistry, and agricultural chemistry. "Instead of the last mentioned study Civil Engineering is pursued by those who prefer it." The third year's program included political economy, "the Federalist," History, natural history, "Natural Theology," natural philosophy, astronomy, and mineralogy. The course of instruction published in 1827 further discloses the pragmatic objectives of the Lyceum:

It is a constant object in instruction at the Lyceum to familiarise the students' minds with the practical application of their lessons. Surveying and Levelling are taught not only in recitation room but in the field; the pupil in chemistry is carried into the laboratory, and allowed to perform experiments; and the classes in Mechanics are exercised in calculating such problems as occur in the practice of the machinist or engineer. Habits are thus formed of great importance to the pupil; and he becomes familiar with those processes of thought which will be necessary to him in active life. His mind is not only stored with the abstract principles of science but he has learned the very distinct and no less difficult lesson, of bringing his knowledge to bear upon any subject, to which it is applicable.[2]

[1] Quoted in Charles Alpheus Bennett, *History of Manual and Industrial Education Up to 1870* (Peoria, Ill., 1926), p. 363.

[2] Ibid., p. 349.

With the withdrawal of state financial support, the Gardiner Lyceum closed its doors after about ten years of operation. The Rensselaer School grew into today's Rensselaer Polytechnic Institute. As in the case of the Lyceum, the Rensselaer School was established to give instruction "in the application of science to the common purposes of·life." It wished in particular to benefit "the sons and daughters of farmers and mechanics" "in the application of experimental chemistry, philosophy, and natural history, to agriculture, domestic economy, the arts, and manufactures." Such was his interest in "useful" knowledge that the benefactor of the school, Stephen Van Rensselaer, provided in the by-laws of the school for "a number of well-cultivated farms and workshops in the vicinity of the school . . . as places of scholastic exercise for students, where the application of the sciences may be most conveniently taught." According to Charles Alpheus Bennett, the school imparted a significant impetus to research, "furnished teachers of applied science to a large number of schools and colleges," and itself functioned as a graduate school, nearly half of its students being at times college graduates. Finally, the Gardiner Lyceum and the Rensselaer School were the forerunners of the Scientific Course opened at Union College in 1845, the Sheffield Scientific School established in connection with Yale College in 1847; the Lawrence Scientific School at Harvard College in 1847; and the Chandler Scientific School at Dartmouth College in 1852.

In addition to these technical institutions of higher learning, the 1820's saw the appearance of mechanics institutes in many of the larger cities. In 1820 the General Society of Mechanics and Tradesmen of the City of New York opened a library for apprentices and established a "mechanics' school." The first important institution of its kind in the United States and one which lasted for thirty-six years, it is less well known than the Franklin Institute of Philadelphia, incorporated in 1824. Resolutions adopted by the latter at its first public meeting disclose the intent of the founders to form a society that "shall consist of Mechanics, Manufacturers, and others friendly to the useful arts" and to promote the same in Philadelphia by means of popular lectures, a library, a collection of models and minerals, and the offering of premiums "on all useful improvements in the Mechanic Arts." In 1826 the institute established a "High School" in which was offered a three-year course of study consisting of English, modern languages, classical studies, and mathematics and "practical sciences." A total of 304 students were in attendance in the fall of 1829. Other mechanics institutes opened during the 1820's in Baltimore (1825), Boston (1827), and Cincinnati (1828).

With the main exception of these essentially secondary institutions, of a very few institutions of higher learning—pre-eminent among which were the Rensselaer School and the United States Military Academy—and very occasionally of the lyceum or lecture system for adult education that rose to swift popularity after the mid-twenties, few formal means of acquiring a technical education existed in the United States in the antebellum period. Indeed, opportunity for formal education at any level must not have been widespread. One reason for believing so is the extent to which leading public men emphasized the need for it. The statements of many of them no doubt partly reflect the explicitly egalitarian values that owed so much to the Revolutionary period. "Promote, then, as an object of primary importance," Washington urged in his first message to Congress, "institutions for the general diffusion of knowledge. In proportion as the structure of government gives force to public opinion, it is essential that public opinion should be enlightened." He said much the same thing in his Farewell Address. In his *Defence of the Constitution of the United States* John Adams declares that all the people must be educated in a republic and that schools must be conveniently located and maintained at public expense. Jefferson, Samuel Adams, Madison, Jay, and many others play variations on the same theme. "To conform the principles, morals, and manners of our citizens to our republican forms of government it is absolutely necessary that knowledge of every kind should be disseminated through every part of the United States," wrote Benjamin Rush. Rush appears to have been the first, but not the last, to propose the founding of a "federal university."

An outburst of what President Ezra Stiles of Yale termed "college enthusiasm" produced seventeen new and lasting colleges before the end of the century, with a dozen being added by 1820. Expansion also occurred on the secondary level with the founding of numerous academies. Academies were generally private schools which "gave opportunity to that middle class of pupils who could afford the time and cost of some schooling above the elementary but who were in many cases not preparing for college." Seventy-five were incorporated in Virginia, Maryland, Pennsylvania, New York, Massachusetts, and Indiana between 1775 and 1800, and by 1860 the total reached 1,261. Unchartered academies were at all times far more numerous than incorporated ones. Common schools and other public institutions, however, fared far less well.

According to Paul Monroe, while other states followed the example of Massachusetts in maintaining free schools on the basis of public taxation, "the value of this achievement was greatly limited by the unwillingness of the local communities to tax themselves to any great extent for this purpose, and by the fact that private schools had a powerful following and a great influence." The principle of the free school was established in Pennsylvania by law in 1834, he adds. "But here as elsewhere a clear distinction must be made between a constitutional provision or a permissive law and an actual system in operation. The Indiana constitution of 1816 made a clear announcement of the free school principle. It was 1871 before the system was an accomplished fact."

As Carl N. Degler expresses it, "the enunciation of a strong belief in the value of education far exceeded the performance. Schools were permitted to decline for lack of funds and repairs; little effort was even made to insure that children would receive the rudiments of reading and writing, nothing was done to secure qualified teachers or even to provide adequate training schools for their recruitment, though the number of children was mounting."

The Pennsylvania Society for the Promotion of Free Schools stated in 1830 that although there were 400,000 children of school age (5 to 16) in the state, not over 150,000 attended schools of any kind. Constance M. Greene comments upon the "illiteracy and ignorance of a considerable segment" of the population of the nation's capital in the 1830's. Charles Alpheus Bennett declares that in New York City early in the nineteenth century there were a few charity schools under denominational or other control, "but a large number of children in the city were not supplied with means of instruction." The children of working people did not have time to attend school for extended periods. Rural opportunities were especially few, particularly as settlements became more and more scattered with the westward movement of the population. H. G. Good succinctly puts the case: the "new nation was educationally underdeveloped and there was need for institutions to cope with growing requirements."

Two developments appear to have been fundamental in increasing the number of public schools and improving their quality. The first was the advent of the so-called Lancasterian system of instruction. Named for the English educator Joseph Lancaster (1778–1838), this monitorial, or mutual instruction, system aimed chiefly at literacy. Narrow and mechanical in concept and operation, it possessed the virtue of bringing a minimal "education" to large numbers at low cost per pupil. In the Lancasterian schools, the first of which opened in New York in 1806, a part or all the teaching was done by the more advanced pupils, called monitors. The only salaried person was the principal, and in schools with 500 or more pupils the expense for each might be as low as $2 or $3 per year. Enjoying a brief but widespread vogue, the movement had become a lost cause before Lancaster's death in 1838. Despite its defects, however, it contributed importantly to the advent of free schools by convincing many people that they could be operated at moderate cost.

The second development was the great wave of reform that moved across the nation in the 1830's and 1840's. In part a reflection of comparable movements in Europe, especially in Great Britain, the causes of woman's rights, temperance, the ten-hour day, debtor relief, Owenite and Fourierist collectivism, abolitionism, and the reform of prisons, houses of correction, almshouses, and insane asylums competed for place in the public conscience. So too did the cause of educational reform. In part the latter took the form of efforts to provide more schools for the deaf and blind and for children of low intelligence. In the main it represented a "gradual but decisive" reversal of the early failure to live up to the widespread belief in public education.

As a result of the dedicated leadership of Horace Mann, Henry Barnard, and others, in the fifties an older system under which parents contributed to the costs of providing an elementary education for their children began increasingly to be replaced by the free public school. The tuition academy dominated secondary education until well after the Civil War, but by 1860 some 320 public high schools were in existence. More than half of them, however, were located in the three states of New York, Massachusetts, and Ohio. The larger growth of the free public high school, like that of free college education under the aegis of the state universities, would come in the post-Civil War years. In fine, the foundations of a free education system were securely laid in the antebellum period, but the height of the superstructure varied from one part of the country to the next.

It was particularly low in the South. In his pioneer study *The Economic Growth of the United States, 1790–1860*,[3] Douglass C. North places a justifiably heavy emphasis upon the small "investment in human capital" made in that region, where in 1840 the ratio of pupils to white population was 5.72 per cent, in comparison to a ratio of 18.41 per cent in the nonslaveholding states. In 1850 the white population of the slaveholding states was nearly half that of the northern states, yet the former had "less than one-third as many public schools, one-fourth as many pupils, one-twentieth as many public libraries, and one-sixth as many volumes in those

[3] Englewood Cliffs, N. J., 1961.

libraries." Similarly, in numbers of schools per one hundred square miles, literacy among the white population, per cent of white children in schools, and tax monies devoted to public education, the West greatly excelled the South. "While the underlying aspirations and motivations of people in American society were important," North concludes, "the investment in human capital was a critical factor both in innovations and in the relative ease with which they could spread. The primary source of this quality of the labor force and entrepreneurial talent was the widespread free education system in the Northeast, although the skills of English and German immigrants were an important supplement." It will be apparent from the foregoing discussion that this is an assessment with which I agree.

Values and Social Structure

In turning now to the "underlying aspirations and motivations of people" and to the structure of the social system under which antebellum Americans lived, it is important to emphasize once again that it is the comparative angle of vision that matters. "Capitalism," to cite again Carl N. Degler's pointed phrase, "came in the first ships," and if first-generation Puritanism sought to contain the challenge of the external world, surely it would be difficult to maintain that Americans turned their backs for long on the materialist promise of a rich land. But this is not to say that they faced that promise with an assiduously rational determination to wring from it a maximum amount of gain. How could they have done so? Some did, as we have seen—those whose geographic or political situation was fortunate—and no doubt few if any scorned an opportunity to turn an extra dollar. But opportunity was the thing: it was, comparatively speaking, circumscribed by small markets, poor transportation, and by other features of the colonial landscape we have sketched. Markets continually expanded throughout the dependent years, but can there be any doubt that the great transportation improvements of the antebellum period widened them far more, especially domestic markets, and thereby produced a far more pronounced "capitalist" permeation of the population than was possible before? And if a greater proportion of an expanding population pursued its material interests more intently, are not the consequences likely to have been favorable to economic growth? The relationship between values and environment is one of mutual interaction, so that both are now cause, now effect. While few if any men wished not to improve their circumstances, the latitude of their opportunity to do so necessarily influenced both the value and quality of economic effort. Congressman Porter's previously cited observation clearly shows what happens to the edge of incentive when external opportunities are not present to hone it to sharpness. As late as 1851 a western newspaper characterized as follows a settler on backlands inaccessible to markets: "He fills up his leisure time by hunting, loses his regular habits, and discouraged and disappointed, ends by doing the little that he had to do to sustain his family, in a slovenly and imperfect manner." "Why is chess so much more popular in Yugoslavia than in the United States?" The answer given this question in 1961 by the American chess champion, Robert Fischer, is this: "Well, you know, in America everybody is interested in making the dollar fast. In Yugoslavia no matter how much you hustle you're not going to get rich, so you might as well play chess." Perhaps one should not illustrate a point from the level of the anecdotal, particularly when sophisticated economic opinion is also available. For in recent testimony before the Joint Economic Committee of the Eighty-sixth Congress, economist Raymond Goldsmith expressed the view that if the American people became convinced that there would be no more swings in the business cycle, the conviction would "change the whole environment for business and consumers, and it is very difficult to foretell what effect that would have on the rate of growth."

What was present in colonial America was more widespread in later America. In 1748 Cadwallader Colden could assert of New York City that "The only principle of life propagated among the young people is to get money, and men are only esteemed according to what they are worth—that is, the money they are possessed of." The prosperity maxims published by Franklin through *Poor Richard's Almanack* (1732–57) are believed by one student to have "probably exerted as much practical influence on Americans as the combined teachings of all the formal philosophers." But it was not till the third decade of the nineteenth century, Irvin G. Wyllie points out, before Franklin's self-help themes were revived by a new generation of success propagandists. Those themes then bore a peculiar relevance to the needs of a nation undergoing a process of rapid growth with inadequate supplies of labor. So too did the values of an even older Protestant ethic, and during the antebellum decades of accelerated growth every major social institution with a role in the formation of public opinion joined in a massive reiteration of the importance of worldly success and of industry, sobriety, and frugality as its necessary and sufficient means.

The cult of the "self-made man," says John William Ward, was universally accepted in America during the years 1815–45. Although it is not without irony that Henry Clay should be credited with having coined the phrase in a speech on behalf of a protective tariff, the age believed that the key to success lay within. American institutions created a fair field for all: it was up to the man. Man was the master of his fate; whether he succeeded or failed was not explicable in terms of heredity or environment but of character and personal determination alone. Yet God played a role in the process "by providing certainty that success went only to the virtuous." The belief of the age in the self-made man was a source of national pride. "The character of the American people," said a Fourth of July orator in 1831, "has been the sole cause of their growth and prosperity. Natural advantages have been elsewhere wasted."

In the inculcation of these beliefs and values the role of the family was probably more fundamental than that of any other institution. In view of the emphasis placed by David C. McClelland upon the importance of "achievement motivation" in economic growth, it is not without interest that "The idea instilled into the minds of most boys, from early life," according to an article published by *Harper's New Monthly Magazine* in 1853, "is that of 'getting on.' The parents test themselves by their own success in this respect; and they impart the same notion to their children." The article reported that to the vast majority of Americans success had long since come to mean achievement in business and in making money. Wyllie finds that wealthy businessmen not only used the mails to urge upon poor nephews the importance to success of industry, sobriety, and frugality but also repeated the same idea at commencement exercises, in newspaper interviews, and in books. Sigmund Diamond concludes that the antebellum press characteristically explained entrepreneurial success in terms of the possession of the same personal qualities.

Many of the leaders of the American cult of self-help were Protestant clergymen. Such men as Henry Ward Beecher and Lyman Abbott preached that "godliness was in league with riches" and "put the sanction of the church on the get-ahead values of the business community." Abbott "rejoiced in the parable of the talents, and used it to justify his claim that Jesus approved the building of great fortunes." Jesus did not condemn wealth, Abbott declared. " 'On the contrary, he approved of the use of accumulated wealth to accumulate more wealth.' " Others said similar things in books. The Reverend Thomas P. Hunt, for example, summarized the case for riches in the title of his work published in 1836, *The Book of Wealth: in Which It Is Proved from the Bible that It is the Duty of Every Man to Become Rich.*

The elementary schools as well as family, church, press, lyceums, and the reading rooms of mercantile library associations served as institutional channels for the theme of self-help. Wyllie points out that the famous readers of William Holmes McGuffey "extolled the glories of labor to several generations of American youth." From 1836 until the end of the century, he estimates, perhaps as many as half the children in America "went to school to McGuffey . . . and learned industry, frugality, and sobriety from him." The

McGuffey readers "contained the same synthesis of Christian and middle-class virtues that could be found in the leading manuals on success."

> Work, work, my boy, be not afraid;
> Look labor boldly in the face;
> Take up the hammer or the spade,
> And blush not for your humble place.[4]

No boy, however poor or unfortunate, had reason to despair as long as he was willing to work. "Persevering industry will enable one to accomplish almost anything," said a New England common school textbook.

To dismiss all this as mere hypocritical rationalization on the part of employers would be unwise. To be sure, there may well have been present in it an element of unconscious rationalization. But it was not hypocritical. Whether because employers had to believe these things in order to convince others they were true or because they repeated them so often they came themselves to believe them, the point is that they did believe them. One reason for thinking they did, is that they seem to have practiced what they preached. It is of course almost impossible to determine how hard businessmen themselves worked or what the relationship was between their industry and their success. But Wyllie points out that foreigners sometimes commented that an "intense work psychology" embraced not only the business community but the entire nation as well. "America seemed to be the only country where a man felt ashamed if he had nothing to do." It will be obvious that the Protestant ethic, particularly the doctrine of the calling, made a vital contribution to this psychology. And it need hardly be added that the shortage of labor in America created a fertile field in which the ethic of work might flourish.

Charles L. Sanford's study of the intellectual origins of New England's textile industry suggests a second reason for not questioning the sincerity of the ethic of work on the part of employers.

[4] Quoted in Irvin G. Wyllie, *The Self-Made Man in America: The Myth of Rags to Riches* (New Brunswick, N. J., 1954), p. 42.

One's initial reaction to the statements and activities of the region's manufacturers, to be sure, might well be unfavorable to that thesis. It is plain that these men faced a twofold problem: that of reducing imports of competing European textiles and that of recruiting a labor supply. They addressed themselves to the problem of competition by memorializing Congress in 1815 to protect American "consumers" from foreign goods, which they said were deceitfully made from "very inferior materials." They also patriotically contrasted American morals and European manners, making such things as "fashionable dress, intellectuality, leisure, and often art into foppish instruments of the devil," while at the same time elevating "the ascetic virtues of simplicity of dress and manner, plainness of speech and thought, modesty, sobriety, manliness, and industry."

The farm daughters of New England provided the answer to their need for labor. As Nathan Appleton later recalled: "There was little demand for female labor, as household manufacture was superseded by the improvements in machinery. Here was in New England a fund of labor, well educated and virtuous." All that was necessary was to convince the girls and their parents that work in the mills was not morally degrading. This the manufacturers did in two ways: they depicted European manufacturing as "presided over by a devilish class of aristocrats," with its urban workforce underpaid and degraded. And, "for moral as well as economic reasons," they established their mills in rural areas where, in many cases, they provided family plots of land, forbade grogshops and taverns, and erected attractive boardinghouses, schools, and churches.

Their efforts were successful: they obtained tariff protection in 1816 and later, and, as Appleton put it, "the daughters of respectable farmers were readily induced to come into these mills for a temporary period."

On the face of it, it would appear to have been a coldly calculated program. We may perhaps add to that appearance by noting Sanford's remark that the manufacturers "exalted the virtues of sobriety, industry, and the like, not merely because they had inherited these as part of the Protestant business ethic, but because these virtues were from the beginning opposed to the urban vices of indolence, drunkenness, and lewdness, which, in turn, were considered vices of a leisured aristocracy." Nevertheless, Sanford justly concludes, "There is every reason to think that American manufacturers believed their own propaganda." Their letters and journals reveal how deeply they held in private the views they spoke in public. For example, when immediate members of the family or business associates took trips to Europe, they were warned by those at home to be wary of the corrosive seductions of foreign cities. And letters from the travelers described spectacles of "pomp and iniquity, extravagance and wretchedness." "Bring home no foreign fancies which are inapplicable to our state of society," Amos Lawrence admonished his son in Paris. There must be no corrupting the Garden of Eden.

It is clear these men conceived themselves as leaders of a great moral crusade to free Americans from a contaminating dependence upon European manufactures. They were "frequently explicit, almost poetic, about their divine mission in America." "God has given us a good land and many blessing," Amos Lawrence wrote his son. "We shall be called to a strict account." Describing his part in the industrial revolution, Nathan Appleton wrote: "Ours is a great novel experiment. . . . Whatever the result, it is our destiny to make it. It is our mission—our care should be to understand it and make it succeed." Looking upon themselves as "servants of the Lord who were setting a national example of manufacturing morality and skill," the textile manufacturers of New England "were often generous in encouraging the establishing of rival factories." Abbott Lawrence wrote to the southerner William C. Rives, "We have not [sic] jealousy, whatever, concerning the establishment of manufactories in all parts of the country." George Cabot "expected that New England operatives would 'diffuse their knowledge and skill through all the States in the Union where manufactories can be carried on.'" Francis Cabot Lowell fostered the growth of manufacturing elsewhere by letting out his patents for the power loom on easy terms. Noted for their philanthropy, these men were yet stern with themselves and with others. "It is on account of so much leisure, that so many fine youths are ruined in this town," Amos Lawrence once told a young Bostonian.

Whether moved by a sense of mission, by the profit motive, or by the desire to "get ahead," the antebellum generation, employers and employees alike, to borrow a phrase by which Glyndon G. Van Deusen characterizes the Jacksonian era, were a "people in motion." Theirs was a striving society, one in which people pushed themselves to make the most of the opportunities opened up by a more rapid pace of economic change, one in which people worked hard, re-summoning their ancient belief in the value of industry and sobriety in order to provide the support of moral justification for the pace at which they worked. What drew them on were not merely economic rewards but social ones as well. There is every reason to believe that the more rapid rate of economic growth was paralleled by a more rapid rate of social change and that the ability to rise to higher levels of status was greater than it had ever been before.

The degree of fluidity of eighteenth century society, it will be remembered, was also marked, at least before its closing decades in New England. The Revolution appears to have recommenced a social transformation that was then carried much further by a subsequent quickening of the pace of horizontal movement, industrialization, and urbanization. Albert Rees has succinctly pointed out one of the principal social and economic effects of industrialization: "Individuals could rise through the skill hierarchy more rapidly in a growing labor force than in a stable one." The rapid urbanization of the antebellum years not only concentrated numerous service occupations connected with trade and industry but also greatly increased those necessary to the sustenance of close community life. One effect of the widening of the market for services was a lowering of the bars of professional standards in the Jacksonian period. In addition, the widening market produced a fissioning of functions formerly performed as a rule by jacks-of-all-trades.

The early nineteenth century witnessed a wide increase in occupational specialization: merchants specialized as importers or exporters, as wholesalers, jobbers, or retailers, while a host of specialists arose to perform business functions ranging from manufacturing to commercial and investment banking and to provide various kinds of insurance and transportation services. In short, society witnessed on its occupational level an increase in productive efficiency which matched that made possible by geographical specialization on the level of physical resources.

The multiplication of occupational opportunities, in combination with the relative ease with which skills and productive property could be acquired, contributed to an unusually high degree of social egalitarianism among white men during the antebellum period. To that egalitarianism the economic growth of the United States owed a great deal. Save for the absurdity of reading into the mind of the past the concerns of the present, it would be tempting to say that Tocqueville understood this well. What he did see very clearly was the psychological connection between the social fact and its economic consequence. In the United States in which he remained for nine months in the early 1830's this most acute of all foreign students of American institutions witnessed and found "difficult to describe the avidity with which the American rushes forward to secure this immense booty that fortune offers. . . . Before him lies a boundless continent, and he urges onward as if time pressed and he was afraid of finding no room for his exertions." Wealth circulated "with inconceivable rapidity, and experience shows that it is rare to find two succeeding generations in the full enjoyment of it." The "commercial activity" of Americans he could describe only as "prodigious," including that of farmers, for "most of them make agriculture itself a trade."

The social fact to which Tocqueville attributed this tremendous economic vitality was the broad equality of social condition which he found to exist in America. Precisely because the distance between man and man in American society was so short, men were extraordinarily sensitive to the inequalities that remained, and they worked hard to remove them. "When inequality of conditions is the common law of society," Tocqueville explained, "the most marked inequalities do not strike the eye." But "when everything is nearly on the same level, the slightest are marked enough to hurt it. Hence the desire of equality always becomes more insatiable in proportion as equality is more complete." This desire generated "an all-pervading and restless activity, a super-abundant force, and an energy which is inseparable from it and which may, however unfavorable circumstances may be, produce wonders." Economic change had quickened the pace of social change, and the latter had turned back upon economic change to drive it at a still faster pace.

The distinguished Frenchman was by no means the only contemporary visitor to America to testify to the existence of a wide degree of social equality. Following a two-year stay between 1834 and 1836, Harriet Martineau recorded that in America "the English insolence of class to class, of individuals towards each other, is not even conceived of, except in the one highly disgraceful instance of people of colour." As did Tocqueville, she pointed out that "In a country where the whole course is open to every one; where in theory, everything must be obtained by merit, men have the strongest stimulus to exert their powers, and try what they can achieve." Mrs. Trollope had a similar comment: "Any man's son may become the equal of any other Man's son, and the consciousness of this is certainly a spur to exertion." To Michael Chevalier, the United States in 1834 was "the land of promise for the labouring class." "The equality of Man is, to this moment," wrote the British traveler Alexander Mackay in 1842, the "cornerstone" of American society.

It is of course hazardous to risk generalization upon the often frail support of travelers' accounts, for they are often—although the essential value of those of Tocqueville and Martineau in particular is not thus impugned—impressionistic and biased. In fact, however, two other kinds of contemporary evidence, as John E. Sawyer has pointed out, sustain the impressions of general travelers.

These are the official reports and unofficial commentaries arising from such international exhibitions as the Crystal Palace Exhibition of 1851, and the various specialized reports of industrial commissions, which began to arrive as early as 1853 for the purpose of studying American manufacturing methods. After careful study of these reports Sawyer reached the following conclusion:

Experts commenting on our machinery or industrial commissions studying our techniques of standardized maufacturing sustain the prevailing themes of the general traveler. In much the same vein and many of the same words, their reports turn to differences in the nature or diffusion of education in America; the absence of rigidities and restraints of class and craft; the freedom from hereditary definitions of the tasks or hardened ways of going about them; the high focus on personal advancement and drives to higher material welfare; and the mobility, flexibility, adaptablility of Americans and their boundless belief in progress. These and closely related patterns are linked directly to economic behavior and economic results—to initiative, originality, systematic effort, and boldness; the "eager resort to machinery" and productive use of small capital, at a time when small capital was decisive; the ceaseless search and ready adoption of the new and more efficient; the intense responsiveness to shifting opportunities and expanding horizons; the "go-aheadism" the visitors from all categories so often placed at the root of the "immense drive" of American maufacturing.[5]

Not all comment, Sawyer points out, was by any means laudatory, and large numbers of observers expressed displeasure or even disgust with American institutions and ways. "But whether they talked of 'a noble desire to elevate one's station' or 'vulgar dollar chasing,' and whether they liked or denounced a society in which business rode high and a wide open social structure fostered mobility, rootlessness, restlessness, and the like, and gave enhanced significance to the visible results of economic success, they were pointing to social values and a social order uniquely favorable to the particular patterns of manufacturing that we have been discussing."

[5] John E. Sawyer, "The Social Basis of the American System of Manufacturing," *Journal of Economic History*, XIV (1954), 376–77.

Once more, it is perfectly true that travelers even before the Revolution saw in the American a "new kind of man," one who was individualistic, optimistic, and enterprising. It should be emphasized again that America never possessed an aristocracy in the European sense. No group had existed that could lay claim to a long tradition of wealth and power, with privileges rooted in the law, with birth rather than achievement the door of entry. Yet just as there is a difference in degree of opportunity between the eighteenth century and the antebellum period, so is there a difference in timbre. It is difficult not to agree with the assessment of Chilton Williamson: the colonial period was predemocratic *in its conscious thought*. There were, to be sure, as Carl N. Degler points out, occasional and moderate expressions of the sentiment of egalitarianism. In the years betwen 1820 and 1860, on the other hand, Americans not only "made it quite clear that theirs was to be an equalitarian and open society." They proclaimed it "blatantly and continuously."

They also acted vigorously on their beliefs, and this blend of idealism with social change that was often consciously sought, did much to produce the egalitarianism so widely noted by contemporaries. By 1810 all but a few states had extended the privilege of voting to either all male taxpayers or to all adult male citizens. This produced no unprecedented swarming to the polls, however. Richard P. McCormick points out that a two-party system to contest elections did not exist in more than half the states till after 1832. With the appearance by 1840 of fairly well-balanced parties in almost every state, there occurred in the national election of that year such a vast outpouring of voters as to prompt McCormick to suggest we substitute the phrase "Tippecanoe Democracy" for "Jacksonian Democracy."

Arguing on the side of tradition, however, is the fact of a rising belief after 1829 that self-government required wide participation by citizens not only in legislative halls but in executive offices. On the level of state and local government, Leonard D. White points out, this belief resulted in the direct election of most officeholders.

In the federal government it resulted in rotation among holders of office. Jackson did not invent the "spoils system," but stability in the administrative services had tended to develop prior to his election in 1828. Indeed, White even speaks of the growth of an "office-holding class." Jackson did not favor long tenure in office, whether by a social elite or a body of bureaucratic specialists. In his first annual message to Congress in December 1829 he expressed his well-known judgment that "The duties of all public offices are, or at least admit of being made, so plain and simple that men of intelligence may readily qualify themselves for their performance, and I can not but believe that more is lost by the long continuance of men in office than is generally to be gained by their experience." "In a country where offices are created solely for the benefit of the people no one man has any more intrinsic right to official station than another." Jackson's actual removals have been exaggerated. They appear to have amounted to less than 10 per cent of all federal officeholders (10,000) during the first eighteen months of the new administration. Still, the number was unprecedented.

There are other evidences of the influence of an enhanced egalitarian spirit during these years, such as the emergence of the theory that the President was as much a direct representative of the people as was Congress. Related to this was the new doctrine that those representatives should regard themselves not as independent decision-makers but as under instructions from the constituency electing them. Jacksonian leaders, Richard Hofstadter points out, encouraged the belief that the "popular will should control the choice of public officers and the formation of public policy." It is a central theme of Marvin Meyers' analysis of the "Jacksonian Persuasion"[6] that with the rise of professional politicians public opinion was heard with a new sensitivity by politicians anxious to win elections. Certainly by the mid-thirties, office seekers were beginning to appeal to the electorate in terms of their humble birth.

If we put these evidences of egalitarian change together with those supplied by our previous discussion of the rising demand for

[6] *The Jacksonian Persuasion: Politics and Beliefs* (Stanford, Calif., 1957).

free, public education and of the contribution made by the Taney Court to the easing of the process of incorporation—to say nothing of the change in the type of officeholder from what White called "trimly-dressed gentlemen of good-breeding to jostling hack politicians from New York and country editors and farmers from the West"—it will be clear how vigorous was the egalitarian impulse of the antebellum period.

A number of other considerations also support the view that, before approximately mid-century, class lines fell lightly over the contours of an essentially fluid society. It was a highly speculative age in which fortunes were made and lost overnight, in which men rose and fell with the dexterous agility depicted in the contemporary pages of Francis Grund. Partnerships and private proprietorships rather than corporations predominated as forms of business enterprise even on the eve of the Civil War, and this suggests that for most purposes the sums required as investment capital to enter business were within the capacities of numerous men. It is especially in the fifties that incorporation and the factory system take their sharp rise, and even then much machinery remained light, wooden, and inexpensive.

Above all, perhaps, Norman Ware's study of the industrial worker concludes that he did not commence until that decade to regard himself as a permanent wage earner. Walter Hugins' recent study of the Workingmen's Movement in New York in the 1830's certainly supports the thesis that workingmen then shared middle-class interests and objectives. Indeed, his analysis of the life histories and occupations of 850 men active in the Workingclass Movement shows that the "working class" was so broad as to include large elements of the *bourgeoisie.*

It is true that Arthur Schlesinger, Jr. maintained in a seminal publication some twenty years ago that "More can be understood about Jacksonian democracy if it is regarded as a problem not of sections but of classes." Schlesinger viewed the Jacksonian movement as one "to control the power of the capitalistic groups, mainly Eastern, for the benefit of noncapitalist groups, farmers and laboring men, East, West, and South." But Clarence H. Danhof's careful study of the costs of farm-making shows that even before the 1850's it is highly questionable whether farmers can be regarded as falling within a "noncapitalist" group. In view of Tocqueville's characterization of his motives, and of other evidence presented in the foregoing pages, it is perhaps not too much to suggest that the great heart of American historiography has bled long enough in the cause of the "poor" farmer. As for labor, Joseph Dorfman has demonstrated that Schlesinger used the term "working men" in a more restricted sense than did the Jacksonian age, which embraced all producers within the approved plural categories of "working classes," "industrious classes," "producing classes," or "useful classes," excluding only bankers and other "political capitalists." And specialized studies of voter behavior in Boston, Philadelphia, and New York by Edward Pessen, William A. Sullivan, and Lee Benson, have demonstrated that to the extent that a "labor movement" can be said to have existed, it did not in general support Jacksonian candidates.

In sum, it would seem to me difficult not to embrace the position of Marvin Meyers, who, accepting Tocqueville's characterization of an essentially homogeneous society, concludes that both political parties "must have reached broadly similar class constituencies to gain, as they did, only a little more or less than half the popular vote" in national elections. As Benson has well said, "Neither Schlesinger's version, nor any other version that assumes there were significant differences in the class nature of party leadership, appears credible. Instead, the evidence indicates that the same socioeconomic groups provided leadership for both parties." Before the 1850's at any rate, a fluid social order, itself in large part a product of broadly egalitarian economic opportunity, made an important contribution to the process of American economic growth.

Epilogue

The preceding discussion has ranged broadly into numerous areas of American life in search of the roots of American economic growth, and has located them in community will and acts of governments, the structure of society and its values, knowledge and education, attitudes toward technological change, the actions of private investors, and the effects of widening markets. Entrepreneurship, it may be noted, has not been singled out for discussion, but this is only because it has been implied in almost everything that has been said. No discussion of American economic growth could omit the quality of entrepreneurship because, essentially, despite the efforts made by Say and others to erect it into a factor of production coequal with land, labor, and capital, it is, in my opinion, nothing more than the desire for efficiency in the use of economic resources. This quality is displayed not only by the private businessman in search of cost-savings via administrative or technological innovation but also by the government administrator seeking ways of widening the tax base for needed public improvements, by the kind of workers found by Nasmyth and other students of American manufacturing methods, and by the kinds of communities whose insistent demands prodded governments into providing social overhead capital necessary to growth. It is a quality of alertness to the possibility of material betterment, and it inheres or fails to inhere in the value system of a culture, although economic change may pave the way for it.

I have tried to make clear that this quality came with the first Americans to these shores, that constriction of environmental opportunity then damped down its efficacy by narrowing its channels of expression, and that with the progressively greater market opportunities provided by both government and private business during the late eighteenth and early nineteenth centuries, it seems increasingly to have permeated the American people. It is tempting to put a special emphasis upon the importance of this progressive permeation, this wide diffusion of the demand for growth. Because of it the "dynamic, innovative activities" productive of revolution in transport, agriculture, and industry were, to cite the language of John E. Sawyer, "sustained by great numbers of people." We became "a nation of 'projectors,' " not a mere "handful of enlightened families or officials or banks, or a scattering of Schumpeterian heroes," but a "population swarming with actual and potential entrepreneurs in all walks of life—multiple centers of initiative, able and motivated to respond, and . . . even to overrespond to the stimuli of the market and of expanding opportunity."

The elevation of a single causal factor to a position of primacy is, however, a procedure fraught with risk. While causal conditions are separable from each other for purposes of analysis, in life they are intimately bound in a net of interdependent relationships. It is this mutual play of the conditions upon each other, conditions that were now cause and then effect, that renders extremely difficult the task of specifying their relative importance. Strictly speaking, none was an independent variable.

Take, for example, the factor of a widening market, which certainly seems to govern the action of many dependent variables. It helped make specialization possible and helped pave the way for technological advance; it increased occupational differentiation and thus helped make possible a greater degree of social mobility; it helped generate a public demand for government aid to internal improvements; it helped attract foreign investments; and so on. But it is obvious that internal improvements also widened the market, as did the income effects of occupational specialization, and the influence of mobility in creating a more standardized demand for products that could be mass-produced by mechanized methods.

Furthermore, if a widening market helped in the achievement of many changes, so too did other factors. The degree of specialization depends not only upon the width of the market but upon the many diversities of human aptitude, opportunity, condition, and interest, and upon the state of knowledge and the facilities for its transmission. Technological advance depends also upon available knowledge, entrepreneurial attitudes, cost-price ratios, the kind of patent laws a nation has (those of the United States, for example, regarded patents as an award to the inventor; in the United Kingdom patents were looked upon as rewards to any person whether inventor or not, for bringing the invention to the attention of the public), and upon still other considerations. To be brief, occupational diversification requires the contribution of education; urbanization, industrialization, westward movement, and much else contributed to social mobility; public demand for internal improvements in part reflected a long colonial tradition of community self-help, and foreign investments in part reflected confidence in American political stability and the credit-worthiness of American governments.

A somewhat different approach to the same problem may prove even more revealing. Let us put the broad question whether it is possible to estimate the relative importance of the contributions made to growth by the public and private sectors of the economy. To do so requires that we be able to estimate the contributions made by the constituent elements of each sector. Let us simplify the problem by asking if it is possible to assign weights to the links of a single causal chain, assuming for this purpose that growth required the traversing of only one causal pathway, that of canal construction, and that other causal pathways, for example those involving changes in social structure, educational opportunity, and intensity of will—pathways that in fact converged upon the process —are irrelevant. Let us simplify still more and assume that such factors as the good credit of state and municipal governments and an established framework of security for investment had nothing to do with the historical fact that "More than ninety percent of the funds [$188,000,000] provided by government" for canal construction in New York, Pennsylvania, Ohio, Indiana, Illinois, and Virginia between 1815 and 1860 "were raised through loans," nearly one-third of which were provided by foreign banking houses, principally in Great Britain. We shall ask one simple, direct causal question: how much weight or causal importance shall we assign the contribution of capital by governments to the economic growth made possible by canals?

I have chosen this problem to illustrate a more general one because four economic historians—Goodrich, Rubin, Cranmer, and Segal—have recently addressed themselves specifically to it. Employing the tool of "modern" benefit-cost analysis, they assume benefits to have been both direct and indirect. Direct benefits conferred by the canals were equal to the savings they effected in moving the nation's commerce. But although these savings were realized initially by the shippers themselves, they were subsequently diffused throughout the economy when the prices of commodities shipped over long distances declined. If canals contributed to economic development, their total benefits exceeded their total costs.

Despite an heroic effort to measure total benefits, it proved impossible to do so. The confession of failure is forthright: "But the most important contribution, in our view, is the one most difficult to measure." The Erie Canal and its tributaries "played a vital role in extending and integrating spatially separated markets" and thus generated large indirect benefits that contributed significantly to economic growth. In sum, the "most important" contribution of the canals was to generate indirect benefits which cannot be measured. If, therefore, we cannot assign a weight to that "importance," how shall we assign weights to the component factors of that importance, to the elements that made it possible? We may justly conclude that the contribution of government formed a necessary condition to economic growth and that the contribution of nonpolitical factors also did. Can we know more than this?

I do not believe we can know more in any precise, numerical sense, but certainly there are excellent reasons for believing that at any given conjuncture of events some factors are "more important" than are others. Comparisons between cases certainly suggests so. Consider, for example, a people's health: the studies of Richard Shryock show the health of the American people sometimes to have been poor enough, yet in general poor health does not appear to have been nearly so important a hindrance to our economic growth as it is likely to prove to that of a number of contemporary nations. Differences in levels of literacy, in cultural values, in technological knowledge and aptitude also immediately appear from comparisons between countries. Nations also have differing resource patterns, or land-man ratios, and are thus differently situated with respect to their ability to attract foreign capital funds or earn them via exports of agricultural surpluses. Comparisons of these kinds make it clear that a given factor in growth cannot everywhere be assigned the same "weight" or degree of importance.

"The influences which are relevant to development," H. J. Habakkuk thoughtfully observes, "combine in many different ways, and each has a different effect according to the combination in which it appears." The available fund of technological knowledge meant less to American growth in 1750 than it did in 1850, and the reason for it is that historical change in the interim altered the combination in which it appeared. Formal, institutional education very probably means a great deal more to American growth in the mid-twentieth century than it did a century ago, and once again it is shift in the balance of factors that explains this. Capital formation as a current condition of growth may be less important than it once was to an underdeveloped nation; at any rate, it is the view of Edward F. Denison that as much as one-half of the productivity change which takes the form of reductions in cost actually reflects managerial and organizational improvements requiring little or no changes in equipment. All of the necessary conditions of growth shift in time in their degree of pertinence, and it is only in the light of particular conjunctures that they can be assessed. But the assessment remains a historical judgment, the validity of which is not at all increased by virtue of its being presented in mathematical form.

In the American economy of the early nineteenth century the shortage of capital funds constitutes a fact of central importance. If growth depended upon industrialization, the latter depended upon a national market, and a national market upon large capital sums for improved transportation. If these are valid assessments, I do not see how a place of central importance in American economic growth can be denied the role of government, because of its contribution to the formation of a national market and the national credit. And if government was as important as it appears to have been, it follows that the achievement of independence was prerequisite to the role it played. This is one of the reasons I have emphasized the American Revolution. Once government had carved out the channels of a national economy, private interest, both domestic and foreign, could pour into those channels a swelling stream of capital funds, manpower, and constant technological change. These were economic rather than political contributions, but to both, as we have seen, must be added the "input" of an insistent community will, the will of an entrepreneurial people who became increasingly better-educated members of a free society.

Douglass C. North nicely illustrates some of the mechanisms of interaction among the economic factors making for growth. Initial developments in manufacturing provided "strong inducements for additional investment in subsidiary or complementary industry," especially consumer goods industries. This forward-reaching "linkage effect" had a counterpart that operated in reverse fashion. The rise of the cotton textile industry, for example, exerted a backward-reaching effect upon demand for textile machinery, iron casting, machine tools, and metal working. And expenditures of income exerted a "multiplier-accelerator effect" upon the level of economic activity in the region where the expenditures were made.

Perhaps unfortunately, it is more difficult to put on display the mechanisms by which technological innovation, skills imparted by education, and incentives deepened and diffused by an open society exerted their linkage effects and suffused the social mass in multiplier-accelerator fashion. Nor can anyone, to my knowledge, disclose with the neat precision of theory the loci, strength, and action of the links between the economic and the noneconomic. One fault of such economic theory as I think I understand is its impounding in a category of *ceteris paribus,* that is to say, among the data given, numerous noneconomic factors that are pertinent to growth, factors whose motions are to be explained rather than assumed. It is true that such factors as social movement and community values are affected by economic change; but the reverse is also true. Perhaps there will someday be elaborated a "general theory of society—specifically some sort of sociology of change," to cite the words of Leland H. Jenks, that will be inclusive of economic and all other major sources of social change. Until the dawn of that doubtful day, only the total resources of the historian, critical and narrative, can succeed in weaving the thread of growth into the richer pattern of human change. His data may often prove unquantifiable, but history is likely to remain the art of weighing the imponderable.

Meanwhile, comparisons are useful because they help provide criteria by which the degree of the probable validity of our hypotheses may be tested. If, for example, one were to assign a high degree of importance in American economic growth to the nation's abundant resources, an elicitation of numerous other instances of growth on the part of countries not in possession of such resources ought to give one pause. Such comparisons cannot disprove a hypothesis, and they do not necessarily weaken it. This is because perfect comparability between cases can never exist. It will always be true that a Collingwoodite immersion in the uniqueness of the particular may disclose differences that may be justified as more important than similarities. Certainty is unattainable, and we may mince nearer the throne only by shuffling between the particular and the general, man and his whole environment, cause and effect.

SELECTED BIBLIOGRAPHY

Abramovitz, Moses. "Economic Growth in the United States: A Review Article," *American Economic Review*, LIII (March 1963).

——, ed. *Capital Formation and Economic Growth*. Princeton, N. J., 1955.

Adelman, Irma. *Theories of Economic Growth and Development*. Stanford, Calif., 1961.

Aitken, Hugh G. J., ed. *The State and Economic Growth*. New York, 1959.

Albion, Robert G. *The Rise of New York Port*. New York, 1939.

Andrews, Charles M. *The Colonial Period in American History: England's Commercial and Colonial Policy*. Vol. IV New Haven, Conn., 1938.

Ashton, T. S. *The Industrial Revolution, 1760–1830*. London, 1948.

Bailyn, Bernard. *The New England Merchants in the Seventeenth Century*. Cambridge, Mass., 1955.

——. *Education in the Forming of American Society*. New York, 1960.

——. "Political Experience and Enlightenment Ideas in Eighteenth Century America," *American Historical Review*, LXVII (January 1962).

——. "Communications and Trade: The Atlantic in the Seventeenth Century," *Journal of Economic History*, XIII (Fall 1953).

——. "Politics and Social Structure in Virginia," in *Seventeenth-Century America: Essays in Colonial History,* ed. James M. Smith. Chapel Hill, N. C., 1959.

Baldwin, John W. "The Medieval Theories of the Just Price," *Transactions of the American Philosophical Society,* Vol. 49 (Philadelphia, 1959).

Baldwin, S. E. "American Business Corporations before 1789," *Annual Report of the American Historical Association,* Vol. I, 1902 (Washington, 1903).

Barber, Bernard. *Social Stratification.* New York, 1957.

Bates, Ralph S. *Scientific Societies in the United States.* New York, 1958.

Baxter, W. T. "Accounting in Colonial America," in *Studies in the History of Accounting,* ed. A. C. Littleton and B. S. Yamey. Homewood, Ill., 1956.

————. *The House of Hancock.* Cambridge, Mass., 1945.

Bennett, Charles Alpheus. *History of Manual and Industrial Education up to 1870.* Peoria, Ill., 1926.

Benson, Lee. *The Concept of Jacksonian Democracy: New York as a Test Case.* Princeton, N. J., 1961.

Berlin, Isaiah. "History and Theory: The Concept of Scientific History," *History and Theory,* I, No. 1 (1961).

Berthoff, Rowland. "The American Social Order: A Conservative Hypothesis," *American Historical Review,* LXV (April 1960).

Bidwell, Percy W., and John I. Falconer. *History of Agriculture in the Northern United States, 1620–1860.* Washington, 1925.

Braithwaite, Richard B. *Scientific Explanation: A Study of the Function of Theory, Probability, and Law in Science.* Cambridge, England, 1959.

Bridenbaugh, Carl. *Cities in Revolt.* New York, 1955.

————. *Cities in the Wilderness.* New York, 1938.

————. *Myths and Realities: Societies of the Colonial South.* Baton Rouge, La., 1952.

Brown, Robert E. "Reinterpretation of the Formation of the American Constitution," *Boston University Law Review,* XLII (Fall, 1962).

————. *Middle Class Democracy and the Coming of the Revolution in Massachusetts.* Ithaca, N. Y., 1955.

————, and B. Katherine Brown. *Virginia, 1705–1786: Democracy or Aristocracy?* East Lansing, Mich., 1964.

Bruce, Philip A. *Economic History of Virginia in the Seventeenth Century.* 2 vols. New York, 1907.

Bruchey, Stuart, *Robert Oliver, Merchant of Baltimore, 1783–1819.* Baltimore, 1956.

————. "Corporation," in *The Encyclopedia Britannica.* Chicago, 1963.

————. "Success and Failure Factors: American Merchants in Foreign Trade in the Eighteenth and Early Nineteenth Centuries," *Business History Review,* XXXII (Autumn 1958).

————. "Douglass C. North on American Economic Growth", *Explorations in Entrepreneurial History,* New Series, I (Winter 1964).

———. "The Forces Behind the Constitution: A Critical Review of the Framework of E. James Ferguson's *The Power of the Purse*", *William and Mary Quarterly*, XIX (July 1962).

Calhoun, Daniel H. *The American Civil Engineer, Origins and Conflict*. Cambridge, Mass., 1960.

Callender, Guy S. "The Early Transportation and Banking Enterprises of the States in Relation to the Growth of Corporations," *Quarterly Journal of Economics*, XVII (November 1902).

Campbell, Mildred. "Social Origins of Some Early Americans," in *Seventeenth-Century America*, ed. James M. Smith. Chapel Hill, N. C., 1959.

Catterall, Ralph. *The Second Bank of the United States*. Chicago, 1902.

Chandler, Alfred D., Jr. "Patterns of American Railroad Finance, 1830–50," *Business History Review*, XXVIII (September 1954).

Chevalier, Michael. *Society, Manners and Politics in the United States*. Boston, 1839.

Chinard, Gilbert. *Thomas Jefferson, The Apostle of Americanism*. 2d. edn. Ann Arbor, Mich., 1957.

Clark, Victor S. *History of Manufactures in the United States*. Vol. I New York, 1949.

Cochran, Thomas C. "The Entrepreneur in American Capital Formation," in *Capital Formation and Economic Growth*, ed. Moses Abramovitz. Princeton, N. J., 1955.

———. "Cultural Factors in Economic Growth," *Journal of Economic History*, XX (December 1960).

———. "The Social Sciences and the Problem of Historical Synthesis," in *The Social Sciences in Historical Research* (Social Science Research Council Bulletin 64). New York, 1954.

Cohen, Morris R. "Method, Scientific," in *Encyclopedia of the Social Sciences*, X (New York, 1937).

Cole, Arthur H. *Wholesale Commodity Prices in the United States, 1700–1861*. Cambridge, Mass., 1938.

———. *The American Wool Manufacture*. 2 vols. Cambridge, Mass., 1926.

Cole, Arthur H. and Harold F. Williamson. *The American Carpet Manufacture*. Cambridge, Mass., 1941.

Cole, Arthur H. "An Approach to the Study of Entrepreneurship: A Tribute to Edwin F. Gay," *Journal of Economic History*, VI (Supplement, 1946).

———. "The Tempo of Mercantile Life in Colonial America, *Business History Review*, XXXIII (Autumn 1959).

Cole, David M. *The Development of Banking in the District of Columbia*. New York, 1959.

Conrad, Alfred H. "Income Growth and Structural Change," in *Ameri-*

can Economic History, ed. Seymour E. Harris. New York, 1961.

————, and John R. Meyer. "Economic Theory, Statistical Inference, and Economic History," *Journal of Economic History*, XVII (December 1957).

Crary, Catherine S. "The Humble Immigrant and the American Dream: Some Case Histories, 1746–1776," *Mississippi Valley Historical Review*, XLVI (June 1959).

Crittenden, Christopher C. *The Commerce of North Carolina, 1763–1789*. New Haven, Conn., 1936.

Cunningham, Noble E., Jr. *The Jeffersonian Republicans: The Formation of Party Organization 1789–1801*. Chapel Hill, N. C., 1957.

Dangerfield, George. *The Era of Good Feelings*. New York, 1952.

Danhof, Clarence H. "Farm-making Costs and the 'Safety-Valve': 1850–1860", *Journal of Political Economy*, XLIX (June 1941).

Davis, Lance E. "Sources of Industrial Finance: The American Textile Industry, A Case Study," *Explorations in Entrepreneurial History*, IX (April 1957).

————, and Peter L. Payne. "From Benevolence to Business: The Story of Two Savings Banks," *Business History Review*, XXXII (Winter 1958).

Davis, Joseph S. *Essays in the Earlier History of American Corporations*. 2 vols. Cambridge, Mass., 1917.

Davis, Kingsley. *The Population of India and Pakistan*. Princeton, N. J., 1951.

Davis, Richard Beale. *William Fitzhugh and His Chesapeake World, 1676–1701*. Chapel Hill, N. C., 1963.

Davison, Robert A. *Isaac Hicks: New York Merchant and Quaker, 1767–1820*. Cambridge, Mass., 1964.

Degler, Carl N. "The Locofocos: Urban 'Agrarians,' " *Journal of Economic History*, XVI (September 1956).

————. *Out of Our Past*. New York, 1959.

Denison, Edward F. *The Sources of Economic Growth in the United States and the Alternatives Before Us* (Committee for Economic Development, Supplementary Paper No. 13). New York, 1962.

Diamond, Sigmund. *The Reputation of the American Businessman*. Cambridge, Mass., 1955.

————. "From Organization to Society: Virginia in the Seventeenth Century," *American Journal of Sociology*, LXIII (March 1958).

Dickerson, Oliver M. *The Navigation Acts and the American Revolution*. Philadelphia, 1951.

Domar, Evsey D. *Essays in the Theory of Economic Growth*. New York, 1957.

Dorfman, Joseph. "The Jackson Wage-Earner Thesis," *American Historical Review*, LIV (January 1949).

————. *The Economic Mind in American Civilization, 1606–1865*. New York, 1946.

Douglas, Paul H. *American Apprenticeship and Industrial Education*. New York, 1921.

Duesenberry, J. S. "Some Aspects of the Theory of Economic Development," *Explorations in Entrepreneurial History*, III (December 1950).

Dwight, Timothy. *Travels: In New England and New York*. 4 vols. New Haven, Conn., 1821.

East, Robert A. "The Business Entrepreneur in a Changing Colonial Economy, 1763–1795," *Journal of Economic History*, VI (Supplement, 1946).

Easterbrook, W. T. "Long-Period Comparative Study: Some Historical Cases," *Journal of Economic History*, XVII (December 1957).

Evans, G. Heberton, Jr. *Business Incorporations in the United States, 1800–1943*. New York, 1948.

Fabricant, Solomon. *Basic Facts on Productivity Change* (National Bureau of Economic Research Occasional Paper 63). New York, 1959.

Fairchild, Byron. *Messrs. William Pepperrell: Merchants of Piscataqua*. Ithaca, N. Y., 1954.

Ferguson, E. James. *The Power of the Purse: A History of American Public Finance, 1776–1790*. Chapel Hill, N. C., 1961.

Fine, Sidney. *Laissez-Faire and the General-Welfare State*. Ann Arbor, Mich., 1956.

Fogel, Robert W. *Railroads in American Economic Growth: Essays in Econometric History*. Baltimore, 1964.

Friis, Herman R. *A Series of Population Maps of the Colonies of the United States, 1620–1790*. New York, 1940.

Gallman, Robert E. "Commodity Output, 1839–1899," in *Trends in the American Economy in the Nineteenth Century*, ed. William N. Parker. Princeton, 1960.

Gatell, Frank Otto. "Spoils of the Bank War: Political Bias in the Selection of Pet Banks," *American Historical Review*, LXX (October 1964).

Gates, Paul W. *The Farmers Age: Agriculture, 1815–1860*. New York, 1960.

Genovese, Eugene D. "The Significance of the Slave Plantation for Southern Economic Development," *The Journal of Southern History*, XXVIII, No. 4 (November, 1962).

Gerschenkron, Alexander. "The Early Phases of Industrialization in Russia and their Relationship to the Historical Study of Economic Growth," in *The Experience of Economic Growth*, ed. Barry E. Supple. New York, 1963.

Gerth, H. H., and C. Wright Mills, eds. *From Max Weber: Essays in Sociology*. New York, 1946.

Gibb, George S. *The Whitesmiths of Taunton*. Cambridge, Mass., 1943.

Goldsmith, Raymond. "National Product and Income: Long-Term Trends," U. S. Congress, Joint Economic Committee, 86th Congress, 1st Session, *Hearings,* Part 2 "Historical and Comparative Rates of Production, Productivity and Prices".

Good, H. G. *A History of American Education.* New York, 1963.

Goodrich, Carter. "American Development Policy: The Case of Internal Improvements," *Journal of Economic History,* XVI (December 1956).

———. *Government Promotion of American Canals and Railroads 1800–1890.* New York, 1960.

Goodrich, Carter, ed. *Canals and American Economic Development.* New York, 1961.

———. and Sol. Davison. "The Wage Earner in the Western Movement," *Political Science Quarterly,* L (June 1935), LI (March 1936).

Gould, Clarence P. *The Land System in Maryland, 1720–1765.* Baltimore, 1913.

———. "The Economic Causes of the Rise of Baltimore," *Essays in Colonial History Presented to Charles McLean Andrews.* New Haven, Conn., 1931.

Govan, Thomas P. *Nicholas Biddle: Nationalist and Public Banker 1786–1844.* Chicago, 1959.

Gray, Lewis C. *History of Agriculture in The Southern States to 1860.* 2 Vols. Gloucester, Mass., 1958.

Greene, Constance M. *Washington, Village and Capital, 1800–1878.* Princeton, 1962.

Greene, Evarts B. *Provincial America, 1690–1740.* New York, 1905.

Grund, Francis J. *Aristocracy in America.* New York, 1959.

Gurley, J. G., and E. S. Shaw. "Money," in *American Economic History* ed. Seymour E. Harris. New York, 1961.

Habakkuk, H. J. *American and British Technology in the Nineteenth Century.* Cambridge, Eng., 1962.

Haller, Willam. *The Rise of Puritanism.* New York, 1957.

Hamilton, Alexander. *The Works of Alexander Hamilton,* ed. Henry Cabot Lodge. 12 vols. New York, 1904.

Hammond, Bray. Review of Arthur Schlesinger Jr.'s, *The Age of Jackson,* in *Journal of Economic History,* VI (May 1946).

———. *Banks and Politics in America from the Revolution to the Civil War.* Princeton, N. J., 1957.

Handlin, Oscar and Mary F. *Commonwealth, A Study of the Role of Government in the American Economy: Massachusetts, 1774–1861.* New York, 1947.

———. "Origins of the American Business Corporation," in *Enterprise and Secular Change,* ed. F. C. Lane and J. C. Riemersma. Homewood, Ill., 1954.

Harper, Lawrence A. *The English Navigation Laws.* New York, 1939.

———. "The Effect of the Navigation Acts on the Thirteen Colonies," in *The Era of the American Revolution,* ed. Richard B. Morris. New York, 1939.

Harper, Lawrence A. "Mercantilism and the American Revolution," *Canadian Historical Review,* XXIII (March 1942).

Harrington, Virginia D. *The New York Merchant on the Eve of the Revolution.* New York, 1935.

Harris, Marshall. *Origin of the Land Tenure System in the United States.* Ames, Iowa, 1953.

Hartz, Louis. *Economic Policy and Democratic Thought: Pennsylvania 1776–1860.* Cambridge, Mass., 1948.

Heath, Milton S. *Constructive Liberalism: The Role of the State in Economic Development in Georgia to 1860.* Cambridge, Mass., 1954.

Heaton, Herbert. "Industrial Revolution," *Encyclopedia of the Social Sciences,* VIII (New York, 1937).

———. "Criteria of Periodization in Economic History," *Journal of Economic History,* XV (September 1955).

Hedges, James B. *The Browns of Providence Plantations, Colonial Years.* Cambridge, Mass., 1952.

Hildreth, Richard. *The History of the United States of America.* Vol. IV New York, 1856.

Hill, Forest G. "Government Engineering Aid to Railroads before the Civil War," *Journal of Economic History,* XI (Summer 1951).

Hofstadter, Richard and C. DeWitt Hardy. *The Development and Scope of Higher Education in the United States.* New York, 1952.

———. *The American Political Tradition.* New York, 1951.

———, and Wilson Smith, eds. *American Higher Education, A Documentary History.* 2 Vols. Chicago, 1961.

Hoselitz, Bert F., ed. *Theories of Economic Growth.* Glencoe, Ill., 1960.

———. "Non-Economic Factors in Economic Growth," *American Economic Review,* XLVII (May 1957).

Hsu, F. L. K. "Social Mobility in China," *American Sociological Review,* XIV (December 1949).

Hugins, Walter. *Jacksonian Democracy and the Working Class.* Stanford, Calif., 1960.

Hunt, Gaillard, ed. *The Journals of the Continental Congress.* Vol. XXII. Washington, 1914.

Hunter, Louis C. "The Influence of the Market upon Technique in the Iron Industry in Western Pennsylvania up to 1860," *Journal of Economic and Business History,* I (February 1929).

———. *Steamboats on the Western Rivers.* Cambridge, Mass., 1949.

Hutcheson, Harold. *Tench Coxe: A Study in American Economic Development*. Baltimore, 1938.

Jefferson, Thomas. *The Works of Thomas Jefferson*, ed. Paul L. Ford. 12 vols. New York, 1905.

Jensen, Arthur L. *The Maritime Commerce of Colonial Philadelphia*. Madison, Wisc., 1963.

Jensen, Merrill. *The New Nation, A History of the United States during the Confederation, 1781–1789*. New York, 1950.

———. *The Articles of Confederation*. Madison, Wisc., 1940.

Johnson, E. A. J. "Federalism, Pluralism, and Public Policy," *Journal of Economic History*, XXII (December 1962).

Kendrick, J. W. *Productivity Trends in the United States*. Princeton, N. J., 1961.

Kirzner, Israel M. *The Economic Point of View: An Essay in the History of Economic Thought*. New York, 1960.

Knight, Edward W. *A Documentary History of Education in the South Before 1860*. 5 Vols. Chapel Hill, N. C., 1949.

Kolko, Gabriel. "Max Weber on America: Theory and Evidence," *History and Theory*, I, No. 2. (1961).

Kuznets, Simon. "Summary of Discussion and Postscript," *Journal of Economic History*, XVII (December 1957).

———. *National Income: A Summary of Findings*. New York, 1946.

———. "Quantitative Aspects of the Economic Growth of Nations: VI. Long-Term Trends in Capital Formation Proportions," *Economic Development and Cultural Change*, IX (July 1961).

———. *Six Lectures on Economic Growth*. Glencoe, Ill., 1959.

———, and Ernest Rubin. *Immigration and the Foreign Born* (National Bureau of Economic Research Occasional Paper 46). New York, 1954.

———. "National Income Estimates for the United States prior to 1870," *Journal of Economic History*, XII (Spring 1952).

Kantor, J. R. *The Logic of Modern Science*. Bloomington, Ind., 1953.

Lane, Frederic C., and Jelle C. Riemersma. "Introduction to Arthur Spiethoff," in *Enterprise and Secular Change*, ed. Lane and Riemersma, Homewood, Ill., 1953.

———. "The Social Sciences and the Humanities," *Proceedings of the American Philosophical Society*, XCII, No. 5 (Philadelphia, 1948).

Lampard, Eric E. *Industrial Revolution: Interpretations and Perspectives*. Washington, 1957.

Lebergott, Stanley. "Wage Trends, 1800–1900," in *Trends in the American Economy in the Nineteenth Century*, ed. William N. Parker. Princeton, N. J., 1960.

Le Duc, Thomas. "Public Policy, Private Investment, and Land Use in American Agriculture, 1825–1875," *Agricultural History*, 37, No. 1 (1963).

Lincoln, Jonathan, T. "Material for a History of American Textile Machinery: The Kilburn-Lincoln Papers," *Journal of Economic and Business History,* IV (February 1932).

Lipset, Seymour M. and Reinhardt Bendix. *Social Mobility in an Industrial Society.* Berkeley, Calif., 1960.

Lively, Robert A. "The American System: A Review Article," *Business History Review,* XXIX (March 1955).

Loehr, Rodney C. "Self-Sufficiency on the Farm," *Agricultural History,* Vol. 26 (April 1952).

MacIver, R. M. *Social Causation.* New York, 1942.

McClelland, David C. *The Achieving Society.* Princeton, N. J., 1961.

McCormick, Richard P. "New Perspectives on Jacksonian Politics," *American Historical Review,* LXV (January 1960).

McGrane, Reginald. *Foreign Bondholders and American State Debts.* New York, 1935.

Malone, Dumas. *Jefferson and the Ordeal of Liberty.* Boston, 1962.

Marshall, Alfred. *Principles of Economics.* 8th edn. London, 1962.

Martin, Robert F. *National Income of the United States, 1799–1938.* New York, 1939.

Martin, Margaret E. *Merchants and Trade of the Connecticut River Valley, 1750–1820,* Smith College Studies in History, XXIV (October 1938–July 1939).

Martineau, Harriet. *Society in America,* ed. by Seymour M. Lipset. New York, 1962.

Meyers, Marvin. *The Jacksonian Persuasion.* Stanford, Calif., 1957.

Miller, John C. *Alexander Hamilton: Portrait in Paradox.* New York, 1959.

Miller, Perry. *The New England Mind, From Colony to Province.* Cambridge, Mass., 1953.

Mills, F. C. *Productivity and Economic Progress* (National Bureau of Economic Research Occasional Paper 38). New York, 1952.

Minsky, Hyman P. "Indicators of the Developmental Status of an Economy," *Economic Development and Cultural Change,* VII (January 1959).

Mitchell, Broadus. *Alexander Hamilton: The National Adventure 1788–1804.* New York, 1962.

Monroe, Paul. *The Founding of the American Public School System: A History of Education in the United States.* Vol. I. New York, 1940.

Morgan, Edmund S. *The Puritan Family.* Boston, 1944.

Morris, Richard B., ed. *Alexander Hamilton and the Founding of the Nation.* New York, 1957.

———. "The Organization of Production During the Colonial Period," in *The Growth of the American Economy,* ed. Harold F. Williamson. Englewood Cliffs, N. J., 1951.

————. *Government and Labor in Early America*. New York, 1946.

————. "Class Struggle and the Revolution," *Willam and Mary Quarterly*, XIX (January 1962).

————. ed. *Era of the American Revolution*. New York, 1939.

Myers, Margaret G. *The New York Money Market*. New York, 1931.

Nef, John U. "The Industrial Revolution Reconsidered," *Journal of Economic History*, III (May 1943).

Nettels, Curtis P. *The Emergence of a National Economy, 1775–1815*. New York, 1962.

————. *The Roots of American Civilization*. New York, 1939.

————. "British Mercantilism and the Economic Development of the Thirteen Colonies," *Journal of Economic History*, XII (Spring 1952).

North, Douglass C. "International Capital Flows and the Development of the American West," *Journal of Economic History*, XVI (December 1956).

————. *The Economic Growth of the United States, 1790 to 1860*. Englewood Cliffs, N. J., 1961.

Nye, Russel B. *The Cultural Life of the New Nation: 1776–1830*. New York, 1960.

Palmer, R. R. *The Age of the Democratic Revolution*. Princeton, N. J., 1959.

Pares, Richard. *Merchants and Planters. Economic History Review*, Supplement No. 4, 1960.

———— *Yankees and Creoles*. Cambridge, England, 1956.

Parker, William N. "The Slave Plantation in American Agriculture," in *Contributions to the First International Conference of Economic History*. Stockholm, 1960.

————, and Franklee Whartenby. "The Growth of Output Before 1840," in *Trends in the American Economy in the Nineteenth Century*, ed. William N. Parker. Princeton, N. J., 1960.

Payne, Peter L., and Lance E. Davis. *The Savings Bank of Baltimore, 1818–1866*. Baltimore, 1954.

Perry, Ralph B. *Puritanism and Democracy*. New York, 1944.

Pessen, Edward. "The Working Men's Party Revisited," *Labor History*, IV. (Fall 1963).

————. "Did Labor Support Jackson? The Boston Story," *Political Science Quarterly*, LXIV (June 1949).

Pierce, Harry H. *Railroads of New York: A Study of Government Aid, 1826–1875*. Cambridge, Mass., 1953.

Plumb, J. H. *England in the Eighteenth Century*. London, 1950.

Price, Jacob M. "The French Farmers-General in the Chesapeake: The MacKercher-Huber Mission of 1737–1738," *William and Mary Quarterly*, XIV (April 1957).

Primm, James N. *Economic Policy in the Development of a Western State: Missouri, 1820–1860*. Cambridge, Mass., 1954.

Ramsay, David. *History of the American Revolution.* 2 vols. Philadelphia, 1789.

Rasmussen, Wayne D. "The Impact of Technological Change on American Agriculture, 1862–1962," *Journal of Economic History,* XXII (December 1962).

Redlich, Fritz. *The Molding of American Banking: Men and Ideas.* 2 vols. New York, 1951.

"Report of the Secretary of State [Jefferson] on the Privileges and Restrictions on the Commerce of the United States in Foreign Countries, Dec. 16, 1793," in *State Papers and Publick Documents of the United States.* Vol. I Boston, 1817.

Rezneck, Samuel. "The Rise and Early Development of Industrial Consciousness in the United States, 1760–1830," *Journal of Economic and Business History,* IV (August 1932).

Robbins, Roy F. *Our Landed Heritage: the Public Domain, 1776–1936.* Princeton, N. J., 1942.

Rogin, Leo. *The Introduction of Farm Machinery in its Relation to the Productivity of Labor in the Agriculture of the United States during the Nineteenth Century.* Berkeley, Calif., 1931.

Rosenberg, Nathan. "Technological Change in the Machine Tool Industry 1840–1910," *Journal of Economic History,* XXIII (December 1963).

Rostow, Walt, W. "The Take-off into Self-Sustained Growth," *Economic Journal,* LXVI (March 1956).

——. "The Interrelation of Theory and Economic History," *Journal of Economic History,* XVII (December 1957).

——. *The Process of Economic Growth.* Oxford, 1960.

——. *The Stages of Economic Growth: A Non-Communist Manifesto.* Cambridge, England, 1960.

Sacks, William S. "Agricultural Conditions in the Northern Colonies Before the Revolution," *Journal of Economic History,* XIII (June 1953).

Sadove, Abraham H. "Transport Improvement and the Appalachian Barrier: a Case study in Economic Innovation." Unpubl. diss. (Harvard University, 1950).

Sanford, Charles L. "The Intellectual Origins and New-Worldliness of American Industry." *Journal of Economic History,* XVIII (March 1958).

Savelle, Max. *Seeds of Liberty.* New York, 1949.

Sawyer, John E. "Entrepreneurship in Periods of Rapid Growth: the United States in the Nineteenth Century," in *Entrepreneurship and Economic Growth.* (Mimeographed). Cambridge, Mass., 1954.

——. "The Social Basis of the American System of Manufacturing," *Journal of Economic History,* XIV (December 1954).

Schachner, Nathan. *Alexander Hamilton.* New York, 1946.

Schlesinger, Arthur M. *The Colonial Merchants and the American Revolution*. New York, 1918.

Schlesinger, Arthur M., Jr. *The Age of Jackson*, Boston, 1946.

Schmidt, Louis B. "Internal Commerce and the Development of a National Economy before 1860," *Journal of Political Economy*, XLVII (December 1939).

Schmookler, Jacob. "Economic Sources of Inventive Activity," *Journal of Economic History*, XXII (March 1962).

Shryock, Richard. *Medicine and Society in America 1660–1860*. New York, 1960.

Schultz, T. W. "Capital Formation by Education." *Journal of Political Economy*, LXVIII (December 1960).

Sebba, Gregor. "The Development of the Concepts of Mechanism and Model in Physical Science and Economic Thought," *American Economic Review*, XLIII (May 1953).

Segal, Harvey H. "Canals and Economic Development," in *Canals and American Economic Development*, ed. Carter Goodrich. New York, 1961.

Sellers, Leila. *Charleston Business on the Eve of the Revolution*. Chapel Hill, N. C., 1934.

Sheffield, Lord John. *Observations on the American States*. London, 1784.

Simpson, Alan. *Puritanism in Old and New England*. Chicago, 1955.

Smith, Adam. *An Inquiry into the Nature and Causes of the Wealth of Nations*. New York reissue, 1937.

Solow, Robert M. "Technical Progress, Capital Formation and Economic Growth," *American Economic Review, Proc.*, (May 1962).

Soltow, James H. "Scottish Traders in Virginia, 1750-1775," *Economic History Review*, XII, No. 1 (1959).

Spengler, Joseph J. "Sociological Value Theory, Economic Analyses, and Economic Policy," *American Economic Review*, XLIII (May 1953).

Spiethoff, Arthur. "The 'Historical' Character of Economic Theories," *Journal of Economic History*, XII (June 1952).

Strassmann, W. Paul. "Creative Destruction and Partial Obsolescence in American Economic Development," *Journal of Economic History*, XIX (September 1959).

————. *Risk and Technological Innovation: American Manufacturing Methods During the Nineteenth Century*. Ithaca, N. Y., 1959.

Studenski, Paul, and Herman E. Kroos. *Financial History of the United States*. New York, 1963.

Sullivan, William A. "Did Labor Support Andrew Jackson?" *Political Science Quarterly*, LXII (December 1947).

Supple, Barry E. "Introduction: Economic History, Economic Theory, and Economic Growth," in *The Experience of Economic Growth:*

Case Studies in Economic History, ed. Barry E. Supple. New York, 1963.

Swisher, Carl B. *Roger B. Taney*. Hamden, Conn., 1961.

Sydnor, Charles S. *The Development of Southern Sectionalism, 1819–1848*. Baton Rouge, La., 1949.

———. *American Revolutionaries in the Making* (former title: *Gentlemen Freeholders*). New York, 1962.

Taussig, F. W. *The Tariff History of the United States*. New York, 1931.

Taylor, George R. *The Transportation Revolution: 1815–1860*. New York, 1951.

Theory and Practice in Historical Study: A Report of the Committee on Historiography (Social Science Research Bulletin 54). New York, 1946.

Thrupp, Sylvia L. "The Role of Comparison in the Development Of Economic Theory," *Journal of Economic History*, XVII (December 1957).

Tocqueville, Alexis de. *Democracy in America*. 2 vols. New York, 1958.

Tolles, F. B. *Meeting House and Counting House, The Quaker Merchants of Colonial Philadelphia, 1682–1763*. Chapel Hill, N. C., 1948.

Tooker, Elva. *Nathan Trotter, Philadelphia Merchant, 1787–1853*. Cambridge, Mass., 1955.

Towne, Marvin W., and Wayne D. Rasmussen. "Farm Gross Product and Gross Investment in the Nineteenth Century," in *Trends in the American Economy in the Nineteenth Century*, ed. William N. Parker. Princeton, N. J., 1960.

Toynbee, Arnold. *The Industrial Revolution*. Boston, 1956.

Trescott, Paul B. *Financing American Enterprise: The Story of Commercial Banking*. New York, 1963.

Trollope, Frances. *Domestic Manners of the Americans*, ed. Donald Smalley. New York, 1949.

Tryon, Rolla M. *Household Manufactures in the United States, 1640–1860*. Chicago, 1917.

U.S. Bureau of the Census. *Historical Statistics of the United States: Colonial Times to 1957*. Washington, D. C., 1960.

Usher, Abbott Payson. "Technical Change and Capital Formation," in *Capital Formation and Economic Growth*. Princeton, N. J., 1955.

———. *The Industrial History of England*. Boston, 1920.

Van Der Kroef, J. M. "The Changing Class Structure of Indonesia," *American Sociological Review*, XXI (April 1956).

Ver Steeg, Clarence L. *Robert Morris*. Philadelphia, 1954.

———. *The American Revolution Considered as an Economic Movement*, Huntington Library Quarterly, XX (Aug. 1957).

Walters, Raymond, Jr. *Albert Gallatin, Jeffersonian Financier and Diplomat*. New York, 1957.

Ward, John William. *Andrew Jackson: Symbol for an Age.* New York, 1962.

Ware, Norman. *The Industrial Worker, 1840–1860.* New York, 1924.

Weaver, Glen. *Jonathan Trumbull, Connecticut's Merchant Magistrate, 1710–1785.* Hartford, Conn., 1956.

Weber, Max. *The Protestant Ethic and the Spirit of Capitalism.* New York, 1958.

Weeden, William B. *Economic and Social History of New England, 1620–1789.* 2 vols. New York, 1890.

White, Leonard D. *The Federalists, A Study in Administrative History.* New York, 1956.

————. *The Jeffersonians, A Study in Administrative History, 1801–1829.* New York, 1956.

————. *The Jacksonians: A Study in Administrative History, 1829–1861.* New York, 1954.

White, Philip L. *The Beekmans of New York in Politics and Commerce, 1647–1877.* New York, 1956.

Williamson, Chilton. *American Suffrage: From Property to Democracy, 1760–1860.* Princeton, N. J., 1960.

Williamson, Harold F. "Mass Production, Mass Consumption, and American Industrial Develoment," in *Contributions to the First International Conference of Economic History.* Stockholm, 1960.

Williston, Samuel. "History of the Law of Business Corporations before 1800," *Harvard Law Review,* Vol. 2 (1889).

Wright, Benjamin F. *The Contract Clause of the Constitution.* Cambridge, Mass., 1938.

Wright, Louis B. *The Colonial Civilization of North America, 1607–1763.* London, 1949.

Wyllie, Irvin G. *The Self-Made Man in America.* New Brunswick, N. J., 1954.

Index

71 72 73   12 11 10 9 8 7 6 5 4 3

ḣarper ♇ ᴛorchbooƙs

American Studies: General

HENRY ADAMS Degradation of the Democratic Dogma. ‡ Introduction by Charles Hirschfeld. TB/1450

LOUIS D. BRANDEIS: Other People's Money, and How the Bankers Use It. Ed. with Intro. by Richard M. Abrams TB/3081

HENRY STEELE COMMAGER, Ed.: The Struggle for Racial Equality TB/1300

CARL N. DEGLER: Out of Our Past: The Forces that Shaped Modern America CN/2

CARL N. DEGLER, Ed.: Pivotal Interpretations of American History
Vol. I TB/1240; Vol. II TB/1241

A. S. EISENSTADT, Ed.: The Craft of American History: Selected Essays
Vol. I TB/1255; Vol. II TB/1256

LAWRENCE H. FUCHS, Ed.: American Ethnic Politics TB/1368

MARCUS LEE HANSEN: The Atlantic Migration: 1607-1860. Edited by Arthur M. Schlesinger. Introduction by Oscar Handlin TB/1052

MARCUS LEE HANSEN: The Immigrant in American History. Edited with a Foreword by Arthur M. Schlesinger TB/1120

ROBERT L. HEILBRONER: The Limits of American Capitalism TB/1305

JOHN HIGHAM, Ed.: The Reconstruction of American History TB/1068

ROBERT H. JACKSON: The Supreme Court in the American System of Government TB/1106

JOHN F. KENNEDY: A Nation of Immigrants. Illus. Revised and Enlarged. Introduction by Robert F. Kennedy TB/1118

LEONARD W. LEVY, Ed.: American Constitutional Law: Historical Essays TB/1285

LEONARD W. LEVY, Ed.: Judicial Review and the Supreme Court TB/1296

LEONARD W. LEVY: The Law of the Commonwealth and Chief Justice Shaw: The Evolution of American Law, 1830-1860 TB/1309

GORDON K. LEWIS: Puerto Rico: Freedom and Power in the Caribbean. Abridged edition TB/1371

RICHARD B. MORRIS: Fair Trial: Fourteen Who Stood Accused, from Anne Hutchinson to Alger Hiss TB/1335

GUNNAR MYRDAL: An American Dilemma: The Negro Problem and Modern Democracy. Introduction by the Author.
Vol. I TB/1443; Vol. II TB/1444

GILBERT OSOFSKY, Ed.: The Burden of Race: A Documentary History of Negro-White Relations in America TB/1405

CONYERS READ, Ed.: The Constitution Reconsidered. Revised Edition. Preface by Richrd B. Morris TB/1384

ARNOLD ROSE: The Negro in America: The Condensed Version of Gunnar Myrdal's An American Dilemma. Second Edition TB/3048

JOHN E. SMITH: Themes in American Philosophy: Purpose, Experience and Community TB/1466

WILLIAM R. TAYLOR: Cavalier and Yankee: The Old South and American National Character TB/1474

American Studies: Colonial

BERNARD BAILYN: The New England Merchants in the Seventeenth Century TB/1149

ROBERT E. BROWN: Middle-Class Democracy and Revolution in Massachusetts, 1691-1780. New Introduction by Author TB/1413

JOSEPH CHARLES: The Origins of the American Party System TB/1049

HENRY STEELE COMMAGER & ELMO GIORDANETTI, Eds.: Was America a Mistake? An Eighteenth Century Controversy TB/1329

WESLEY FRANK CRAVEN: The Colonies in Transition: 1660-1712† TB/3084

CHARLES GIBSON: Spain in America † TB/3077

CHARLES GIBSON, Ed.: The Spanish Tradition in America + HR/1351

LAWRENCE HENRY GIPSON: The Coming of the Revolution: 1763-1775. † Illus. TB/3007

JACK P. GREENE, Ed.: Great Britain and the American Colonies: 1606-1763. + Introduction by the Author HR/1477

AUBREY C. LAND, Ed.: Bases of the Plantation Society + HR/1429

JOHN LANKFORD, Ed.: Captain John Smith's America: Selections from his Writings ‡ TB/3078

LEONARD W. LEVY: Freedom of Speech and Press in Early American History: Legacy of Suppression TB/1109

PERRY MILLER: Errand Into the Wilderness TB/1139

PERRY MILLER T. H. JOHNSON, Eds.: The Puritans: A Sourcebook of Their Writings
Vol. I TB/1093; Vol. II TB/1094

† The New American Nation Series, edited by Henry Steele Commager and Richard B. Morris.
‡ American Perspectives series, edited by Bernard Wishy and William E. Leuchtenburg.
a History of Europe series, edited by J. H. Plumb.
§ The Library of Religion and Culture, edited by Benjamin Nelson.
‖ Researches in the Social, Cultural, and Behavioral Sciences, edited by Benjamin Nelson.
Σ Harper Modern Science Series, edited by James A. Newman.
° Not for sale in Canada.
+ Documentary History of the United States series, edited by Richard B. Morris.
# Documentary History of Western Civilization series, edited by Eugene C. Black and Leonard W. Levy.
ʌ The Economic History of the United States series, edited by Henry David et al.
¶ European Perspectives series, edited by Eugene C. Black.
** Contemporary Essays series, edited by Leonard W. Levy.
* The Stratum Series, edited by John Hale.

EDMUND S. MORGAN: The Puritan Family: *Religion and Domestic Relations in Seventeenth Century New England*   TB/1227
RICHARD B. MORRIS: Government and Labor in Early America   TB/1244
WALLACE NOTESTEIN: The English People on the Eve of Colonization: 1603-1630. † *Illus.*
TB/3006
FRANCIS PARKMAN: The Seven Years War: *A Narrative Taken from* Montcalm and Wolfe, The Conspiracy of Pontiac, *and* A Half-Century of Conflict. *Edited by John H. McCallum*   TB/3083
LOUIS B. WRIGHT: The Cultural Life of the American Colonies: 1607-1763. † *Illus.*
TB/3005
YVES F. ZOLTVANY, Ed.: The French Tradition in America +   HR/1425

American Studies: The Revolution to 1860

JOHN R. ALDEN: The American Revolution: 1775-1783. † *Illus.*   TB/3011
MAX BELOFF, Ed.: The Debate on the American Revolution, 1761-1783: *A Sourcebook*
TB/1225
RAY A. BILLINGTON: The Far Western Frontier: 1830-1860. † *Illus.*   TB/3012
STUART BRUCHEY: The Roots of American Economic Growth, 1607-1861: *An Essay in Social Causation. New Introduction by the Author.*
TB/1350
WHITNEY R. CROSS: The Burned-Over District: *The Social and Intellectual History of Enthusiastic Religion in Western New York, 1800-1850*   TB/1242
NOBLE E. CUNNINGHAM, JR., Ed.: The Early Republic, 1789-1828 +   HR/1394
GEORGE DANGERFIELD: The Awakening of American Nationalism, 1815-1828. † *Illus.*   TB/3061
CLEMENT EATON: The Freedom-of-Thought Struggle in the Old South. *Revised and Enlarged. Illus.*   TB/1150
CLEMENT EATON: The Growth of Southern Civilization, 1790-1860. † *Illus.*   TB/3040
ROBERT H. FERRELL, Ed.: Foundations of American Diplomacy, 1775-1872   HR/1393
LOUIS FILLER: The Crusade against Slavery: 1830-1860. † *Illus.*   TB/3029
DAVID H. FISCHER: The Revolution of American Conservatism: *The Federalist Party in the Era of Jeffersonian Democracy*   TB/1449
WILLIAM W. FREEHLING, Ed.: The Nullification Era: *A Documentary Record* ‡   TB/3079
WILLIM W. FREEHLING: Prelude to Civil War: *The Nullification Controversy in South Carolina, 1816-1836*   TB/1359
PAUL W. GATES: The Farmer's Age: *Agriculture, 1815-1860* ∆   TB/1398
FELIX GILBERT: The Beginnings of American Foreign Policy: *To the Farewell Address*
TB/1200
ALEXANDER HAMILTON: The Reports of Alexander Hamilton. ‡ *Edited by Jacob E. Cooke*
TB/3060
THOMAS JEFFERSON: Notes on the State of Virginia. ‡ *Edited by Thomas P. Abernethy*
TB/3052
FORREST MCDONALD, Ed.: Confederation and Constitution, 1781-1789 +   HR/1396
BERNARD MAYO: Myths and Men: *Patrick Henry, George Washington, Thomas Jefferson*
TB/1108
JOHN C. MILLER: Alexander Hamilton and the Growth of the New Nation   TB/3057
JOHN C. MILLER: The Federalist Era: 1789-1801. † *Illus.*   TB/3027

RICHARD B. MORRIS, Ed.: Alexander Hamilton and the Founding of the Nation. *New Introduction by the Editor*   TB/1448
RICHARD B. MORRIS: The American Revolution Reconsidered   TB/1363
CURTIS P. NETTELS: The Emergence of a National Economy, 1775-1815 ∆   TB/1438
DOUGLASS C. NORTH & ROBERT PAUL THOMAS, Eds.: *The Growth of the American Economy to 1860* +   HR/1352
R. B. NYE: The Cultural Life of the New Nation: 1776-1830. † *Illus.*   TB/3026
GILBERT OSOFSKY, Ed.: Puttin' On Ole Massa: *The Slave Narratives of Henry Bibb, William Wells Brown, and Solomon Northup* ‡
TB/1432
JAMES PARTON: The Presidency of Andrew Jackson. *From Volume III of the* Life of Andrew Jackson. *Ed. with Intro. by Robert V. Remini*   TB/3080
FRANCIS S. PHILBRICK: The Rise of the West, 1754-1830. † *Illus.*   TB/3067
MARSHALL SMELSER: The Democratic Republic, 1801-1815 †   TB/1406
TIMOTHY L. SMITH: Revivalism and Social Reform: *American Protestantism on the Eve of the Civil War*   TB/1229
JACK M. SOSIN, Ed.: The Opening of the West +   HR/1424
GEORGE ROGERS TAYLOR: The Transportation Revolution, 1815-1860 ∆   TB/1347
A. F. TYLER: Freedom's Ferment: *Phases of American Social History from the Revolution to the Outbreak of the Civil War. Illus.*
TB/1074
GLYNDON G. VAN DEUSEN: The Jacksonian Era: 1828-1848. † *Illus.*   TB/3028
LOUIS B. WRIGHT: Culture on the Moving Frontier   TB/1053

American Studies: The Civil War to 1900

W. R. BROCK: An American Crisis: *Congress and Reconstruction, 1865-67* °   TB/1283
T. C. COCHRAN & WILLIAM MILLER: The Age of Enterprise: *A Social History of Industrial America*   TB/1054
W. A. DUNNING: Reconstruction, Political and Economic: 1865-1877   TB/1073
HAROLD U. FAULKNER: Politics, Reform and Expansion: 1890-1900. † *Illus.*   TB/3020
GEORGE M. FREDRICKSON: The Inner Civil War: *Northern Intellectuals and the Crisis of the Union*   TB/1358
JOHN A. GARRATY: The New Commonwealth, 1877-1890 †   TB/1410
JOHN A. GARRATY, Ed.: The Transformation of American Society, 1870-1890 +   HR/1395
HELEN HUNT JACKSON: A Century of Dishonor: *The Early Crusade for Indian Reform.* † *Edited by Andrew F. Rolle*   TB/3063
ALBERT D. KIRWAN: Revolt of the Rednecks: *Mississippi Politics, 1876-1925*   TB/1199
ARTHUR MANN: Yankee Reforms in the Urban Age: *Social Reform in Boston, 1800-1900*
TB/1247
ARNOLD M. PAUL: Conservative Crisis and the Rule of Law: *Attitudes of Bar and Bench, 1887-1895. New Introduction by Author*
TB/1415
JAMES S. PIKE: The Prostrate State: *South Carolina under Negro Government.* ‡ *Intro. by Robert F. Durden*   TB/3085
WHITELAW REID: After the War: *A Tour of the Southern States, 1865-1866.* ‡ *Edited by C. Vann Woodward*   TB/3066
FRED A. SHANNON: The Farmer's Last Frontier: *Agriculture, 1860-1897*   TB/1348

2

VERNON LANE WHARTON: The Negro in Mississippi, 1865-1890   TB/1178

American Studies: The Twentieth Century

RICHARD M. ABRAMS, Ed.: The Issues of the Populist and Progressive Eras, 1892-1912 +   HR/1428
RAY STANNARD BAKER: Following the Color Line: American Negro Citizenship in Progressive Era. ‡ Edited by Dewey W. Grantham, Jr. Illus.   TB/3053
RANDOLPH S. BOURNE: War and the Intellectuals: Collected Essays, 1915-1919. ‡ Edited by Carl Resek   TB/3043
A. RUSSELL BUCHANAN: The United States and World War II. † Illus.
Vol. I TB/3044; Vol. II TB/3045
THOMAS C. COCHRAN: The American Business System: A Historical Perspective, 1900-1955   TB/1080
FOSTER RHEA DULLES: America's Rise to World Power: 1898-1954. † Illus.   TB/3021
JEAN-BAPTISTE DUROSELLE: From Wilson to Roosevelt: Foreign Policy of the United States, 1913-1945. Trans. by Nancy Lyman Roelker   TB/1370
HAROLD U. FAULKNER: The Decline of Laissez Faire, 1897-1917   TB/1397
JOHN D. HICKS: Republican Ascendancy: 1921-1933. † Illus.   TB/3041
ROBERT HUNTER: Poverty: Social Conscience in the Progressive Era. ‡ Edited by Peter d'A. Jones   TB/3065
WILLIAM E. LEUCHTENBURG: Franklin D. Roosevelt and the New Deal: 1932-1940. † Illus.   TB/3025
WILLIAM E. LEUCHTENBURG, Ed.: The New Deal: A Documentary History +   HR/1354
ARTHUR S. LINK: Woodrow Wilson and the Progressive Era: 1910-1917. † Illus. TB/3023
BROADUS MITCHELL: Depression Decade: From New Era through New Deal, 1929-1941 ∧   TB/1439
GEORGE E. MOWRY: The Era of Theodore Roosevelt and the Birth of Modern America: 1900-1912. † Illus.   TB/3022
WILLIAM PRESTON, JR.: Aliens and Dissenters: Federal Suppression of Radicals, 1903-1933   TB/1287
WALTER RAUSCHENBUSCH: Christianity and the Social Crisis. ‡ Edited by Robert D. Cross   TB/3059
GEORGE SOULE: Prosperity Decade: From War to Depression, 1917-1929 ∧   TB/1349
GEORGE B. TINDALL, Ed.: A Populist Reader: Selections from the Works of American Populist Leaders   TB/3069
TWELVE SOUTHERNERS: I'll Take My Stand: The South and the Agrarian Tradition. Intro. by Louis D. Rubin, Jr.; Biographical Essays by Virginia Rock   TB/1072

Art, Art History, Aesthetics

CREIGHTON GILBERT, Ed.: Renaissance Art ** Illus.   TB/1465
EMILE MALE: The Gothic Image: Religious Art in France of the Thirteenth Century. § 190 illus.   TB/344
MILLARD MEISS: Painting in Florence and Siena After the Black Death: The Arts, Religion and Society in the Mid-Fourteenth Century. 169 illus.   TB/1148
ERWIN PANOFSKY: Renaissance and Renascences in Western Art. Illus.   TB/1447
ERWIN PANOFSKY: Studies in Iconology: Humanistic Themes in the Art of the Renaissance. 180 illus.   TB/1077

JEAN SEZNEC: The Survival of the Pagan Gods: The Mythological Tradition and Its Place in Renaissance Humanism and Art. 108 illus.   TB/2004
OTTO VON SIMSON: The Gothic Cathedral: Origins of Gothic Architecture and the Medieval Concept of Order. 58 illus.   TB/2018
HEINRICH ZIMMER: Myths and Symbols in Indian Art and Civilization. 70 illus. TB/2005

Asian Studies

WOLFGANG FRANKE: China and the West: The Cultural Encounter, 13th to 20th Centuries. Trans. by R. A. Wilson   TB/1326
L. CARRINGTON GOODRICH: A Short History of the Chinese People. Illus.   TB/3015
DAN N. JACOBS, Ed.: The New Communist Manifesto and Related Documents. 3rd revised edn.   TB/1078
DAN N. JACOBS & HANS H. BAERWALD, Eds.: Chinese Communism: Selected Documents   TB/3031
BENJAMIN I. SCHWARTZ: Chinese Communism and the Rise of Mao   TB/1308
BENJAMIN I. SCHWARTZ: In Search of Wealth and Power: Yen Fu and the West   TB/1422

Economics & Economic History

C. E. BLACK: The Dynamics of Modernization: A Study in Comparative History   TB/1321
STUART BRUCHEY: The Roots of American Economic Growth, 1607-1861: An Essay in Social Causation. New Introduction by the Author.   TB/1350
GILBERT BURCK & EDITORS OF Fortune: The Computer Age: And its Potential for Management   TB/1179
JOHN ELLIOTT CAIRNES: The Slave Power. ‡ Edited with Introduction by Harold D. Woodman   TB/1433
SHEPARD B. CLOUGH, THOMAS MOODIE & CAROL MOODIE, Eds.: Economic History of Europe: Twentieth Century #   HR/1388
THOMAS C. COCHRAN: The American Business System: A Historical Perspective, 1900-1955   TB/1180
ROBERT A. DAHL & CHARLES E. LINDBLOM: Politics, Economics, and Welfare: Planning and Politico-Economic Systems Resolved into Basic Social Processes   TB/3037
PETER F. DRUCKER: The New Society: The Anatomy of Industrial Order   TB/1082
HAROLD U. FAULKNER: The Decline of Laissez Faire, 1897-1917 ∧   TB/1397
PAUL W. GATES: The Farmer's Age: Agriculture, 1815-1860 ∆   TB/1398
WILLIAM GREENLEAF, Ed.: American Economic Development Since 1860 +   HR/1353
J. L. & BARBARA HAMMOND: The Rise of Modern Industry. || Introduction by R. M. Hartwell   TB/1417
ROBERT L. HEILBRONER: The Future as History: The Historic Currents of Our Time and the Direction in Which They Are Taking America   TB/1386
ROBERT L. HEILBRONER: The Great Ascent: The Struggle for Economic Development in Our Time   TB/3030
FRANK H. KNIGHT: The Economic Organization   TB/1214
DAVID S. LANDES: Bankers and Pashas: International Finance and Economic Imperialism in Egypt. New Preface by the Author TB/1412
ROBERT LATOUCHE: The Birth of Western Economy: Economic Aspects of the Dark Ages   TB/1290

3

4

History: Renaissance & Reformation

JACOB BURCKHARDT: The Civilization of the Renaissance in Italy. *Introduction by Benjamin Nelson and Charles Trinkaus. Illus.* Vol. I TB/40; Vol. II TB/41

JOHN CALVIN & JACOPO SADOLETO: A Reformation Debate. *Edited by John C. Olin* TB/1239

FEDERICO CHABOD: Machiavelli and the Renaissance TB/1193

THOMAS CROMWELL: Thomas Cromwell. *Selected Letters on Church and Commonwealth, 1523-1540.* ¶ *Ed. with an Intro. by Arthur J. Slavin* TB/1462

R. TREVOR DAVIES: The Golden Century of Spain, 1501-1621 ° TB/1194

J. H. ELLIOTT: Europe Divided, 1559-1598 α ° TB/1414

G. R. ELTON: Reformation Europe, 1517-1559 ° α TB/1270

DESIDERIUS ERASMUS: Christian Humanism and the Reformation: *Selected Writings. Edited and Translated by John C. Olin* TB/1166

DESIDERIUS ERASMUS: Erasmus and His Age: *Selected Letters. Edited with an Introduction by Hans J. Hillerbrand. Translated by Marcus A. Haworth* TB/1461

WALLACE K. FERGUSON et al.: Facets of the Renaissance TB/1098

WALLACE K. FERGUSON et al.: The Renaissance: *Six Essays. Illus.* TB/1084

FRANCESCO GUICCIARDINI: History of Florence. *Translated with an Introduction and Notes by Mario Domandi* TB/1470

WERNER L. GUNDERSHEIMER, Ed.: French Humanism, 1470-1600. * *Illus.* TB/1473

MARIE BOAS HALL, Ed.: Nature and Nature's Laws: *Documents of the Scientific Revolution #* HR/1420

HANS J. HILLERBRAND, Ed., The Protestant Reformation HR/1342

JOHAN HUIZINGA: Erasmus and the Age of Reformation. *Illus.* TB/19

JOEL HURSTFIELD: The Elizabethan Nation TB/1312

JOEL HURSTFIELD, Ed.: The Reformation Crisis TB/1267

PAUL OSKAR KRISTELLER: Renaissance Thought: *The Classic, Scholastic, and Humanist Strains* TB/1048

PAUL OSKAR KRISTELLER: Renaissance Thought II: *Papers on Humanism and the Arts* TB/1163

PAUL O. KRISTELLER & PHILIP P. WIENER, Eds.: Renaissance Essays TB/1392

DAVID LITTLE: Religion, Order and Law: *A Study in Pre-Revolutionary England. § Preface by R. Bellah* TB/1418

NICCOLO MACHIAVELLI: History of Florence and of the Affairs of Italy: *From the Earliest Times to the Death of Lorenzo the Magnificent. Introduction by Felix Gilbert* TB/1027

ALFRED VON MARTIN: Sociology of the Renaissance. ° *Introduction by W. K. Ferguson* TB/1099

GARRETT MATTINGLY et al.: Renaissance Profiles. *Edited by J. H. Plumb* TB/1162

J. E. NEALE: The Age of Catherine de Medici ° TB/1085

J. H. PARRY: The Establishment of the European Hegemony: 1415-1715: *Trade and Exploration in the Age of the Renaissance* TB/1045

J. H. PARRY, Ed.: The European Reconnaissance: *Selected Documents #* HR/1345

BUONACCORSO PITTI & GREGORIO DATI: Two Memoirs of Renaissance Florence: *The Diaries of Buonaccorso Pitti and Gregorio Dati. Edited with Intro. by Gene Brucker. Trans. by Julia Martines* TB/1333

J. H. PLUMB: The Italian Renaissance: *A Concise Survey of Its History and Culture* TB/1161

A. F. POLLARD: Henry VIII. *Introduction by A. G. Dickens.* ° TB/1249

RICHARD H. POPKIN: The History of Scepticism from Erasmus to Descartes TB/1391

PAOLO ROSSI: Philosophy, Technology, and the Arts, in the Early Modern Era 1400-1700. || *Edited by Benjamin Nelson. Translated by Salvator Attanasio* TB/1458

FERDINAND SCHEVILL: The Medici. *Illus.* TB/1010

FERDINAND SCHEVILL: Medieval and Renaissance Florence. *Illus.* Vol. I: *Medieval Florence* TB/1090

Vol. II: *The Coming of Humanism and the Age of the Medici* TB/1091

R. H. TAWNEY: The Agrarian Problem in the Sixteenth Century. *Intro. by Lawrence Stone* TB/1315

H. R. TREVOR-ROPER: The European Witch-craze of the Sixteenth and Seventeenth Centuries and Other Essays ° TB/1416

VESPASIANO: Rennaissance Princes, Popes, and XVth Century: *The Vespasiano Memoirs. Introduction by Myron P. Gilmore. Illus.* TB/1111

History: Modern European

RENE ALBRECHT-CARRIE, Ed.: The Concert of Europe # HR/1341

MAX BELOFF: The Age of Absolutism, 1660-1815 TB/1062

OTTO VON BISMARCK: Reflections and Reminiscences. *Ed. with Intro. by Theodore S. Hamerow* ¶ TB/1357

EUGENE C. BLACK, Ed.: British Politics in the Nineteenth Century # HR/1427

EUGENE C. BLACK, Ed.: European Political History, 1815-1870: *Aspects of Liberalism* ¶ TB/1331

ASA BRIGGS: The Making of Modern England, 1783-1867: *The Age of Improvement* ° TB/1203

ALAN BULLOCK: Hitler, A Study in Tyranny. ° *Revised Edition. Illus.* TB/1123

EDMUND BURKE: On Revolution. *Ed. by Robert A. Smith* TB/1401

E. R. CARR: International Relations Between the Two World Wars. 1919-1939 ° TB/1279

E. H. CARR: The Twenty Years' Crisis, 1919-1939: *An Introduction to the Study of International Relations* ° TB/1122

GORDON A. CRAIG: From Bismarck to Adenauer: *Aspects of German Statecraft. Revised Edition* TB/1171

LESTER G. CROCKER, Ed.: The Age of Enlightenment # HR/1423

DENIS DIDEROT: The Encyclopedia: *Selections. Edited and Translated with Introduction by Stephen Gendzier* TB/1299

JACQUES DROZ: Europe between Revolutions, 1815-1848. ° *a Trans. by Robert Baldick* TB/1346

JOHANN GOTTLIEB FICHTE: Addresses to the German Nation. *Ed. with Intro. by George A. Kelly* ¶ TB/1366

ROBERT & ELBORG FORSTER, Eds.: European Society in the Eighteenth Century # HR/1404

C. C. GILLISPIE: Genesis and Geology: *The Decades before Darwin §* TB/51

Literature & Literary Criticism

Philosophy

ERNST CASSIRER: Rousseau, Kant and Goethe.
Intro. by Peter Gay   TB/1092
FREDERICK COPLESTON, S. J.: Medieval Philosophy   TB/376
F. M. CORNFORD: From Religion to Philosophy:
A Study in the Origins of Western Speculation §   TB/20
WILFRID DESAN: The Tragic Finale: An Essay on
the Philosophy of Jean-Paul Sartre TB/1030
MARVIN FARBER: The Aims of Phenomenology:
The Motives, Methods, and Impact of Husserl's Thought   TB/1291
MARVIN FARBER: Basic Issues of Philosophy: Experience, Reality, and Human Values
                                       TB/1344
MARVIN FARBERS: Phenomenology and Existence:
Towards a Philosophy within Nature TB/1295
PAUL FRIEDLANDER: `Plato: An Introduction
                                       TB/2017
MICHAEL GELVEN: A Commentary on Heidegger's
"Being and Time"   TB/1464
J. GLENN GRAY: Hegel and Greek Thought
                                       TB/1409
W. K. C. GUTHRIE: The Greek Philosophers:
From Thales to Aristotle °   TB/1008
G. W. F. HEGEL: On Art, Religion Philosophy:
Introductory Lectures to the Realm of Absolute Spirit. || Edited with an Introduction
by J. Glenn Gray   TB/1463
G. W. F. HEGEL: Phenomenology of Mind. ° ||
Introduction by George Lichtheim   TB/1303
MARTIN HEIDEGGER: Discourse on Thinking.
Translated with a Preface by John M. Anderson and E. Hans Freund. Introduction by
John M. Anderson   TB/1459
F. H. HEINEMANN: Existentialism and the Modern Predicament   TB/28
WERER HEISENBERG: Physics and Philosophy:
The Revolution in Modern Science. Intro. by
F. S. C. Northrop   TB/549
EDMUND HUSSERL: Phenomenology and the
Crisis of Philosophy. § Translated with an
Introduction by Quentin Lauer   TB/1170
IMMANUEL KANT: Groundwork of the Metaphysic of Morals. Translated and Analyzed by
H. J. Paton   TB/1159
IMMANUEL KANT: Lectures on Ethics. § Introduction by Lewis White Beck   TB/105
WALTER KAUFMANN, Ed.: Religion From Tolstoy
to Camus: Basic Writings on Religious Truth
and Morals   TB/123
QUENTIN LAUER: Phenomenology: Its Genesis
and Prospect. Preface by Aron Gurwitsch
                                       TB/1169
MAURICE MANDELBAUM: The Problem of Historical Knowledge: An Answer to Relativism
                                       TB/1198
H. J. PATON: The Categorical Imperative: A
Study in Kant's Moral Philosophy   TB/1325
MICHAEL POLANYI: Personal Knowledge: Towards a Post-Critical Philosophy   TB/1158
KARL R. POPPER: Conjectures and Refutations:
The Growth of Scientific Knowledge TB/1376
WILLARD VAN ORMAN QUINE: Elementary Logic
Revised Edition   TB/577
WILLARD VAN ORMAN QUINE: From a Logical
Point of View: Logico-Philosophical Essays
                                       TB/566
JOHN E. SMITH: Themes in American Philosophy: Purpose, Experience and Community
                                       TB/1466
MORTON WHITE: Foundations of Historical
Knowledge   TB/1440
WILHELM WINDELBAND: A History of Philosophy
Vol. I: Greek, Roman, Medieval   TB/38
Vol. II: Renaissance, Enlightenment, Modern
                                       TB/39

LUDWIG WITTGENSTEIN: The Blue and Brown
Books °   TB/1211
LUDWIG WITTGENSTEIN: Notebooks, 1914-1916
                                       TB/1441

Political Science & Government

C. E. BLACK: The Dynamics of Modernization:
A Study in Comparative History   TB/1321
DENIS W. BROGAN: Politics in America. New
Introduction by the Author   TB/1469
CRANE BRINTON: English Political Thought in the
Nineteenth Century   TB/1071
ROBERT CONQUEST: Power and Policy in the
USSR: The Study of Soviet Dynastics °
                                       TB/1307
ROBERT A. DAHL & CHARLES E. LINDBLOM: Politics,
Economics, and Welfare: Planning and Politico-Economic Systems Resolved into Basic
Social Processes   TB/1277
HANS KOHN: Political Ideologies of the 20th
Century   TB/1277
ROY C. MACRIDIS, Ed.: Political Parties: Contemporary Trends and Ideas **   TB/1322
ROBERT GREEN MC CLOSKEY: American Conservatism in the Age of Enterprise, 1865-1910
                                       TB/1137
MARSILIUS OF PADUA: The Defender of Peace.
The Defensor Pacis. Translated with an Introduction by Alan Gewirth   TB/1310
KINGSLEY MARTIN: French Liberal Thought in
the Eighteenth Century: A Study of Political
Ideas from Bayle to Condorcet   TB/1114
BARRINGTON MOORE, JR.:Political Power and
Social Theory: Seven Studies || TB/1221
BARRINGTON MOORE, JR.: Soviet Politics—The
Dilemma of Power: The Role of Ideas in
Social Change || TB/1222
BARRINGTON MOORE, JR.: Terror and Progress—
USSR: Some Sources of Change and Stability
JOHN B. MORRALL: Political Thought in Medieval
Times   TB/1076
KARL R. POPPER: The Open Society and Its
Enemies Vol. I: The Spell of Plato TB/1101
Vol. II: The High Tide of Prophecy: Hegel,
Marx, and the Aftermath   TB/1102
CONYERS READ, Ed.: The Constitution Reconsidered. Revised Edition, Preface by Richard
B. Morris   TB/1384
JOHN P. ROCHE, Ed.: Origins of American Political Thought: Selected Readings   TB/1301
JOHN P. ROCHE, Ed.: American Political
Thought: From Jefferson to Progressivism
                                       TB/1332
HENRI DE SAINT-SIMON: Social Organization, The
Science of Man, and Other Writings. ||
Edited and Translated with an Introduction
by Felix Markham   TB/1152
CHARLES SCHOTTLAND, Ed.: The Welfare State **
                                       TB/1323
JOSEPH A. SCHUMPETER: Capitalism, Socialism
and Democracy   TB/3008

Psychology

ALFRED ADLER: The Individual Psychology of
Alfred Adler: A Systematic Presentation in
Selections from His Writings. Edited by
Heinz L. & Rowena R. Ansbacher   TB/1154
LUDWIG BINSWANGER: Being-in-the-World: Selected Papers. || Trans. with Intro. by Jacob
Needleman   TB/1365
HADLEY CANTRIL: The Invasion from Mars: A
Study in the Psychology of Panic || TB/1282
MIRCEA ELIADE: Cosmos and History: The Myth
of the Eternal Return §   TB/2050
MIRCEA ELIADE: Myth and Reality   TB/1369

7

MIRCEA ELIADE: Myths, Dreams and Mysteries: *The Encounter Between Contemporary Faiths and Archaic Realities* § TB/1320
MIRCEA ELIADE: Rites and Symbols of Initiation: *The Mysteries of Birth and Rebirth* § TB/1236
HERBERT FINGARETTE: The Self in Transformation: *Psychoanalysis, Philosophy and the Life of the Spirit* ‖ TB/1177
SIGMUND FREUD: On Creativity and the Unconscious: *Papers on the Psychology of Art, Literature, Love, Religion.* § *Intro. by Benjamin Nelson* TB/45
J. GLENN GRAY: The Warriors: *Reflections on Men in Battle. Introduction by Hannah Arendt* TB/1294
WILLIAM JAMES: Psychology: *The Briefer Course. Edited with an Intro. by Gordon Allport* TB/1034
C. G. JUNG: Psychological Reflections. *Ed. by J. Jacobi* TB/2001
KARL MENNINGER, M.D.: Theory of Psychoanalytic Technique TB/1144
JOHN H. SCHAAR: Escape from Authority: *The Perspectives of Erich Fromm* TB/1155
MUZAFER SHERIF: The Psychology of Social Norms. *Introduction by Gardner Murphy* TB/3072
HELLMUT WILHELM: Change: *Eight Lectures on the* I Ching TB/2019

Religion: Ancient and Classical, Biblical and Judaic Traditions

W. F. ALBRIGHT: The Biblical Period from Abraham to Ezra TB/102
SALO W. BARON: Modern Nationalism and Religion TB/818
C. K. BARRETT, Ed.: The New Testament Background: *Selected Documents* TB/86
MARTIN BUBER: Eclipse of God: *Studies in the Relation Between Religion and Philosophy* TB/12
MARTIN BUBER: Hasidism and Modern Man. *Edited and Translated by Maurice Friedman* TB/839
MARTIN BUBER: The Knowledge of Man. *Edited with an Introduction by Maurice Friedman. Translated by Maurice Friedman and Ronald Gregor Smith* TB/135
MARTIN BUBER: Moses. *The Revelation and the Covenant* TB/837
MARTIN BUBER: The Origin and Meaning of Hasidism. *Edited and Translated by Maurice Friedman* TB/835
MARTIN BUBER: The Prophetic Faith TB/73
MARTIN BUBER: Two Types of Faith: *Interpenetration of Judaism and Christianity* ° TB/75
MALCOLM L. DIAMOND: Martin Buber: *Jewish Existentialist* TB/840
M. S. ENSLIN: Christian Beginnings TB/5
M. S. ENSLIN: The Literature of the Christian Movement TB/6
ERNST LUDWIG EHRLICH: A Concise History of Israel: *From the Earliest Times to the Destruction of the Temple in A.D. 70* ° TB/128
HENRI FRANKFORT: Ancient Egyptian Religion: *An Interpretation* TB/77
ABRAHAM HESCHEL: The Earth Is the Lord's & The Sabbath. *Two Essays* TB/828
ABRAHAM HESCHEL: God in Search of Man: *A Philosophy of Judaism* TB/807
ABRAHAM HESCHEL: Man Is not Alone: *A Philosophy of Religion* TB/838
ABRAHAM HESCHEL: The Prophets: *An Introduction* TB/1421

T. J. MEEK: Hebrew Origins TB/69
JAMES MUILENBURG: The Way of Israel: *Biblical Faith and Ethics* TB/133
H. J. ROSE: Religion in Greece and Rome TB/55
H. H. ROWLEY: The Growth of the Old Testament TB/107
D. WINTON THOMAS, Ed.: Documents from Old Testament Times TB/85

Religion: General Christianity

ROLAND H. BAINTON: Christendom: *A Short History of Christianity and Its Impact on Western Civilization. Illus.*
Vol. I TB/131; Vol. II TB/132
JOHN T. MCNEILL: Modern Christian Movements. *Revised Edition* TB/1402
ERNST TROELTSCH: The Social Teaching of the Christian Churches. *Intro. by H. Richard Niebuhr* Vol. TB/71; Vol. II TB/72

Religion: Early Christianity Through Reformation

ANSELM OF CANTERBURY: Truth, Freedom, and Evil: *Three Philosophical Dialogues. Edited and Translated by Jasper Hopkins and Herbert Richardson* TB/317
MARSHALL W. BALDWIN, Ed.: Christianity through the 13th Century # HR/1468
W. D. DAVIES: Paul and Rabbinic Judaism: *Some Rabbinic Elements in Pauline Theology. Revised Edition* ° TB/146
ADOLF DEISSMAN: Paul: *A Study in Social and Religious History* TB/15
JOHANNES ECKHART: Meister Eckhart: *A Modern Translation by R. Blakney* TB/8
EDGAR J. GOODSPEED: A Life of Jesus TB/1
ROBERT M. GRANT: Gnosticism and Early Christianity TB/136
WILLIAM HALLER: The Rise of Puritanism TB/22
GERHART B. LADNER: The Idea of Reform: *Its Impact on the Christian Thought and Action in the Age of the Fathers* TB/149
ARTHUR DARBY NOCK: Early Gentile Christianity and Its Hellenistic Background TB/111
ARTHUR DARBY NOCK: St. Paul ° TR/104
GORDON RUPP: Luther's Progress to the Diet of Worms ° TB/120

Religion: The Protestant Tradition

KARL BARTH: Church Dogmatics: *A Selection. Intro. by H. Gollwitzer. Ed. by G. W. Bromiley* TB/95
KARL BARTH: Dogmatics in Outline TB/56
KARL BARTH: The Word of God and the Word of Man TB/13
HERBERT BRAUN, et al.: God and Christ: *Existence and Province. Volume 5 of Journal for Theology and the Church, edited by Robert W. Funk and Gerhard Ebeling* TB/255
WHITNEY R. CROSS: The Burned-Over District: *The Social and Intellectual History of Enthusiastic Religion in Western New York, 1800-1850* TB/1242
NELS F. S. FERRE: Swedish Contributions to Modern Theology. *New Chapter by William A. Johnson* TB/147
WILLIAM R. HUTCHISON, Ed.: American Protestant Thought: *The Liberal Era* † TB/1385
ERNST KASEMANN, et al.: Distinctive Protestant and Catholic Themes Reconsidered. *Volume 3 of Journal for Theology and the Church,*

9